MW00720796

CC

THE ESSENTIALS

OTHER BOOKS BY ALAN TWIGG

Tibetans in Exile: The Dalai Lama & The Woodcocks

Full-Time: A Soccer Story

*Thompson's Highway: British Columbia's Fur Trade, 1800–1850:
The Literary Origins of British Columbia, Vol. 3*

Understanding Belize: A Historical Guide

Aboriginality: The Literary Origins of British Columbia, Vol. 2

101 Top Historical Sites of Cuba

First Invaders: The Literary Origins of British Columbia, Vol. 1

Intensive Care: A Memoir

Cuba: A Concise History for Travelers

Twigg's Directory of 1001 BC Writers

Strong Voices: Conversations with 50 Canadian Writers

Vander Zalm: From Immigrant to Premier

Vancouver and its Writers

Hubert Evans: The First Ninety-Three Years

For Openers: Conversations with 24 Canadian Writers

THE ESSENTIALS

150 Great B.C. Books & Authors

ALAN TWIGG

RONSDALE

The Essentials
Copyright © 2010 Alan Twigg

All rights reserved. No part of this publication may be reproduced, stored in a retrieval system, or transmitted, in any form or by any means, without prior written permission of the publisher, or, in Canada, in the case of photocopying or other reprographic copying, a license from Access Copyright (the Canadian Copyright Licensing Agency).

RONSDALE PRESS
3350 West 21st Avenue
Vancouver, B.C., Canada V6S 1G7
www.ronsdalepress.com

Typesetting: Get To The Point Graphics, in New Baskerville 11 pt on 14.1
Cover Design: David Lester
Paper: Ancient Forest Friendly Rolland ST50 – 50% post-consumer waste, totally chlorine-free and acid-free

Photos from/by Alan Twigg, Laura Sawchuk, UBC Rare Books & Special Collections (Ralph Stanton), Vancouver Public Library (Paul Whitney), *B.C. BookWorld* archives or courtesy of Canadian publishers and authors.

Cover images: painting by bill bissett, self-portrait; photos of E. Pauline Johnson (VPL), Douglas Coupland (James O'Mara), Alice Munro (Sheila Munro), Malcolm Lowry (UBC Rare Books & Special Collections), W.P. Kinsella and CBC studio (Laura Sawchuk).

About the author: www.alantwigg.com

Ronsdale Press wishes to thank the following for their support of its publishing program: the Canada Council for the Arts, the Government of Canada through the Canada Book Plan, the British Columbia Arts Council and the Province of British Columbia through the Book Publishing Tax Credit program.

Library and Archives Canada Cataloguing in Publication

Twigg, Alan, 1952-
The essentials: 150 great BC books & authors / Alan Twigg.

ISBN-13: 978-1-55380-108-5

1. Canadian literature–British Columbia–History and criticism. I. Title.

PS8131.B7T95 2010   C810.9   C2010-904860-1

At Ronsdale Press we are committed to protecting the environment. To this end we are working with Canopy (formerly Markets Initiative) and printers to phase out our use of paper produced from ancient forests. This book is one step towards that goal.

Printed in Canada by AGMV Marquis

To David Lester,
for friendship and creativity

A MATTER OF REJOICING

"Without Homer, the Greeks would amount to bugger all."
— ROBERT SWANSON, LOGGING POET

"When I first came to Vancouver in the early 1950s it was a lonely place with few fellow writers, with no publishers, and with one slender poetry magazine, Alan Crawley's Contemporary Verse. *Now Vancouver is the centre of a province inhabited by hundreds of professional writers, with scores of publishing houses large and small, and many literary magazines, some of them with national and even international reputations. It poses a growing rivalry to the older literary centres of Eastern Canada. This is a matter for rejoicing."*
— GEORGE WOODCOCK, ACCEPTANCE SPEECH, FREEDOM OF THE CITY, VANCOUVER CITY COUNCIL CHAMBERS, 1994

"Back in Toronto they make jokes like, 'The continent slopes to the west and all the nuts roll to the West Coast.' That's a crock. We know the nuts roll as far as the Rocky Mountains. That's why we put them there. Only the crafty ones make it through to the other side."
— ANNE CAMERON, LETTER TO ALAN TWIGG

"There's nothing British about it."
— TOMMY GREGORY, OKANAGAN ELDER, AS REPEATED BY JEANNETTE ARMSTRONG TO ALAN TWIGG, INTERVIEW, PENTICTON, 1995

CONTENTS

IV. 1950s

V. 1960s

VI. 1970s

IX. NEW MILLENNIUM

GENERATION X

"A groundbreaking novel."

—Los Angeles Times

TALES FOR AN ACCELERATED CULTURE

DOUGLAS COUPLAND

Cover art for Douglas Coupland's first book, Generation X: Tales for an Accelerated Culture *(1991), an audaciously original novel that could replace Malcolm Lowry's* Under the Volcano *as the most famous book ever written in British Columbia*

TURNING UP THE VOLUMES

D ouglas Coupland has added "Generation X" to the English lexicon. W.P. Kinsella gave us "Build it and they will come." Malcolm Lowry wrote his classic novel *Under the Volcano* in a squatter's shack in North Vancouver. Pauline Johnson led the way for aboriginal writers. Alice Munro, of West Vancouver, Victoria and Comox, is often regarded as the world's best short story writer.

But the vast majority of B.C. authors remain unknown.

For more than a century, the most significant writing from British Columbia was etched on a rock in Elcho Harbour, near the mouth of the Bella Coola River, by the first European to cross the North American continent, an intrepid Scottish businessman who used a mixture of grease and vermilion paint to leave his inadvertently haiku-like message:

> *Alex Mackenzie*
> *From Canada by land*
> *22nd July 1793*

Thereafter, most British Columbians who wanted their words viewed in a book were dependent on literary gatekeepers in faraway places, mainly London, New York or Toronto.

There were few bookstores and no British Columbia–based publishing houses with national distribution. Self-publishing evolved as a necessary B.C. tradition. During the 1960s, most books from B.C. were printed for independent authors by Mitchell Press in Vancouver or Morriss Printing in Victoria.

The dividing point between literary famine and literary feast was the formation of the Association of Book Publishers of British Columbia in 1974, exactly 200 years after Juan Pérez became the first European to make contact with Haida in B.C. waters in 1774.

By the 1980s, there were approximately 25 publishing houses. Like the Picts in Scotland behind Hadrian's Wall, B.C.'s independent booksellers developed a series of fortresses on the west side of the Rockies, unconquered by the invading chain stores owned from afar. A splendid outpouring ensued. By the early 1990s, federal surveys revealed B.C. had the highest book-reading rate per capita in Canada.

British Columbia has been a literary hotspot of North America ever since.

The Essentials is an invitation to visit 150 literary markers for a journey—or pilgrimage—to discover the nature of our collective story as British Columbians.

To prevent this book from turning into a doorstopper, authors who have mainly achieved prominence elsewhere, such as Milton Acorn, Margaret Atwood, Pierre Berton, James Clavell, Raymond Chandler, Margaret Laurence, Al Purdy, Sinclair Ross, Robert Service and Carol Shields, have been excluded—along with about 9,000 others.

Where is my good friend and colleague Jean Barman, the historian who gave us *The West Beyond the West*, the standard history of our province? Where is Edith Iglauer, who wrote *Fishing with John?*

Carol Shields   Robert Service   Margaret Laurence

Where are Robin Skelton and George Fetherling, who have written almost 50 books each?

Where is Andreas Schroeder, who almost single-handedly gave us Public Lending Right legislation in Canada? Where are Michael Turner, Robert Bateman, Patrick Lane, Lorna Crozier, Morris Panych, Bill New, Marilyn Bowering, John Gray, Terry Glavin, L.R. Wright, Peter Trower, P.K. Page, Phyllis Webb, Robert Harlow, R.M. Patterson and all the others whose names would fill two pages?

A panoramic approach, in a wide variety of genres, from 1774 to 2010, necessarily omits hundreds of books and authors. The remarkable outpouring of recent decades will appear under-represented to those who wish to see their reflections in this mirror. But public usefulness takes precedence: people must know they have a literary past.

British Columbia has a collective story, seldom told or understood. In an attempt to give an over-arching impression of what it means to be a British Columbian, the broad spectrum of literature has been illuminated.

Originality and historical significance are two criteria for inclusion. I have also selected authors whose overall bodies of work and personal lives are significant, rather than restrict this collection of entries to specific titles.

The Essentials is for those who care about British Columbia, whether they are self-styled literati or not. It is also for people who

Jean Barman   Edith Iglauer   Andreas Schroeder

know little about literary activity west of the Rockies. It is my hope that *The Essentials* will contribute to the knowledge of those who feel qualified to decide on the "best" books or authors in Canada. I strongly believe B.C. deserves more attention in this regard.

———————

I wish to thank David Lester for designing another book for me, Noah Moscovitch and Erinna Gilkison for their diligence, and publisher Ron Hatch for having the gumption to publish my on-going series of titles about the literature of British Columbia.

As well, I wish to acknowledge the collegial friendship of Sheryl MacKay, host of CBC Radio's *North by Northwest*. My off-the-cuff conversations with Sheryl over the past three years, in a segment we call *Turning Up the Volumes*, have been an important catalyst for this non-Oxford guide to literature west of the Rockies.

I hope *The Essentials* will get more people talking about more B.C. books and authors in much the same spirit as *Turning Up the Volumes*.

— A.T.

I
1774–1850

Artist's exoticised rendering of a Haida with a labret (lip piece) from George Dixon's *A Voyage Round the World: But More Particularly to the North-West Coast of America* **(1789).**

"The women are well dressed and covered the same as the men. They wear hanging from the lip a round piece of very thin wood which makes them very ugly, for at a distance it looks as though they have their tongues hanging out. They manage it with great facility and simply by a movement of the lip they raise it and cover the mouth and part of the nose. Those who saw them nearer by said they have the lip pierced and hang the piece of wood from it. We do not know what their purpose is, whether it be to make themselves ugly or to adorn themselves. I am inclined to the latter."

– *Fray Juan Crespi, Thursday, July 21, 1774. From* Missionary Explorer on the Pacific Coast, 1769–1774 *(University of California Press, 1927).*

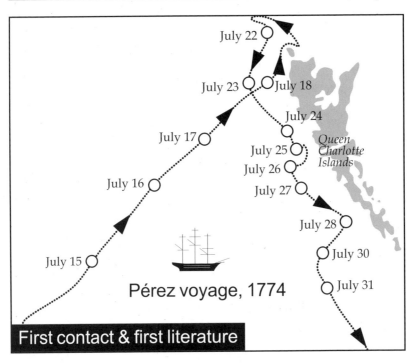

July 22

July 23   July 18

July 24

July 17   *Queen Charlotte Islands*

July 25

July 26

July 16

July 27

July 28

July 15

July 30

July 31

Pérez voyage, 1774

First contact & first literature

JUAN CRESPI & JUAN PÉREZ

Juan Pérez on the Northwest Coast: Six Documents of His Expedition in 1774 (1989), edited by Herbert K. Beals

The beginning of B.C. literature—words on paper originating from British Columbia territory—is unheralded and obscure. It dates back to the afternoon of July 19, 1774, when the first known European visitors to B.C. waters saw an approaching canoe near Langara Island, at the north end of Haida Gwaii. The Spanish sea captain Juan Pérez, his second-in-command Esteban José Martínez and the priests aboard the 82-foot frigate *Santiago* kept diaries that recorded this encounter.

Aboriginals, most likely Haida, greeted the newcomers with music. "While they were still some distance from the barque," wrote the priest Juan Crespi, "we heard them singing. . . . They drew near the frigate and we saw that there were eight men and a boy in the canoe, seven of them rowing, while the eighth, who was painted, was standing up in the attitude of dancing, and, throwing feathers on the water."

Crespi's diaries were published in Spanish in 1857, leading to H.E. Bolton's *Fray Juan Crespi: Missionary Explorer on the Pacific Coast 1769–1774* (1927).

The Pérez expedition opened the world's last unmapped temperate zone to exploration. His voyage produced the first crude map of the B.C. coastline from eyewitness experience, but British Columbians remain mostly unaware of Pérez because the early Spanish history of B.C. was expunged by British colonialism. As well, Spanish historians dismissed Pérez because he failed to place a cross and claim sovereignty for Spain, and he failed in his mission to detect Russian incursions in northern waters.

Original documents from Pérez's voyage ended up in the Archivo General de la Nación in Mexico City and the Naval Museum in Madrid, but were ignored for more than a century until a doctoral student named Olive Johnson undertook some preliminary translations in 1911. Portland historian Herbert K. Beals translated and annotated *Juan Pérez on the Northwest Coast: Six Documents of His Expedition in 1774* (1989) for the Oregon Historical Society, providing the first account in English of the *Santiago*'s seven-month voyage.

Pérez and Crespi were first. There is no evidence that a monk from China named Hui Shen reached the west coast in the fifth century or that a Greek-born sailor named Valerianos, a.k.a. Juan de Fuca, reached the strait that now bears his name. Also, scholars in the Drake Navigators Guild have debunked claims that Sir Francis Drake reached the coast of what we now call British Columbia.

For other authors associated with "Spanish Columbia," see the abcbookworld entries (without Spanish accents) for Baird, John Edward; Bartroli, Tomas; Beals, Herbert K.; Bodega y Quadra, Juan Francisco de la; Bolton, Herbert E.; Caamano, Jacinto; Campa Cos, Miguel de la; Cook, Warren L.; Cutter, Donald C.; de Suria, Tomas; de Viana, Francisco J.; Efrat, Barbara S.; Engstrand, Iris H.H.; Espinosa y Tello, Jose de; Galiano, Dionisio Alcalá; Galvin, John; Griffin, George Butler; Hezeta, Bruno de; Inglis, Robin; Jane, Cecil; Kendrick, John; Little, C.H.; Malaspina, Alejandro; Martinez, Estevan Jose; Mathes, W. Michael; Mathes, W.M.; McDowell, Jim; Mourelle, Francisco; Pena, Tomas de la; Perez, Juan; Quimper, Manuel; Sierra, Benito de la; Thurman, Michael E.; Wagner, Henry Raup.

First Nations people greeted newcomers with singing near Langara Island, Haida Gwaii, in 1774. This drawing by John Webber in 1778 is the earliest depiction of contact with Europeans, from the Captain Cook expedition, at Nootka Sound.

JOSÉ MOZIÑO

Noticias de Nutka (1913) by José Moziño

The first important anthropological work about British Columbia is *Noticias de Nutka* by José Mariano Moziño, a botanist who accompanied Captain Bodega y Quadra to Nootka Sound in 1792. Moziño was sufficiently adept at languages to glean verification of Pérez's visit to San Lorenzo (Nootka Sound) in 1774.

Moziño frankly describes the nature of relations between the Spanish and the Nuu-chah-nulth. His comrades "insulted them at various times, crippled some and wounded others, and did not fail to kill several." Moziño also noted that aboriginals were consumed by venereal diseases, "which the sailors of our ships have spread among them."

Moziño was the first of many to mention the practice of polygamy among Northwest Coast aboriginals and to report on birth practices, fertility and sexuality. "As soon as they throw off the afterbirth, they run into the sea and swim with great resolution. What is strange is that after a son is born, if his father is a *tais* [meaning "chief"], he has to enclose himself in the lodge, seeing neither the sun nor the waves. He is fearful of gravely offending Qua-utz, who would leave both him and his son without life in punishment of his sin. . . . Names are changed according to one's age, and in this matter each new one is solemnized with greater luxury and magnificence than the first one. . . . As soon as the menstrual flow appears in a girl for the first time, they celebrate in the same manner, and her name is also changed. If by chance she is the daughter of the principal chief of the *taises*, this proclamation occurs on the same day. We were present to congratulate Maquinna for that of his daughter Izto-coti-clemot, who before this time was called Apenas."

Born of Spanish-born parents in Temascaltepec, Mexico, in 1757, Moziño was at Nootka Sound in 1792 from April 29 to September 21. Moziño's study was augmented by the first Nootkan-Spanish dictionary, catalogues of plants and animals, and paintings by Atanasio Echeverría.

A copy of his manuscript—not the missing original—was recovered from a Mexican library in 1880, without drawings, and was republished in 1913 with a minimal print run of perhaps 100 copies. It remained long ignored by scholars in English. A few other copies are now known to exist in Paris, Madrid, Yale University Library and a private collection. The 1913 version from Mexico City was later translated and edited by Iris Higbie Wilson, a San Diego historian.

JOHN JEWITT

A Journal, Kept at Nootka Sound by John R. Jewitt,
One of the Surviving Crew of the Ship Boston, *of Boston, John Salter,*
Commander, Who Was Massacred on 22d of March, 1803;
Interspersed with Some Account of the Natives, Their Manners
and Customs (1807) by John Jewitt

The most famous book of pre-Confederation British Columbia is the memoir of young American blacksmith named John Jewitt who survived a massacre in 1803 and remained in captivity for nearly three years with the Mowachaht (of the Nuu-chah-nulth) on the west coast of Vancouver Island. By 1931, only seven copies of Jewitt's original 1807 version of his journal were known to exist but an expanded and embellished account by Richard Alsop, *A Narrative of the Adventures and Sufferings of John R. Jewitt* (1815), has remained in print ever since.

Blacksmith John Jewitt wrote the first commercially successful book about B.C.

Jewitt arrived at Friendly Cove (Nootka Sound) aboard the *Boston* on March 12, 1803. The following day, Maquinna, the *tyee* of the nearby Yuquot settlement, led a flotilla of canoes to visit the *Boston*, greeting Captain John Salter in English. Ostensibly to avenge a verbal insult from Salter, Maquinna and the Mowachaht later returned and killed 25 crewmembers of the *Boston*, including Salter, having first invited Salter to send some of his men away from the ship to go fishing. Jewitt was severely injured and took refuge below deck. John Thompson, a sailmaker, hid in the hold and was found the following day.

Maquinna had observed Jewitt at his forge as an "armourer" and recognized his value as a blacksmith. To remain alive, Jewitt had to promise to be a good slave and make Maquinna weapons and tools. Jewitt saved Thompson, 20 years his senior, by telling Maquinna that Thompson was his father. After Jewitt was asked to identify the severed heads of his former shipmates, the ship was ransacked and burned.

Thompson remained estranged from their captors. Jewitt was adopted into the tribe and chose a young wife, Eu-stoch-ee-exqua, the daughter of Upquesta, a chief. According to Jewitt, an affectionate relationship ensued. Jewitt bided his time until July 19, 1805, when another trading brig, the *Lydia*, approached Friendly Cove. Jewitt wrote a note to Captain Hill of the *Lydia* and duped Maquinna into delivering it. His message begged Hill to invite Maquinna aboard, capture him, and demand the release of Thompson and himself. Jewitt and Thompson were successfully traded for Maquinna.

Jewitt claims he made ink for his journal by boiling and filtering a blend of plant and berry juices with powdered coal. *A Journal, Kept At Nootka Sound* (1807) was printed by Jewitt soon after the *Lydia* returned to Boston, via China. Hartford merchant Richard Alsop overcame Jewitt's "small capacity as a narrator" by conducting interviews with Jewitt, using Daniel Defoe's *Robinson Crusoe* as his model for a ghostwritten version that referred to Jewitt as the lone survivor of the massacre in its title.

Jewitt was not the first white man to reside in British Columbia for more than a year. That distinction belongs to John MacKay, assistant "surgeon" on the fur trading brig *Captain Cook*, who reached Nootka Sound under Captain Strange in 1786. To learn the local language and gain an advantage in future trading, MacKay volunteered to remain as Maquinna's guest at Yuquot and Tahsis from the summer of 1786 to the autumn of 1787. MacKay's adventures remain little-known.

UBC Rare Books & Special Collections has a microfilm copy of Jewitt's original journal that was made by the Canadian Institute for Historical Microreproductions from an original held at the Provincial Archives of British Columbia. There are digital copies in the Google Books collection from sources uncredited.

For other authors with books pertaining to British Columbia published or written between 1800 and 1850, see abcbookworld entries for Banks, Charles A.; Barneby, William Henry; Belcher, Edward; Blanchet, Francis; Bowes, Gordon Emerson; Brink, Nicky L.; Burley, David; Burley, Edith I.; Corney, Peter; Cox, Ross; Cullen, Mary K.; Evans, Elwood; Fleurieu, Charles; Franchère, Gabriel; Gibson, James R.; Horetzky, Charles; Irving, Washington; Jessett, Thomas E.; Johnson-Dean, Christina B.; Langsdorff, George H. Von; Mofras, Eugene Duflot (de); Patterson, Samuel; Reynolds, Stephen; Ridley, William; Rodney, William; Roquefeuil, Camille (de); Ross, Alexander; Wallace, J.N. (James Nevin); Wilkes, Charles; Woollen, William Watson.

DANIEL HARMON

A Journal of Voyages and Travels in the Interiour of North America
(1820) by Daniel Harmon

Of the men who established 50 trading forts west of Alberta prior to 1850, next to David Thompson, whose remarkable life was transcontinental in scope, the best writer of that "Scottish Columbia" era was Daniel Harmon, whose lucid journals of New Caledonia still make for palatable reading. The Harmon family monument in Mount Royal Cemetery in Montreal can be found near the grave of David Thompson. Both men were unprejudiced and discerning humanists who remained faithful to their Métis "country wives."

Born in 1778, the fourth son of a tavern-keeper in Vermont, Harmon was a Bible reader who married fourteen-year-old Lisette in 1805. She was the daughter of a French-Canadian voyageur and a "Snare" (Snake Indian) woman. Lisette would bear him fourteen children, bury all but two, and remain at Harmon's side until the end of his days.

After several years in the Athabasca district, the Harmons were relocated to New Caledonia (the "Siberia of the fur trade" in northern B.C.), where they mainly lived at Fort St. James and Fort Fraser from 1810 to 1819.

Craving serious conversation about religion and literature, Harmon was nicknamed "the priest" by his peers. In 1813, while stationed at Stuart Lake, he wrote: "Few of us are employed more, and many of us much less, than one fifth of our time, in transacting the business of the Company. The remaining four-fifths are at our own disposal. If we do not, with such an opportunity, improve our understandings, the fault must be our own; for there are few posts which are not tolerably well supplied with books. These books are not, indeed, all of the best kind; but among them are many which are valuable. If I were deprived of these silent companions, many a gloomy hour would pass over me. Even with them, my spirit at times sinks, when I reflect on the great length of time which has elapsed, since I left the land of my nativity, and my relatives and friends, to dwell in this savage country."

In 1819, Harmon decided to forsake New Caledonia, but not his Métis wife. He wrote: "We have wept together over the departure of several children. . . . We have children still living who are equally dear to both of us. How could I spend my days in the civilized world and leave my beloved children in the wilderness? How could I tear them from a mother's love and leave her to mourn over their absence to the day of her death? How could I think of her in such circumstances without anguish?"

When the Harmons reached Fort William in 1819, they were married in a Christian ceremony at the North West Company headquarters. Five days later, Lisette gave birth to another son, John. Two days after this birth, the family departed for Montreal.

The Harmons completed their 4,000-mile exodus from New Caledonia to Vermont, crossing most of the continent, in only 11 weeks. Later Daniel Harmon co-founded Harmonville (now called Coventry) in Vermont, where he served as a church deacon and set a penalty for drunkenness: the clearing of one stump. Thereafter the price for pulling out one stump was set at one pint of rum.

Daniel Harmon

In 2006, with support from the Friends of Fort St. James National Historic Site, Daniel Harmon's great-great-great-grandson, Graham Ross of Victoria, arranged for re-publication of Harmon's journal using a version edited by W.K. Lamb.

II
1850–1900

Artist's rendering of prospectors panning for gold from Matthew Macfie's
Vancouver Island and British Columbia *(1865).*

ALFRED WADDINGTON

The Fraser Mines Vindicated; or, the History of Four Months (1858)
by Alfred Waddington

U sually cited as B.C.'s first author (of a non-governmental book), Alfred Penderell Waddington came to Victoria in 1858, attracted by gold fever, at the relatively old age of 57. Even though his gold panning expertise was negligible, he hastily wrote *The Fraser Mines Vindicated; or, the History of Four Months* (1858) to affirm gold deposits were still plentiful in the lower Fraser River.

Waddington falsely boasted in his preface that his was "the first book published on Vancouver Island." In fact, David Cameron's *The Rules of Practice and the Forms to be used in the Superior and Inferior Courts of Civil Justice of Vancouver Island* was published a month earlier by the *Victoria Gazette*. Cameron would produce a similar guide to Supreme Court practices in 1865, published by the Vancouver Printing and Publishing Company.

Waddington is more widely remembered as a progressive politician and a disastrous land developer. It was his bold plan to build a faster route to the Cariboo goldfields, via Bute Inlet, south of Knight Inlet, that prompted the so-called Chilcotin War of 1864. In 1861, Waddington sent his surveyor Robert Homfray to Bute Inlet to examine the feasibility of a "gold road" or toll road from the mouth of the Klinaklini River, into the Homathko River Valley, and then on to Barkerville. Aboriginals were forewarned they would die of smallpox if they interfered. In response, eight members of the Tsilhqot'in (Chilcotin) First Nation attacked one of Waddington's work camps in the Homathko Canyon in 1864 and killed 14 members of the survey expedition. The overall death toll rose to 19 "white" men and four aboriginals by year's end.

Alfred Waddington is usually cited as B.C.'s first author.

Five Tsilhqot'in aboriginals were sentenced to death by Judge Matthew Begbie and hanged at Quesnellemouth. A sixth man was later hanged in New Westminster. The Chilcotin War, as it became known, remained a divisive racial issue in B.C. for more than a century. Eventually the province's NDP government formally apologized for territorial infringements of Waddington's men, as well as the procedural shortcomings of the trial and hangings.

Waddington's effort to open a new road to the Cariboo ruined him financially, but the highest peak entirely within provincial boundaries, Mount Waddington (13,260 ft.), located 300 kilometres north of Vancouver, is named in his honour.

Alfred Waddington was still lobbying for his Bute Inlet route to the Cariboo when he died at age 71—of smallpox—in Ottawa in 1872.

For related titles, see abcbookworld entries for E.S. Hewlett's *The Chilcotin Uprising: A Study of Indian-White Relations in Nineteen Century British Columbia* (1972), Mel Rothenburger's *The Chilcotin War* (1978), Terry Glavin's *Nemiah: The Unconquered Country* (1992), Judith Williams' *High Slack: Waddington's Gold Road and the Bute Inlet Massacre of 1864* (1996) and Rich Mole's *The Chilcotin War: A Tale of Death and Reprisal* (2009).

THOMAS N. HIBBEN

Originally from North Carolina, British Columbia's first noteworthy bookstore owner, Thomas Napier Hibben, started the venerable B.C. tradition of publishers who are credited as authors. Hibben first learned printing and bookselling in San Francisco. According to the memoirs of Edgar Fawcett, Hibben's business in Victoria was opened, as early as 1855, as Hibben & Carswell, in the Fardon Building, next to the Bank of British North America, the pioneer bank in the city. The first Masonic lodge of the Free-masons of Victoria was established above Hibben & Carswell's, on Yates Street, in 1860. Hibben's English-born partner, James Carswell, left for Toronto where he established the Carswell Company in 1864, still operational as Canada's pioneer law publishing house. (Hibben was not the province's first publisher. Waddington's *The Fraser Mines Vindicated* was printed in 1858 by Paul de Garro.)

Hibben has been credited as the author of *Dictionary of Indian Tongues, Containing Most of the Words and Terms Used in the Tshimpsean, Hydah, & Chinook, With Their Meaning or Equivalent in the English Language* (1862) and *A Dictionary of the Chinook Jargon* (1871). A copy of Hibben's rare *Dictionary of Indian Tongues* now sells for more than $3,000. Hibben's oft-reprinted *A Dictionary of the Chinook Jargon* was cribbed from a work published by George Gibbs in 1863. In addition, Hibben printed an uncredited 408-page volume called *Guide to the Province of British Columbia for 1877-8* (1877) containing advertisements and a Chinook dictionary.

The Chinook trading language (an amalgam of aboriginal, English and French terms) was used in trials in B.C., such as the prosecution of Chilcotin chiefs following the so-called Chilcotin War in 1864, as well as the prosecution of Tshuanahusset, who was charged with the 1868 murder of black Salt Spring Island pioneer William Robinson. It was officially used as late as 1913–1916 for the McKenna-McBride Commission. By 1962, the Summer Institute of Linguistics estimated that approximately 100 Chinook speakers remained in North America. By 1990, the language was considered nearly extinct.

Decades after Hibben's book, the Oblate missionary Jean-Marie Raphael Le Jeune, namesake for the lakeside resort community of Lac Le Jeune, became one of the foremost progenitors of Chinook jargon. Stationed at Kamloops and Williams Lake, he published *Chinook Rudiments* (1924) and a remarkable mimeographed Chinook newsletter, the *Kamloops Wawa*, which described itself as "the queerest newspaper in the world."

First published on May 2, 1891, the *Wawa* was "Indian news" printed in both the English alphabet and a bizarre form of short-

hand developed in 1867 by two French clerics, the Duploye brothers. As a result of the *Wawa*'s wide circulation, many Native and
non-Natives in the B.C. Interior became literate as Duployan readers. Le Jeune didn't realize Duployan shorthand could be transfer-
able to his followers until a cripple named Charley-Alexis Mayoos,
from the Lower Nicola, noticed some of Le Jeune's Duployan notes
and immediately grasped its fundamentals. He, in turn, began spreading the "phonography" to members of the Coldwater Indian band.
Le Jeune published his last issue of the *Kamloops Wawa* in September of 1904.

Other authors who produced Chinook guides include Gabriel Franchère (1810), John
Dunn (1844), Blanchet (1852), Alexander Caulfield Anderson (1858), William Carew
Hazlitt (1858), Theodore Winthrop (1862), Francis Norbert Blanchet (1852), George Gibbs
(1863), Duncan George Forbes Macdonald (1863), William F. Sturgis (1864), Granville
Stuart (1865), Christopher Knipe (1868), James Constantine Pilling (1868), Modeste
Demers (1871), Louis Napoleon St. Onge (1871), M. Stannard (1873), John Kaye Gill
(1878), Myron Eells (1878), John Booth Good (1880), Paul Durieu (1886), Jean-Marie
Raphael Le Jeune (1886), Thomas Wickham Prosch (1888), Charles Montgomery Tate
(1889), Horatio Hale (1890), James Constantine Pilling (1893), Franz Boas (1894), Alexander Alfred Boddy (1896), Alexander Ross (1904), Joel Palmer (1906), Frederick J. Long
(1909), George C. Shaw (1909) and Walter Shelley "Chinook" Phillips, a.k.a. El Commancho
(1913). For other authors pertaining to the Chinook language, see abcbookworld entries
for Glavin, Terry; Howay, F.W.; Jacobs, Melville; Lang, Georg; Lillard, Charles; Thomas, Edward
Harper; Verne, Ray; Walker, Alexander; Zimmerman, Heinrich.

RICHARD HENRY ALEXANDER

*The Diary and Narrative of Richard Henry Alexander in a Journey
Across the Rocky Mountains* (1973) by Richard Henry Alexander

When the Thomas McMicking expedition bound for the
Cariboo gold fields departed from Fort Garry at the outset
of June in 1862, it left behind various parties who would follow
thereafter. These individuals formed three contingents: a group
of 20 led by an American doctor named Symington, a minor group

of five people known as the Rennie party, and a larger group of 63 people ostensibly led by police sergeant Stephen Redgrave. According to Joanne Leduc, editor of McMicking's memoirs, republished as *Overland from Canada to British Columbia: By Mr. Thomas McMicking of Queenston, Canada West* (1981), the leader of the largest "after-party" was actually an American adventurer named Timolean Love and two "half-breed" guides. Included in this Redgrave/Love cavalcade were the artist William G.R. Hind and Richard Henry Alexander. The latter produced a diary that remained as a manuscript in the provincial archives until it was published in a limited edition of 500 copies as *The Diary and Narrative of Richard Henry Alexander In a Journey Across the Rocky Mountains* (1973).

Born in Edinburgh in 1844, Richard Henry Alexander, the son of a wine merchant, was brought to Toronto by his parents in 1855. To reach the Cariboo gold fields, Alexander and others believed they could save time by going directly overland and not using the Panama route or the Oregon Trail, but Alexander's diary and letters reveal he and his companions almost starved to death in order to complete their Alexander Mackenzie–like overland quest in mid-November of 1862.

Alexander's diary is significant as one of the earliest literary accounts of a migrant settler arriving overland to British Columbia. Millions have since followed Alexander to Lotusland to escape the harshness of winters in the other provinces, flying for a few hours instead of tramping through the wilderness for almost six months.

Upon his arrival in B.C., Alexander worked briefly for John Robson, editor of the *British Columbian*. He also mined briefly at Williams Creek, returned south to Victoria, and later took charge of the Hastings Mill Store, Vancouver's first retail outlet, opened in 1856. He began working there as an accountant and rose to the position of manager upon the death of Captain James Raymur. Located at the foot of present-day Dunlevy Street, the store also served as a meeting place and post office. It survived the great fire of 1886 and was moved to its present site at the foot of Alma Street in Kitsilano in 1930. Alexander also served as a justice of the peace and a member of the Granville school board. He ran for mayor of Vancouver in the first civic election of May 3, 1886, but his arrogance made voters choose a newcomer, Malcolm Alexander MacLean, a realtor who won by 17 votes. At the time Richard Henry Alexander was the biggest employer in Granville, as Vancouver was then known. He died in Seattle in 1915.

WALTER CHEADLE

The North-West Passage by Land (1865) by Walter Cheadle

From the 1860s to World War One, B.C. literature largely consisted of British travel memoirs reporting on exotic British Columbia. Few are readable today. One of the earliest and best of this genre was written by English physician Walter Butler Cheadle. He and companion William Fitzwilliam (Viscount Milton) have been dubbed Canada's first "transcontinental tourists." Three years earlier, Charles Edward Barrett-Lennard had published *Travels in British Columbia, With the Narrative of a Yacht Voyage Round Vancouver Island* (1862), but Cheadle was an "overlander" whose perspective was unusually unfettered by the need to cast himself as an expert.

Almost half of Cheadle's lively and literate two-year chronicle in *The North-West Passage by Land* (1865), later republished as *Cheadle's Journal of Trip Across Canada, 1862–1863*, describes adventures in B.C. From Edmonton, Cheadle and Fitzwilliam crossed the Rockies through the uncharted Yellowhead Pass, rafting the Thompson River to Kamloops. They then toured New Westminster, Victoria and the Cariboo. They were greatly assisted by their Assiniboine Métis guide, Louis Battenotte, who brought along his family. The journal concludes with events in California and at sea;

Walter Cheadle (centre) was one of the earliest "tourists" to write a book about B.C..

it reveals Cheadle as a shrewd observer of human nature, whether in the bush or the ballroom.

The North-West Passage by Land originally was falsely credited to Viscount Milton. By 1891 the book had run to nine printings. In its current edition, historian Stephen R. Bown claims, "It is a book that no lover of the west can ignore."

British Columbia has been the subject for comments and books by dozens of writers who have mostly revealed their ignorance in the process.

Rudyard Kipling was swindled when he bought some property in Vancouver, but he gave confident opinions on both Victoria and Vancouver as he passed through, claiming Canadians were far more law-abiding than Americans. Frances Macnab, the pseudonym of globe-trotting journalist Agnes Fraser, reached B.C. via the new rail line in 1897. Like Kipling, she warned against the influx of invading Americans in her 369-page *British Columbia for Settlers: Its Mines, Trade and Agriculture* (1898).

Without first-hand knowledge, Jules Verne wrote a cautionary Klondike gold rush novel, partially set in B.C., *Le Volcan d'or* (*The Golden Volcano*), unpublished until 1989.

For some other authors who were transient authorities on B.C., see abcbookworld entries for Adams, Emma; Adney, Tappan; Angelo, Charles Aubrey; Assher, Ben; Aubertin, John; Ballantyne, Robert Michael; Ballou, Maturin; Barneby, William Henry; Bates, Emily; Bealby, J.T.; Bell, Archie; Biggar, Emerson; Black, Jack; Blakiston, Thomas Wright; Boddam-Whetham, J.W.; Borel, Andre; Briggs, Horace; Brittain, Harry; Burall, W.T.; Burlet, Lucien de; Carmichael, Dean; Church, Herbert; Collis, Septima M.; Cornwallis, Kinahan; Croasdaile, Henry; DeGroot, Henry; Dufferin, Lady; Duncan, Sinclair; Eardley, Wilmot; Fleming, Sandford; Fraser, Esther; Friesach, Carl; Galloway, C.F.J.; Garner, Charles; Graham, Harry; Grant, George M.; Harrison, Carter; Hoagland, Edward; Holitscher, Arthur; Huleatt, Hugh; Jenkinson, Anthony; Johnson, R. Byron; Johnston, Lukin; Keith, Agnes Newton; Lees, James; Macfie, Matthew; McEvoy, Bernard; Outram, James; Roper, Edward; Stark, Freya; Sykes, Ella; Tanner, Henry; Warren, C. Henry; Wilby, Thomas W.

JAMES ANDERSON

Sawney's Letters; or Cariboo Rhymes from 1864–1868 (1868)
by James Anderson

The first poetry book printed in British Columbia was written by James Anderson, since dubbed the "Robert Service of the Cariboo gold rush."

Born in Perthshire, Scotland, in either 1838 or 1839, Anderson sought his fortune in the Cariboo in 1863, but he never struck it rich. Concurrent with his activities in the Cariboo Glee Club, Anderson issued a weekly newspaper with a friend that contained lyrical materials about the mining life. Much of his writing was ostensibly addressed to someone back in Scotland named Sawnee, or Sawney, explaining life in the gold fields, but it is not known whether such a person was real or an artistic contrivance. Read aloud in coffee saloons, Anderson's poetry contained references to the great Barkerville fire of 1868 and legendary characters such as Cariboo Cameron. James Anderson left the Cariboo in 1871 and returned to live on one of his father's properties in Fifeshire.

Anderson first published parts of his *Sawney's Letters* in the *Cariboo Sentinel* in 1865 and 1866. It was printed as a separate folder on June 22, 1868, known for archival purposes as *Sawney's Letters; or Cariboo Rhymes from 1864-1868*. No copy of this original 1868 version advertised in the *Cariboo Sentinel* has been found. A second edition printed in 1868 is worth approximately $2,500. A third, enlarged edition of Cameron's booklet appeared in 1869 under the title *Sawney's Letters and Cariboo Songs*. A fourth and larger edition at 49 pages was published in 1895 by W.S. Johnston & Company of Toronto. A mimeographed version of the 1868 version was printed in 1950 by the Bibliographical Society of Canada titled simply *Sawney's Letters* with an introduction by William Kaye Lamb. In 1960, Lamb and Michael R. Booth contributed the text for a new version of *Sawney's Letters, or Cariboo Rhymes* published in the *British Columbia Library Quarterly*. *Sawney's Letters and Cariboo Rhymes* was issued by the Barkerville Restoration Advisory Committee, printed in Victoria, in 1962, with an introduction by Willard E. Ireland.

It is possible James Anderson's work was originally printed on the first printing press brought into British Columbia, but this is a matter of some debate. Some believe the first B.C. printing press was originally sent to San Francisco from Paris by the Society for the Propagation of the Gospel, then sent to Victoria in 1858 to publish the *Vancouver Island Gazette* and a French newspaper that folded after two issues. Roman Catholic Bishop Demers then sold the press to Amor De Cosmos, who published the *British Colonist* with it. In 1863, De Cosmos sold it to George Wallace, who had it shipped to Williams Creek in pieces on the backs of men, before the Cariboo Wagon Road was built. He sold his operation after one year to Allan and Lambert. Robert Halloway became the next owner and operator in 1868, running the print shop in Barkerville until the great fire. Supposedly he moved it to Richfield. After the *Cariboo Sentinel* closed, the printing press was used in Kamloops and Yale for Interior papers. In 1887, the press went to the Sisters of St. Anne in Kamloops, who later placed it in the St. Ann's Academy Museum in Victoria.

GEORGE MERCER DAWSON

Scrupulously private and excessively modest, the hunchbacked bachelor poet and explorer George Mercer Dawson ought to be revered as a Canadian hero.

Born into a Scottish-Presbyterian family in Pictou, Nova Scotia, in 1849, Dawson suffered from Pott's Disease as a child and never grew larger than a ten-year-old. He suffered severe migraine headaches all his life but never complained and rarely made any mention of his spinal deformity. Despite his physical limitations, Dawson was capable of feats of endurance that intimidated larger men. He covered more territory than any other surveyor for the Geological Survey of Canada. He was also a superb geologist, a paleontologist, an ethnographer, a pioneer photographer, a botanist and an excellent descriptive writer.

Dawson discovered much of the coal reserves of B.C.; he was one of the three men primarily responsible for mapping the area that attracted the Klondike Gold Rush; and he published extensively about the Interior Salish, the Haida and the Kwakwaka'wakw of British Columbia. He also undertook the first extensive surveys of the Yukon and Peace River districts, drew attention to the Crow's Nest Pass region, explored the Shuswap, Kamloops, Okanagan and West Kettle valleys, and spent a year on the Bering Sea to co-author a pelagic sealing industry report with Sir George Baden-Powell that led to an international settlement of a dispute with the Russians. Dawson published vocabularies of the Haida, Kwakwaka'wakw, Yukon and Secwepemc. A linguist, he also pondered the similarities of the Carrier and Chilcotin languages and speculated that the original inhabitants of North America might have come from Asia.

Dawson was first employed in Canada as a geologist and bota-

George Mercer Dawson, B.C.'s most significant geologist

nist. He undertook the first survey of the Queen Charlotte Islands and took invaluable photographs of Haida totems in the 1870s. Amateur and professional anthropologists who later used cameras to record Aboriginal culture in British Columbia included Harlan I. Smith, Franz Boas, Charles Frederick Newcombe, Samuel Barrett, Albert Parker Niblack, George T. Emmons, Marius Barbeau and Edward Sheriff Curtis—but Dawson led the way.

Comrades were always amazed by George Dawson's stamina and zest for research. For example, setting out in May of 1887, he ascended the Stikine by canoe to Telegraph Creek, walked over the divide to Dease Lake, travelled down the Dease River to Lower Post, went up the Liard and Frances rivers to Frances Lake in the eastern Yukon, walked 70 miles overland to Pelly River, built a canvas canoe and then a wooden boat, ascended the Lewes River, reached and crossed the Chilkoot Pass, and returned to the coast in September—thereby completing a round-trip that encompassed 63,200 square miles of territory. George Mercer Dawson died in Ottawa, at age 52, in 1901. Dawson Creek, Dawson City and a school in Masset bear his name, but few realize he was a prolific author.

George Mercer Dawson's publications pertaining to B.C. include *On the Superficial Geology of British Columbia* (1878), *Report on the Queen Charlotte Islands, 1878* (1880), *Report on an Exploration from Port Simpson on the Pacific Coast, to Edmonton on the Saskatchewan, Embracing a Portion of the Northern Part of British Columbia and the Peace River Country, 1879* (1881), *Comparative Vocabularies of the Indian Tribes of British Columbia, co-written with William Fraser Tolmie* (1884), *Report on an Exploration in the Yukon District, N.W.T., and Adjacent Northern Portion of British Columbia* (1888), *Notes and Observations on the Kwakiool People of Vancouver Island* (1888), *Glaciations of British Columbia and Adjacent Regions* (1889), *On the Earlier Cretaceous Rocks of the Northwestern Portion of the Dominion of Canada* (1889), *On the Later Physiographical Geology of the Rocky Mountain Region in Canada, with Special Reference to Changes in Elevation and the History of the Glacial Period* (1890), *Notes on the Shuswap People of British Columbia* (1891). Douglas Cole and Bradley Lockner have edited his journals.

FRANZ BOAS

Franz Boas secured his reputation as the greatest pioneer anthropologist of British Columbia while making seven trips to gather research in B.C. from 1886 to 1890, then three more between 1914 and 1931.

Boas' career was triggered by a visit to Berlin in 1885 by Chief Tom Henry and nine members of his Bella Coola band, brought to Europe as performers by a young Norwegian, Bernard Fillip Jacobsen. This troupe of Nuxalk entertainers toured through Europe for a year, much to the delight of Boas, who spent as much time with the "dear Indians" as he could manage.

Originally a geographer, Boas had done field work for a year on Baffin Island in 1883–84, but the "severe sobriety" of the Inuit had failed to impress him. The artistry and the "wealth of thought" contained in the dances and masks of the Bella Coola performers, in contrast, immediately enchanted him. He visited their lodgings near the Reichstag, recording their songs and studying their language. He joined in their dances, almost stripping naked to do so.

With letters of introduction from George Mercer Dawson, Boas reached Victoria in 1886, hoping to finance his research trip by buying Native artifacts cheaply and selling them at a profit to German and American museums. After three weeks in Victoria, Boas took a steamer north to Alert Bay, returning by way of Quamichan, Comox and Nanaimo. En route, he saw potlatches, gathered stories and witnessed a shamanic healing. He paid $120 for his collectibles and eventually resold most of them for $600.

By 1888, Boas was back in B.C. taking physical measurements of aboriginals (often in jails), collecting skulls and sometimes stealing skeletons from graves. If required, he paid $20 for a skeleton and $5 for a skull.

By 1891, he was positioned to plan some of the ethnology displays for the 1893 Chicago World's Fair. Under the aegis of its Columbian Exhibit to honour the 400th anniversary of Columbus' supposed discovery of America, Boas' Pacific Northwest exhibition concentrated on the Fort Rupert Kwakwaka'wakw.

The first of Boas' numerous published works related to B.C., *Chinook Texts*, appeared in 1894.

As the first professor of anthropology at Columbia University, he became increasingly reliant on George Hunt and James Teit for research and artifacts—most notably the Whalers' Washing House from an island in Jewett's Lake, near Friendly Cove, that was secured, en masse, by Hunt in 1904.

Boas realized that the construction of railways would soon bring more collectors to western North America and felt great urgency to proceed with his groundbreaking work. He once boasted as an anthropologist, "No one here [in North America] has accomplished as much as I have."

And he was correct.

Born in Minden, Germany, in 1858, Franz Boas died in New York in 1942.

Douglas Cole of Simon Fraser University spent 17 years working on *Franz Boas: The Early Years, 1858–1906* (1999), the first biography to draw on a large collection of Boas family letters at the American Philosophical Society in Philadelphia. In the biography, Boas emerges as a likeable person, loyal to friends and devoted to his family, although he was sometimes overzealous in pursuit of his scientific goals. For a list of books by Franz Boas, many of which pertain to B.C., consult his entry at abcbookworld.

Franz Boas (above) relied on George Hunt and James Teit for research.

HUBERT HOWE BANCROFT

*The History of the Pacific States, Vol. XXVII British Columbia
1792–1887* (1887) by Hubert Howe Bancroft

Hubert Howe Bancroft of California can be viewed as the grandfather of B.C.'s historians, just as Oregonian fur trader John McLoughlin was the grandfather of B.C. politics by tutoring James Douglas. Bancroft stands tall as the most remarkable historian, publisher and book collector on the Pacific Coast.

Bancroft was a co-author of the first full-fledged history of British Columbia, which his biographer claims was written mainly by Bancroft. Various factbooks, guidebooks and travelogues about B.C. had appeared prior to Bancroft's history but these were mainly attempts to take advantage of curiosity abroad. At 792 pages, *The History of the Pacific States, Vol. XXVII British Columbia 1792–1887* [credited to Bancroft, Amos Bowman Nemos and Alfred Bates] (1887) was published in San Francisco by Bancroft's History Company as part of a series intended to establish his intellectual domain over most of western North America. It was preceded by a two-volume *History of the Northwest Coast* that had examined events up to 1846.

Bancroft and his wife visited Victoria in 1878 to begin research for the project, gaining access to Hudson's Bay Company (HBC) accounts and government records, as well as the private papers of James Douglas, Simon Fraser, John Stuart and other fur traders. They also interviewed HBC stalwarts such as John Tod, Roderick Finlayson and A.C. Anderson, but took care to also incorporate the viewpoints of Amor De Cosmos, Gilbert Sproat, Edward Cridge and John Good.

Bancroft summarized the significance of North West Company

Hubert Howe Bancroft

and HBC forts west of the Rockies as "depots of compressed power."

Having arrived from Ohio in 1852, Bancroft opened a book and stationery shop in San Francisco in 1856. It became the largest store of its kind west of Chicago. This bookstore served as the catalyst for a publishing program that would net Bancroft more than one million dollars in subscription-based sales of his historical works. By selling subscriptions to his readers, Bancroft compiled a comprehensive 39-volume history of Western America, writing four of the weighty tomes himself. Of the hundreds of men employed in Bancroft's "history factory" only about a dozen did the actual writing. Bancroft organized the research, accumulating knowledge, not always scrupulously, but omnivorously.

As a bookseller, Bancroft specialized in books about the Pacific area from Alaska to Patagonia, gathering a library of 60,000 volumes that was moved to the University of California in 1905. This California-centred library became the main resource for research into western American history. As Bancroft's biographer wrote in 1946, "In the historiography of western America, no name is writ larger than Hubert Howe Bancroft's." He was also one of the first intellectuals to characterize the West Coast of North America as its own psychological and sociological region, a zone where, he prophesied, one could witness a "worn-out world re-animated." Of the approximately 30 efforts to follow in Bancroft's large footsteps, currently the most-used is Jean Barman's *The West Beyond the West: A History of British Columbia* (1991).

For other authors who have written histories of B.C, see abcbookworld entries for Akrigg, George Philip Vernon; Anderson, Alexander Caulfield; Angus, H.F.; Anstey, Arthur; Begg, Alexander; Bennett, William; Boam, Henry J.; Bowering, George; Brown, Ashley; DeGroot, Henry; Denton, V.L.; Fladmark, Knut; Goodchild, Fred H.; Gosnell, R.E.; Gough, John; Griffin, Harold; Hibben, T.N.; Hocking, Anthony; Howay, F.W.; Johnston, Hugh; Lane, Myrtle E.; Lawson, Maria; Macfie, Matthew; McKelvie, B.A.; Molyneux, Geoffrey; Morice, Adrien Gabriel; Nuffield, Edward; Odlum, Edward Faraday; Ormsby, Margaret Anchoretta; Robin, Martin; Roy, Patricia; Sage, W.N.; Scholefield, E.O.S.; Stephen, Pamela; Tod, John; Woodcock, George.

British Columbia's first novelist Morley Roberts remains unheralded.

MORLEY ROBERTS

Morley Roberts wrote the first B.C. novel of outstanding liter-ary merit, *The Prey of the Strongest* (1906), as well as the first B.C., a potboiler called *The Mate of the Vancouver* (1892). Despite having written more than 80 books, Roberts is only rarely cited in B.C. literary history for his travelogue of his ramblings in western North America during 1884–1885, *The Western Avernus: Toil and Travel in Further North America* (1887). About half of this highly readable account concerns B.C. It kindled the imagination of a young banking apprentice in Glasgow, Scotland, named Robert Service, who, after reading *The Western Avernus,* quit his job and came to Vancouver Island.

Roberts was attracted to B.C. as "almost the farthest place from anywhere in the world," but he subsequently observed, "Men wander to and fro like damned souls or migratory salmon or caribou." Having arrived in New Westminster with 25 cents in his pocket, he took a job in the Dominion sawmill, working from 6 a.m. to 6 p.m. for thirty dollars a month, plus board. He was discharged from the mill in April of 1885 following a fist fight at dinner with a Chinese waiter. He set off for Kamloops, taking with him Virgil, Horace, Coleridge and Keats as companions. A second altercation with a different "Mongolian" in New Westminster forced a hasty exit via Victoria.

Back in England, Roberts conducted an affair with a married woman, Alice Selous, whom he eventually married in 1893. A year later he visited Robert Louis Stevenson in the South Pacific. He also published a fictionalized biography of his lifelong friend, George Gissing, *The Private Life of Henry Maitland* (1912), and a study of another literary friend, *W.H. Hudson: A Portrait* (1924). Morley Roberts returned to B.C. for a second visit in 1926, described in *On the Old Trail* (1927), in which he looks askance at B.C.'s attempts at social progress. In his later years, Roberts turned increasingly towards pathology and sociology, enquiring into the nature and causes of cancer.

Charles Lillard once described *The Prey of the Strongest* (1906) as "our first accurate portrayal of life in the mills, in the woods and gambling halls; as well it is our first novel to honestly place the Indian and Oriental within B.C.'s labouring-class society." Certainly it provides a rare, authentic account of working class life in late 19th-century B.C. based on Roberts' sophisticated perceptions and his "school-of-hard-knocks" experiences.

Almost two-thirds of Roberts' melodramatic earlier novel, *The Mate of the Vancouver* (1892), is set in B.C. Thomas Ticehurst, a semi-reluctant sailor, sails from England on the *Vancouver* in 1881 to accompany his brother to the West Coast. He falls in love with a passenger named Elsie, is rejected by her and is stabbed in San Francisco by a villain named Matthias. Matthias goes to jail but vows revenge. Ticehurst recovers and follows Elsie northward. Ticehurst vanquishes Matthias and marries Elsie in Thomson Forks (ie. Kamloops).

Here is Roberts' description of the Dominion sawmill in 1885, likened to an orchestra: "The whole Mill was a tuned instrument, a huge sounding board. There was no discord, for any discord played its part, it was one organic harmony, pleasing, fatiguing, satisfying; any dropped note was missed: if the Lath Mill stayed in silence, something was wanting, when the Shingler said nothing, the last fine addition to the music fell away. And yet the one harmony of the Mill was a background for the soloes of the Saws, for the great diapason of the Hoes, for the swifter speech of the Pony, for the sharp cross notes of the Trimmers. The saws sang according to the log, to its nature, to its growth: either for the butt or the cleaner wood." Born in London in 1857, Morley Roberts died there in 1942. He published almost 100 books, some of which are available via the internet, including *The Western Avernus*.

MARGARET MCNAUGHTON

Overland to the Cariboo: An Eventful Journey of Canadian Pioneers to the Gold-Fields of British Columbia in 1862 (1896), by Margaret McNaughton

The first female author of B.C. was Lily Alice Lefevre (neé Cooke) whose 95-page collection of poetry *The Lions' Gate and Other Verses* (1895) was printed in Victoria. Margaret McNaughton's (neé Peebles) historical narrative *Overland to the Cariboo: An Eventful Journey of Canadian Pioneers to the Gold-Fields of British Columbia in 1862* (1896) was the first significant non-fiction book by a B.C. woman. It summarizes the unprecedented journey of Thomas McMicking and his approximately 150 companions in a caravan from Fort Garry (later called Winnipeg) to the gold-fields of British Columbia. Thousands of gold seekers reached the Cariboo goldfields by sea; only a few hundred risked travelling by land from eastern Canada.

Among the overlanders was Archibald McNaughton, from Montreal, who became Margaret McNaughton's husband. Her concise account is not eyewitness reportage. Augmented by details provided by her husband, the text followed a serialized narrative that McMicking published in 14 instalments in the *British Columbian* from November 29, 1862, to January 23rd, 1863, after Archibald McMicking had befriended John Robson, editor of the *British Columbian*, in New Westminster. McMicking drowned in the Fraser River in 1886 during an unsuccessful attempt to save his six-year-old son.

The main party of gold seekers departed on July 5th from Long Lake, just west of Fort Garry, and reached Fort Edmonton on July 21st. McMicking's caravan consisted entirely of men with the exception of Irish-born Catherine Schubert, who travelled in a horse and buggy with her German-born husband Augustus Schubert and their three children. McMicking crossed the Rockies via the Yellowhead Pass to reach the upper Fraser River and Tête Jaune Cache where a band of Secwepemcs saved them from starvation. McMicking later wrote, "We found the red men of the prairies to be our best friends." A splinter group proceeded via the North Thompson River, where two travellers drowned. Assisted by a First Nations midwife, Catherine Schubert gave birth to her fourth child, Rose, the first "white girl" born in the B.C. Interior, at Thompson's River Post (later called Kamloops) in October. Everyone arrived too late for the gold rush, and few of the adventurers ever staked a claim.

Margaret McNaughton, the second female author in British Columbia

McNaughton's account of the five-and-a-half-month expedition across a *terra incognita* is even-handed like a ship's log: "The average rate of speed was two-and-a-half miles an hour and ten hours' was accomplished each time." These were God-fearing, courageous people who ventured into a vast unknown where "they had bound themselves to rest on the Sabbath, and the rule was scrupulously observed." Along the way, McNaughton does provide a few deft sentences as a storyteller: "The mosquitoes swarmed in myriads, causing both man and beast the utmost torture." McNaughton's version of events was republished in 1973 as one of the early titles from J.J. Douglas Ltd., a company that would grow into Douglas & McIntyre, Western Canada's largest publishing company.

Female travellers who produced published descriptions of British Columbia prior to books by McNaughton and Lefevre include M. Stannard (1873), Caroline C. Leighton (1884), Eliza Ruhamah Scidmore (1885), Emily Katharine Bates (1887), Ellen Elizabeth Spragge (1887), Emma Hildreth Adama (1888), Emily Katharine Bates (1889), Abby Woodman (1889), Mrs. Algernon St. Maur (1890), Lady Dufferin (1891), Emily Headland (1891) and Lady Aberdeen (1893).

CLIVE PHILLIPPS-WOLLEY

With Kiplingesque bravado, Sir Clive Phillipps-Wolley was a great white hunter who epitomizes an era of British Columbian literature that portrayed B.C. as a rough Eden that only required English pluck and perseverance to be tamed.

Born Edward Clive Oldnall Long Phillips in 1853 in Dorset, England, Phillipps-Wolley was a distant relative of Lord Robert Clive, knighted for his military and administrative roles during the subjugation of Bengal in the 18th century. As Phillips, he successfully petitioned for the inheritance of his great-grandfather's estate, dropped the first name Edward in favour of Clive, changed his last name to Phillipps-Wolley, took up the study of law, married 16-year-old Janie Fenwick, taught musketry and then managed to

Clive Phillipps-Wolley, the only B.C. author ever to be knighted, is buried in Duncan on Vancouver Island.

practise law for less than a year. In 1881, he published *Sport in the Crimea and Caucasus,* based on his time hunting in Russia. *Trottings of a Tenderfoot: A Visit to the Columbian Fiords* (1888) is mostly about his two-month hunting trip to B.C., mainly on Vancouver Island. "I came across no place in America in which I would be so content to stay as in Victoria," he wrote. He returned in 1886 on a game hunting expedition, described in *A Sportsman's Eden* (1888), after which he settled in Victoria in 1890. "You could not pay me to come back to the old country," he said in an interview with the *London Mining Journal.*

Phillipps-Wolley followed his hastily written novel about a remittance man on Vancouver Island, *One of the Broken Brigade* (1897), with *The Chicamon Stone* (1900), a novel that includes a heroic Tahltan named Siyah Joe who knows the secret location of gold on McDame Creek. (Chicamon means gold.)

Phillipps-Wolley had some commercial success with *Gold, Gold in Cariboo!* (1894), a young adult novel, set in 1862, warning against the folly of gold fever, and proved himself popular as a public speaker, although he repeatedly failed in his attempts to gain election as a politician.

As a provincial sanitary inspector, he described Nelson as a disaster area and criticized B.C.'s Chinese as living cheaply in unsanitary conditions to compete in the labour market. "Wherever I have been in British Columbia I have found Chinamen living like sewer rats, a grave danger to white men's health." He concluded, "Nanaimo Chinatown can be cured in only one way—by fire." He equally despised Americans. "Canada's danger is a moral, not a physical one," he decreed. "If you should allow your newspapers to draw their news, as they copy their style, from the Yankees, annexation will soon follow."

Warning of an expanding German navy, Phillipps-Wolley began

urging Canada to build warships for England in 1908. At his own expense, he published a pamphlet containing his speeches, entitled *The Canadian Naval Question*. Phillipps-Wolley's son Clive Jr. was killed as a young soldier in 1914, days after England declared war on Germany. Phillipps-Wolley was knighted in 1915. Two years later he dedicated the poems in *Songs from a Young Man's Land* to his dead son.

Phillipps-Wolley died of a cerebral hemorrhage in 1918 and was buried in the St. Peter's Anglican Church cemetery in Duncan.

JULIA HENSHAW

British Columbia's first female novelist was an extraordinary outdoorswoman, naturalist and high society figure who published her first novel, *Hypnotized* (1898), under the pen of Julian Durham, adding one letter to her given name Julia and adopting the name of the town where she was born. Julia Henshaw also published newspaper columns under the pseudonym G'wan and worked as a literary and theatre critic for the *Vancouver Province*.

Born in Durham, England, in 1869, Julia Wilmotte Henderson married Charles Grant Henshaw, a well-connected investment broker, and they arrived in Vancouver in the late 1880s. She claimed they reached the source of the Columbia River in 1896 and became the first couple to drive a motor car across the Rocky Mountains in 1914. Whether or not this is true, it is certain that Henshaw had an audacious spirit.

While visiting Field, B.C., Henshaw availed herself of the knowledge gathered by botanist Charles Schaffer and his wife Mary Schaffer Warren to publish *Mountain Wildflowers of America* in 1906, essentially co-opting the Schaffers' work. Henshaw wrote two more books on wildflowers and took credit for the discovery of the pink lady's slipper, or *Cypripedium acuale*. She has also been credited

Julia Henshaw, B.C.'s first female novelist

with co-founding the Georgian Club, the first women's social club in Vancouver.

Hypnotized: Or the Experiment of Sir Hugh Galbraith; A Romance (1898) was published from Ontario and dubbed by one critic as the "Canadian book of the year." Possibly Henshaw's status as a high society wife had something to do with the praise it received. Canadian literary critic Lawrence J. Burpee described the work as "a study of what may be called unconscious hypnotism," but suggested Mrs. Henshaw could do better.

Henshaw's follow-up novel, *Why Not, Sweetheart?* (1901), opens at the provincial asylum for the insane, overlooking the Fraser River. A Dr. Dufft of the Mind Ease Asylum mentions a hereditarily insane Englishman, Christopher Sabel, to a visiting sportsman named Jack Maclyn.

The sportsman Maclyn proceeds to fall in love with the roommate of a progressive and caustic journalist named Agnes Arbuckle. Her shy roommate named Naomi has a jealous guardian named Professor Cyr who declares himself to be Naomi's fiancé.

Eventually madman Sabel and the evil professor struggle and drown together in a river in the B.C. interior. Naomi is free to explain to Maclyn that she went to the altar with Sabel when she was 17 but he went insane during the ceremony, leaving her half-married to him. Agnes marries a politician; Maclyn marries Naomi. All's well that ends well.

Henshaw cannot easily be dismissed as a mere dabbler in the arts. She reputedly mapped the interior of Vancouver Island in 1910–1911 and accompanied the Swiss guide Edward Feuz to the summit of Asulkan Pass, at 7,716 feet, in 1910.

In 1914, when Charles Henshaw was a recruiting officer in Vancouver's Victory Square, Julia Henshaw went overseas to work with an ambulance and food unit. For helping to evacuate several towns under enemy fire, she was awarded the Croix de Guerre with a gold star. The French government later presented her with an enormous painting of Napoleon.

Having lived on Robson Street in Vancouver's West End, she moved to Caulfeild in West Vancouver where she died in 1937.

JAMES TEIT

When Franz Boas met James Teit in the summer of 1894, he hired him immediately. "The young man, James Teit, is a treasure!" he wrote. Educated in Scotland until only age 16, Teit nonetheless became fluent in several First Nations languages. In addition, he spoke some German, Dutch, French and Spanish. This fluency enabled Teit to become the first literate activist for aboriginal rights in B.C.

The chiefs of British Columbia referred to Teit as their "hand." When Prime Minister Wilfrid Laurier visited Kamloops in 1910, it was James Teit who prepared the official response on behalf of the Secwepemc, Okanagan and Nlaka'pamux nations, delivered by Chief Louis of Kamloops, to assert rights to their traditional lands. Teit also accompanied the delegation of 96 chiefs from 60 B.C. bands who met with Premier Richard McBride and his cabinet in Victoria in 1911. In 1912, he went to Ottawa with nine chiefs to meet with newly elected Conservative Prime Minister Robert Borden, during which time Teit translated the four speeches made by John Chilahitsa (Okanagan), Basil David (Secwepemc), John Tedlenitsa (Nlaka'pamux) and James Raitasket (Sta'atl'imx). Teit delivered a statement to Borden for the delegation: "We find ourselves practically landless, and that in our own country, through no fault of ours, we have reached a critical point, and, unless justice comes to the rescue, we must go back and sink out of sight as a race." He returned to Ottawa with eight chiefs in 1916.

When the 1912–1916 Royal Commission issued its report on aboriginal grievances, the Allied Tribes opposed it, and again it was James Teit who replied on their behalf, "The Indians see nothing of value to them in the work of the Royal Commission. Their crying needs have not been met." In 1917, Teit and Reverend

Peter Kelly sent a telegram to Borden to oppose conscription for aboriginal men, likening it to enslavement, because the land question remained unresolved and aboriginals were being denied their basic rights as citizens. At Teit's urging, an order-in-council was passed on January 17, 1918, to exempt aboriginals from conscription. Teit and Kelly also published a 6,000-word pamphlet to formally reject the McKenna-McBride report on behalf of the Allied Indian Tribes of British Columbia, an organization Teit co-founded. In 1920, he circulated a document in Ottawa to members of parliament entitled *A Half-Century of Injustice toward the Indians of British Columbia.*

A self-taught botanist, Teit also worked as an entomologist, a

photographer and an anthropologist who published 2,200 pages of ethnological material and also produced almost 5,000 pages of unpublished manuscript material (according to University of Victoria historian Wendy Wickwire in the *Canadian Historical Review*, Vol. 79, No. 2, 1998). His first of eleven significant anthropological publications was *Traditions of the Thompson River Indians of British Columbia* (1898). The owner of a wax cylinder recording machine, Teit also recorded local singers and identified them with catalogued photographs.

Linguist and anthropologist James Teit, seen here with his first wife, Antko, served tirelessly as B.C.'s first influential exponent of First Nations political rights, writing articulate and passionate appeals.

Born on the Shetland Islands, Scotland, in 1864, Teit immigrated to Spences Bridge in the Fraser Canyon in 1884 to help manage a store on the estate owned by his uncle, John Murray, at which time Teit reverted to the Norse spelling of his surname, Tate. He married a member of the Nlaka'pamux nation, Susanna Lucy Antko, with whom he lived happily for twelve years until her death in 1899. After Teit remarried in 1904, his six children received Scandinavian names. It is seldom noted that Teit became a member of the Socialist Party of Canada, reading socialist books by American and German authors as early as 1902. James Teit died in 1922, in Merritt.

"Unlike [Franz] Boas," Wickwire writes, "who viewed Native peoples as remnants of the past—academic subjects of study or anthropological 'informants' through whom he could reconstruct an image of the pre-contact past—Teit viewed Native peoples as his contemporaries—friends, relatives, and neighbours who lived a lifestyle similar to his own."

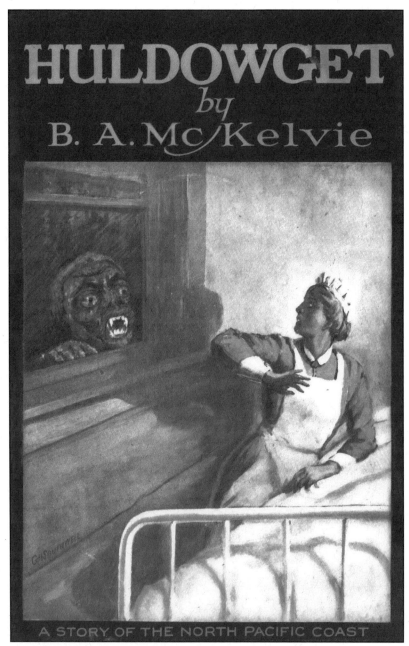

Cover art for B. A. McKelvie's Huldowget: A Story of the North Pacific Coast *(1926)*

III
1900–1950

MARTHA DOUGLAS HARRIS

History and Folklore of the Cowichan Indians (1901)
by Martha Douglas Harris

The youngest daughter of Sir James Douglas, the most pow-
erful man in British Columbia for almost two decades, Martha
Douglas Harris became the first female author to be born in B.C.
As a storyteller, she was greatly influenced by her half-Cree mother,
Lady Amelia Douglas, from whom she inherited a respect for abo-
riginal legends.

Out of deference to her parents' sensitivities about their mixed-
race backgrounds, Harris waited until both her parents had died
before adapting six of her mother's Cree stories and 14 Cowichan
stories for *History and Folklore of the Cowichan Indians* (1901), the
first collection of aboriginal stories to be commercially published
from B.C.

Harris stated she compiled the 20 stories to protect and recall
the "native dignity and wholesome life" of the Cowichan band on
Vancouver Island. This collection predated Pauline Johnson's better-known *Legends of Vancouver* by ten years.

Martha Harris's affinity for aboriginal culture was not merely
sentimental. Harris maintained friendships with families living on
the Songhees Reserve, and her collection of aboriginal basketry is
now housed at the Royal British Columbia Museum. In response
to the relocation of the Songhees people to Esquimalt, following
the government acquisition of the valuable Songhees Reserve lands,
Harris openly expressed her dismay and consternation in a letter
to the editor of the *Daily Colonist* in 1912.

Born in 1854, three years after her father became Governor of
the Colony of Vancouver Island, Martha Douglas married colonial

Accomplished at arts and crafts, Martha Douglas Harris became one of B.C.'s first transcribers of First Nations stories for literary purposes. Her book appeared in 1901.

official Dennis Reginald Harris during a lavish wedding in 1878. As a member of the Vancouver Island Arts and Crafts Society, she exhibited her still lifes and portraits as a "paintress." Also a wood-carver and lacemaker, she co-founded the Lace Club of Victoria in 1919. Other charter members of the club included Emily Carr and photographer Hannah Maynard. To promote hand spinning with B.C. wool, Harris taught other women how to weave and encouraged the local production of spinning wheels in Victoria. Her own spinning wheel was donated to Helmcken House in the 1930s.

Harris learned to apply native plant dyes to wool acquired from sheep breeders in Summerland, Chilliwack and on Vancouver Island, leading to the formation of the Women's Institute Weavers' Guild, later known as the Victoria Handweavers' and Spinners' Guild. She also laid the groundwork for the Island Weavers Plant, a commercial undertaking created by Enid Murray at Esquimalt in 1933, the same year that Harris died.

A.G. MORICE

The History of the Northern Interior of British Columbia, Formerly New Caledonia, 1660–1880 (1904) by A.G. Morice

Brilliant and often described as egotistical, Father Adrien-Gabriel Morice is second only to William Duncan as the most remarkable missionary in B.C. history. In the early 1900s, he established a printing operation from a cabin behind his church at Fort St. James, communicating with the outside world via the post office at Quesnel. Morice produced a collection of his essays, printed in British Columbia by his own Stuart Lake Mission Press, in 1902. Hence an argument can be made that British Columbia's first truly independent publishing house was at Fort St. James and Morice was B.C.'s first self-publisher.

Born in France in 1859, Morice was inspired by Father Émile Petitot to join the Oblates of Mary Immaculate in 1879. His best-known work in English, *The History of the Northern Interior of British Columbia, Formerly New Caledonia, 1660–1880* (1904), is the classic history of the trading area known as New Caledonia. Morice's history comprises oral accounts and makes clear how alcohol was deliberately introduced by the fur trade to weaken the resistance of aboriginals. The preface confidently states, "The record of these times has never been written, not to say published, and the only author who has ever touched on some of the events with which we will soon entertain the reader, Hubert Howe Bancroft, is so irretrievably inaccurate in his remarks that his treatment of the same might be considered well-nigh worthless."

Morice arrived in B.C. in 1880, and began to learn both Chilcotin and Carrier languages at St. Joseph's School in Williams Lake. Ordained in 1882, he was reprimanded for rebelliousness and sent to Fort St. James as punishment in 1885. He was thrilled. For ten years Morice worked with the Carrier First Nation and invented a syllabic script for the Dene language. With his health shattered, Morice was sent in 1904 to New Westminster. After four years of recuperation, Morice moved to St. Boniface, Manitoba, where he spent the rest of his life as a scholar and writer, publishing a history of Catholicism in Western Canada but estranged from church authorities. He published an autobiography, *First Years in Western Canada* (1930), and his two-volume *The Carrier Language: A Grammar and Dictionary* (1932). Morice died in 1938. Moricetown on the Bulkley River is named in his honour, as well as Morice Lake, Morice River and the Morice Range. David Mulhall has written a biography, *Will to Power: The Missionary Career of Father Morice* (1986).

For other literary works associated with missionaries, see abcbookworld entries for Andersen, Doris; Annett, Kevin Daniel; Arctander, John William; Bagshaw, Roberta; Beaver, Herbert; Bischoff, William Norbert; Blackburn, Carole; Blanchet, Francis; Boddy, Alexander Alfred; Bolduc, Jean-Baptiste; Bolt, Clarence Ralph; Bolton, Herbert E.; Brabant, Augustin Joseph; Brown, R.C. Lundin; Brown, Robert C.L.; Burnham, Lem; Burridge, Kenelm; Christophers, Brett; Coccola, Nicolas; Collison, William; Craven, Margaret; Crespi, Juan; Cronin, Kay; Crosby, Emma; Crosby, Thomas; Davis, George T.B.; De Coccola, Raymond; Demers, Modeste; Down, Sister Mary; Duchaussois, Reverend P.; Dunlop, Herbert Francis; Durieu, Paul; Furtwangler,

Albert; Garraghan, Gilbert Joseph; Garrioch, A.C.; Good, John Booth; Gould, S.; Gowen, Hubert H.; Grant, James; Hadley, Michael; Haicks, Charles; Hall, Alfred; Harrison, Charles; Hasell, F.H. Eva; Hills, George; Huel, R.; Jackson, Sheldon; James, George; Jennings, Dennis; Johnson, M.E.; Jujut, Abbe; Keenleyside, Vi; Keller, W. Phillip; Kelm, Mary-Ellen; Knipe, Christopher; Lamirande, Emilien; Large, Richard Geddes; Lascelles, Thomas A.; Laveille, E.; Le Jeune, Jean-Marie; Lillard, Charles; Maes, Yvonne; Margaret, Helene; McCullagh, James B.; McKellar, Hugh; McKervill, Hugh; McNally, Vincent J.; Mercier, Anne; Moeran, J.W.W.; Morley, Alan; Morris, Wilfred H.; Morton, W.L.; Moser, Reverend Chas; Mulhall, David; Munro, John; Neylan, Susan; Pandosy, Father; Patterson, E. Palmer II; Pena, Tomas de la; Pierce, William H.; Prang, Margaret; Raley, G.H.; Scott, Robert; Sheepshanks, John; Sinclair, James; Smet, Pierre-Jean De; Solverson, Howard; St. Onge, Louis Napoleon; Stackhouse, Cyril; Steckler, Gerard; Stock, Eugene; Stursberg, Peter; Tomlinson, Robert; Usher, Jean; Van Der Heyden, Joseph; Ward, N. Lascelles; Weir, Joan Sherman; Wellcome, Henry; Whitehead, Margaret; Williams, Cyril E.H.

M.A. GRAINGER

Woodsmen of the West (1908) by M.A. Grainger

The classic work of early B.C. logging literature is M.A. Grainger's only novel *Woodsmen of the West* (1908). Its narrator describes working in a logging camp in Coola Inlet that is operated by a jack-of-all-trades from Nova Scotia named Carter. A co-worker named Bill Allen admires Carter as "a black figure of activity" who succeeds with his "desperate drive-her-under pigheadedness." The narrator is an aloof observer of the action who nonetheless conveys admiration for the remarkable terrain and the industry of man. The story and setting are derived from Grainger's own experiences at Knight Inlet.

Born in London in 1874, Martin Allerdale Grainger grew up in Australia, won a scholarship to Cambridge, excelled at mathematics, graduated in 1896, set out for the Klondike, became stranded in B.C.'s Cassiar region, worked as a backpacker for the Hudson's Bay Company, looked after horses in order to gain his passage to South Africa, enlisted in Lord Roberts' Horse to fight in the Boer

War and then returned to B.C. He also worked as a placer miner around Atlin and Dease Lake, then as a logger in the Minstrel Island area.

Grainger met Mabel Higgs, the sister of his closest friend, on one of the Gulf Islands. After she returned to England, he followed and proposed. *Woodsmen of the West* earned him the $300 he needed to finance his steerage passage, and his wife's first-class passage, back to Canada.

Having served as secretary on a Royal Commission in 1910 to investigate logging practices, Grainger was the main author of the Forest Act of 1912, the basis for B.C.'s forestry policies. He also helped H.R. Macmillan gain the position of Chief Forester. Grainger himself became Acting Chief Forester and was named Chief Forester in 1917.

From 1920 onwards, Grainger worked in the private sector, forming the Timberland Investigation and Management Company in 1922 with Aird Flavelle and Frank Pendleton. It became M.A. Grainger Co. Ltd., headquartered in Vancouver's Metropolitan Building.

Never a slave to convention, Grainger had his secretary draw an outline of the sole of his foot on a piece of paper each year and then had the diagram dispatched to an Indian village to have three pairs of moccasins made. When Grainger was introduced to King George V in 1920, he wore his moccasins.

Grainger travelled extensively in the wilderness northeast of Hope, writing in a cabin he built near Princeton and lobbying for the creation of a wilderness preserve.

Although the Hope-Princeton Highway was not completed until 1949, Manning Park was created, as he hoped, in June of 1941, four months before Grainger died.

Roderick Haig-Brown and Bertrand Sinclair have also written novels that portray life in the logging camps, as does Bus Griffiths' one-of-a-kind *Now You're Logging* (1978), a graphic novel about two young men learning truck-logging during the Dirty Thirties. The "logger-poet" Peter Trower has also written many fine poems and three novels featuring loggers and logging, following in the footsteps of Robert Swanson. For more logging fiction, see abcbookworld entries for Cushman, Dan; Fairlie, Jock; Godwin, George; Goodchild, George; Ostos, Quoron; Roberts, Morley.

AGNES DEANS CAMERON

The New North: Being Some Account of a Woman's Journey Through Canada to the Arctic (1910) by Agnes Deans Cameron

The first celebrated author who was born in B.C., male or female, was Agnes Deans Cameron, born in Victoria in 1863. Her funeral cortege in 1912 was the largest the city of Victoria had ever witnessed. Upon her death, the *Daily Colonist* of Victoria declared, "It is possible that when the history of British Columbia comes to be written the name of Agnes Deans Cameron will be inscribed therein as the most remarkable woman citizen of the province." Cameron was most widely known for her journalism and her crusading social spirit, but she wrote one significant book about her adventures, *The New North: Being Some Account of a Woman's Journey through Canada to the Arctic* (1910).

With an unwavering belief in equal rights and female suffrage, Cameron became British Columbia's first female high school teacher in 1890 and its first female principal in 1894. She and her niece were also the first white women to reach the Arctic overland in 1908.

Cameron was also one of British Columbia's first female journalists, publishing extensively in Canadian and American magazines such as *Pacific Monthly, The Canadian Magazine, Saturday Evening Post, Educational Journal of Western Canada* and *The Coast.* She wrote and published fiction as early as 1903 and became a perceptive observer of Inuit and Chipewyan culture and women. She travelled extensively in later years promoting immigration to western Canada and addressing audiences at Oxford, Cambridge, St. Andrew's University and the Royal Geographical Society. However, precious few know her name now.

The number of books that relate to the rise of feminism within B.C., or celebrate women's extraordinary achievements, is vast and they merit consideration as a genre of their own. For example, the prairie reformer and author Nellie McClung is seldom recognized as a British Columbian, but she lived in Victoria from 1935 until her death in 1951.

For some other authors pertaining to women's issues and lives in British Columbia, see abcbookworld for Aberdeen, Lady; Acker, Alison; Adams, Amanda; Aguirre, Carmen; Allan, Elaine; Allison, Susan; Amberston, Celu; Andersen, Doris; Andersen, Marnie; Angus, Julie; Armstrong, Luanne; Arnott, Joanne; Artz, Sibylle; Backhouse, Frances; Baker, Marie Annharte; Barkley, Frances; Barman, Jean; Barnsley, Jan; Barnwell, Leslie; Baxter, Sheila; Beck, Lily Adams; Billy, Mary; Birchwater, Sage; Blackman, Margaret; Blackwood, Margaret; Blair, Hilary; Blanchet, M. Wylie; Boissery, Beverley; Bourgeois-Doyle, Richard I.; Boyd, Susan; Bramham, Daphne; Bridge, Kathryn; Brown, Audrey Alexandra; Brown, Jennifer; Callison, Daisy Elizabeth; Cameron, Anne; Cameron, June Carey, Betty; Carpenter, Cecilia Svinth; Carr, Emily; Cash, Gwen; Chase, Gillean; Chong, Denise; Chunn, Dorothy; Clarkes, Lincoln; Cobb, Myrna; Cohen, Marjorie Griffin; Coleman, Anne; Collis, Septima M.; Converse, Cathy; Cracroft, Sophia; Crosby, Emma; Crossland, Jackie; Crowie, Jasana; Cruikshank, Julie; Culhane, Dara; Currie, Dawn; Czajkowski, Chris; Daniel, Barbara; Daniluk, Judith; Davidson, Florence; Day, Shelagh; Dean, Misao; Delany, Sheila; Diamond, Sara; Dossa, Parin; Douglas, Amelia; Douglas, Gilean; Dowse, Sara; Dragu, Margaret; Duder, Cameron; Dufferin, Lady; Duffus, Maureen; Duncan, (Sandy) Frances; Dutton, Donald; Edwards, Anne; Edwards, Isabel; Elliott, Marie Anne; Faith, Karlene; Ferguson, Marjorie; Fertig, Mona; Finlay, K.A.; Flood, Cynthia; Flynn, Bethine; Forbes, Elizabeth; Forsberg, Tor; Foubister, Linda; Fraser, Clara; Fraser, Marian; Gerson, Carole; Gibson, Valerie; Gilbert, Lara; Glick-Reiman, Beth; Goldsmith, Penny; Gough, Lyn; Gould, Jan; Graydon, Shari; Greene, Trevor; Greenslade, Frances; Grey, Jan; Grey, Winifred; Griffin, Betty; Guiled, Brenda; Hall, Jane; Halliday, Linda; Hankivsky, Olena; Hardwick, Joan; Harrison, Eunice; Hastings, Margaret Lang; Henshaw, Julia; Hessing, Melody; Hodgson, Barbara; Hollingsworth, Margaret; Holmes, Tori; Holt, Simma; Howard, Cori; Howard, Irene; Howarth, Jean; Hudson, Elizabeth; Hume, Stephen; Ingram, Susan; Jackel, Susan; Jensen, Vickie; Jewett, Pauline; Johnson, Peter; Jones, Beverley; Jones, Jo Fraser; Jordan, Rosa; Joussaye, Marie; Kawatski, Deanna; Kemper, Margaret; Kennedy, Louise; Kerr, Luella; Kingscote, Barbara; Kivi, K. Linda; Klassen, Ingrid; Knickerbocker, Nancy; Krawczyk, Betty; Kwa, Lydia; Lacombe, Danny; Lakeman, Lee; Lam, Fiona; Landale, Zoe; Latham, Barbara; Laur, Darren; Lee, Nancy; Lefevre, Lily Alice; LeGates, Marlene; Levy, Paul; Lewis, Norah L.; Lewis, S.P.; Lockharte, Susan; Long, Wendy; Lowman, John; Lowther, Pat; Lugrin, Nora de Bertrand; Luke, Pearl; MacGill, Elsie Gregory; Mackay, Isabel Ecclestone; MacLaren, Sherrill; MacPhee, Rosalind; Maes, Yvonne; Maguire, Diane; Manji, Irshad; Marlatt, Daphne; McClean, Sylvie; McKowan, Evah; McLaughlin, Karen; McLennan, Emily Augusta; McMaster, Lindsey; Meraw, Ann Mundigel; Minkus, Kim; Mitchell, Margaret; Moir, Rita; Moore, Mandy; Morra, Linda; Morrow, Marina; Morton, W.L.; Murphy, Claire Rudolph; Murphy, Emily Gowan; Neering, Rosemary; Nichols, Marjorie; Nickerson, Betty; Norcross, Elizabeth Blanche; Norton, Wayne; Ormsby, Margaret Anchoretta; Page, Lafern; Palmer, Debbie; Parr, Joy; Penrose, Evelyn; Perrin, Dave; Perry, Adele; Phillips, Elizabeth; Potvin, Liza; Preece, Alison; Press,

K.I.; Price, Lisa A.; Radha, Swami Sivananda; Raglon, Rebecca; Ravenhill, Alice; Reeve, Phyllis; Rink, Deborah; Roberts, Anita; Robideau, Henri; Robinson, Cass; Roger, Gertrude Minor; Roy, Carole; Rutherdale, Myra; Sager, Ed; Samant, Ganesh; Sarsfield, Mairuth Hodge; Schellenberg, Betty A.; Schwartz, Ellen; Scoones, Anny; Scott, Jean; Simpson, Elizabeth; Skinner, Constance Lindsay; Smith, Cyndi; Smith, Jessie Ann; Smith-Ayala, Emilie; Snowber, Celeste; Stanwell-Fletcher, Theodora; Stewart, Lee; Stewart, Mary Lynn; Stonehouse, Cathy; Stonier-Newman, Lynne; Storrs, Monica; Strong-Boag, Veronica; Sykes, Ella; Taylor, Dianne; Taylor, Georgina; Thobani, Sunera; Thompson, Dawn; Thomson, Ann; Townsend, Lorna; Trebett, Margaret; Trudeau, Margaret; Tuele, Nicholas; van Deusen, Kira; Van Kirk, Sylvia; Van Luven, Lynne; Vernon, Lorraine; Vertinsky, Patricia; Vries Maggie de; Warland, Betsy; Whelan, Dianne; White, Evelyn; Wilks, Claire Weissman; Williams, Carol; Wilson, Robert; Woodley, Barbara; Wright, Sunny; Young, Clair.

E. PAULINE JOHNSON

Legends of Vancouver (1911) by E. Pauline Johnson

Pauline Johnson is widely accepted as the starting point for aboriginal writing in B.C. although she never learned to speak an aboriginal language and most of her poetry was not about First Nations people.

As of 1895, Emily Pauline Johnson or "Tekahionwake" toured extensively, often wearing European clothing for one half of her performances on stage and "Indian" clothing for the other half. Historian Daniel Francis has suggested in *The Imaginary Indian: The Image of the Indian in Canadian Culture* (1992), that the "need to satisfy the demands of a White audience stultified Pauline Johnson's development as a writer and limited her effectiveness as a spokesperson for Native people." She is mostly remembered for her poems "The Song My Paddle Sings" and "The Legend of the Qu'Appelle," as well as *Legends of Vancouver* (1911).

When visiting the West Coast, Pauline Johnson usually stayed at the Hotel Vancouver. Increasingly troubled by ill health, she announced before an appreciative audience at the Pender Auditorium in 1909 her intention to live permanently in Vancouver. She

Mary Anne Capilano was an uncredited co-author of Legends of Vancouver.

took an apartment at 1117 Howe Street and concentrated on her writing, increasingly turning her hand to essays and short fiction.

In 1910, Johnson began publishing prose pieces in the *Saturday Province Magazine*, edited by Lionel Maskovski, and these stories led to *Legends of Vancouver* (1911). It contains her versions of stories told to her by Chief Capilano and Mary Capilano of the Squamish Band, including the well-known story "The Siwash Rock" about the rock in Stanley Park near Lions Gate Bridge. Pauline Johnson wanted their collaboration to be called "Legends of the Capilanos." Unfortunately she did not get her wish and Joe and Mary Capilano are rarely, if ever, credited as First Nations authors.

A follow-up volume, *Flint and Feather* (1912), combining poetry from her first two books, has proven to be one of the most reprinted poetry collections in Canadian history, rivalling the works of Robert Service.

Suffering from painful and inoperable breast cancer, Johnson expressed her desire to be buried in Stanley Park. Wary of setting precedents, civic authorities agreed to Johnson's request with the proviso that she be cremated. She died on March 7, 1913, just three days before her 52nd birthday. Thousands of people lined Georgia Street to witness her funeral procession. She had lived in Vancouver for four years. Two more prose collections, *The Moccasin Maker* (1913) and *The Shagganappi* (1913), were released to ensure her debts were paid. Johnson had requested that no structure be raised in her memory. However, the Women's Canadian

Club began its campaign to erect a stone monument for her ashes, near Third Beach, in 1914. Construction was not completed until 1922. Initial response to the monument was mixed. The face and braided hairstyle of her image are not representative of her appearance, and Johnson's right profile is depicted looking away from her beloved Siwash Rock. It has nonetheless remained Vancouver's only well-known monument to a local writer.

JOHN VOSS

The Venturesome Voyages of Captain Voss (1913) by John Voss

Prior to Thor Heyerdahl and the *Kon-Tiki*, there was John Voss and the *Tilikum*, a 50-year-old dugout canoe that was transformed into an ocean-going vessel that sailed from Vancouver Island to London from 1901 to 1904.

The story goes that an intrepid Winnipeg-born reporter named Norman Luxton met hardened sailor John Claus Voss in a Victoria beer parlour and they started talking about the seaworthiness of local aboriginal dugout canoes made of red cedar. In 1901, for $80, Voss purchased an old Nuu-chah-nulth dugout. Apparently a bottle of rye sealed the deal. Voss and a shipwright named Harry Vollmer prepared their 32-foot craft in the hopes of emulating the first solo circumnavigation of the world by Nova Scotian–born Joshua Slocum in his 37-foot sloop *Spray* (1895–1898). At the time, Slocum's memoir was a bestseller. Luxton would accompany Voss in the hopes of writing a similar account. Voss and Vollmer built up the sides of the *Tilikum* by seven inches and added three masts, oak frames, a set of close-hauled sails totalling 230 square feet of canvas, a cockpit for steering, a half ton of ballast, 400 pounds of sand for trimming ballast and a five-foot by eight-foot cabin. Vollmer's wife sewed the sails on her sewing machine.

With its unpredictable captain, the Tilikum *prepares to embark from Victoria in 1901.*

Voss was apparently an excessively volatile character, prone to drunken rages. On their way to Samoa the much younger Luxton had to threaten Voss with a .22 calibre Stevens pistol and keep him locked in the cabin. On Samoa they visited the tomb of Robert Louis Stevenson and Luxton had a fling with a woman named Sadie Thompson with "legs like mutton and breasts like huge cabbages."

Prior to their departure for Fiji, Luxton made Voss sign a document, witnessed by a storekeeper named Swan, in which Voss agreed to submit to a judicial enquiry if for any reason Luxton did not survive the next leg of the voyage. Luxton disembarked at Fiji but planned to rejoin Voss in Sydney and share in whatever celebratory honours might accrue. Suffering from exposure upon his arrival in Sydney, Voss was hospitalized for several weeks, reportedly due to "sickness he contracted through the women on the islands."

The pair of adventurers were feted in Australia, but Luxton opted not to continue from Melbourne, suspecting Voss had tossed his replacement overboard. Adopting the name McVoss, the German- or Danish-born sailor stubbornly crossed the Indian Ocean to the Cape of Good Hope, sailed up the west coast of Africa, via the Azores, and arrived at the mouth of the Thames River in September of 1904, having had 11 different mates pass through his command during his 40-month adventure.

Voss published his memoir as *The Venturesome Voyages of Captain Voss* (1913). Its current republished title is *40,000 Miles in a Canoe and Sea Queen*. The *Tilikum* was sold several times, then left to decay in a Thames shipyard. Luxton failed to publish his side of the story during his lifetime, but his daughter edited his notes and photographs, added biographical sketches, and eventually published *Tilikum: Luxton's Pacific Crossing* (1971). The *Tilikum* was retrieved from England in the 1920s and has been a permanent exhibit of the Maritime Museum of B.C. since 1965. Someone should make a movie.

F.W. HOWAY

British Columbia from the Earliest Times to the Present (1914)
by F.W. Howay & E.O.S. Scholefield

The most important collector of local literature in the first half of the 20th century, F.W. Howay was a giant of northwest coast history and literature, but few know his name today.

Frederic William Howay was born near London, Ontario, in 1867 and brought to B.C. as a child. With his lifelong friend Robie Reid and future B.C. premier Richard McBride, Howay entered Dalhousie University to study law in 1887. He graduated in 1890 along with Richard McBride and another future premier of British Columbia, W.J. Bowser.

Howay returned to B.C. and opened a joint legal practice with Reid in 1893. The first article in the first issue of the *British Columbia Historical Quarterly* in 1937 is by Howay, a longtime supporter of the publication. Howay co-wrote a four-volume history, *British Columbia from the Earliest Times to the Present* (1914), with E.O.S. Scholefield, followed by *British Columbia: The Making of a Province* (1928), effectively replacing Hubert Howe Bancroft's history for four decades.

Howay was the first president of the B.C. Historical Association, the B.C. representative on the Historic Sites and Monuments Board of Canada and a member of the Art, Historical and Scientific Association of Vancouver. He was also a longtime Freemason who hobnobbed with the upper class as a member of both the Terminal City Club in Vancouver and the Pacific Club in Victoria. Howay was narrowly defeated in a 1906 election as a Liberal candidate running against his friend, Premier Richard McBride, and was appointed Judge of the County Court of New Westminster in 1907. He would serve as a county judge for 30 years, severely intolerant of labour unrest, until he retired in 1937.

Howay was continuously engaged as a maritime historian, and as B.C.'s most active regional scholar he was elected as president of the Royal Society of Canada in 1941. He was a UBC Senator from 1915 to 1942, first chairman of the New Westminster Library and a recipient of the King's Silver Jubilee Medal. He was a good friend and benefactor of William Kaye Lamb who inherited Howay's mantle as the foremost archivist of British Columbia's literary culture. He died in New Westminster in 1943. His private collection of literature and papers was donated to UBC where it remains, in conjunction with the valuable collection of Robie Reid.

F.W. Howay was the first significant scholar chiefly concerned with B.C. history.

EDWARD S. CURTIS

The North American Indian, Being a Series of Volumes Picturing
and Describing the Indians of the United States and Alaska
(1907–1930) by Edward S. Curtis

Pioneer photographer Edward Sheriff Curtis produced 20 volumes of text and original photography in *The North American Indian, Being a Series of Volumes Picturing and Describing the Indians of the United States and Alaska* (1907–1930) in keeping with his gargantuan goal of recording on film, and documenting with text, all possible information on aboriginals west of the Mississippi. Curtis also wrote a frontier opera and two bestsellers, *Indian Days of Long Ago* (1914) and *Land of the Head Hunters* (1915). Volumes 9 (Salishan), 10 (Kwakiutl) and 11 (Haida and Nootka) of his series are directly related to B.C. The largest of the 20 volumes concerns the Kwakwaka'wakw. When the first two volumes of his photos were published in 1907, the *New York Herald* hailed the work of Curtis as "the most gigantic undertaking in the making of books since the King James edition of the Bible." Curtis visited 80 tribes and took more than 40,000 photographs.

Believing aboriginals of Western North America were doomed to vanish provided Curtis with his mandate to generate a massive archive of images that were frequently staged for effect. In response, Métis playwright Marie Clements published her play, *The Edward Curtis Project: A Modern Picture Story* (2010), staged coincidentally with the 2010 Olympics, to examine Curtis' hubris. Rodger Touchie simultaneously published a non-fiction appreciation of Curtis' photos above the 49th parallel, *Edward S. Curtis Above the Medicine Line* (2010) to celebrate the remarkable breadth and dramatic impact of his work.

Edward S. Curtis was the most significant photographer of First Nations in B.C.

Born in Wisconsin in 1868, Edward Curtis first arrived in the villages of Puget Sound at age 19. One of his first subjects was "Princess Angeline," the daughter of Chief Seattle. In his twenties, Curtis was a photographer for some of the world's leading scientists on a two-month scientific voyage from Seattle to the Bering Sea. This was the catalyst for his 30-year obsession with portraying the aboriginal spirit and ostensibly eradicating false notions of aboriginal life. Curtis contributed to *Scribner's Magazine*, and his early exhibitions at New York's Waldorf-Astoria earned him the support of Theodore Roosevelt and the patronage of J. Pierpoint Morgan. Despite these connections, Curtis' Seattle studio was chronically short of money as he struggled to complete his journeys to all tribes west of the Mississippi from New Mexico to Alaska.

For 20 years Curtis was greatly assisted by the mostly unknown W.E. Meyers, a former reporter for the *Seattle Star* newspaper, who took notes by shorthand and assembled the narratives of ethnographic materials. Curtis' work in B.C. was also assisted by the interpreter George Hunt, son of a Tsimshian woman and a Hudson's Bay Company employee, who lived for 60 years among the Kwakwaka'wakw. In 1920, Curtis moved to Los Angeles and assisted Cecil B. Demille in the making of *The Ten Commandments*. Curtis died of a heart attack in 1952 at age 84. An original edition of *The North American Indian* sells for more than $80,000.

FREDERICK NIVEN

Frederick Niven was British Columbia's first professional man of letters and the first significant literary figure of the Kootenays. He lived by his wits, as an independent writer, mainly on the outskirts of Nelson, from 1920 until 1944. Although some of his more than 40 titles were written to keep the wolf from the door, such as *Cinderella of Skookum Creek* (1916), by contrast, Niven's collection of 16 short stories called *Above Your Heads* (1911) consisted exclusively of stories rejected by editors who believed their content would be "over the heads" of readers.

Born to Scottish parents in Valparaiso, Chile, in 1878, Frederick Niven was raised in Glasgow, from age five. At age 20, Niven was sent to the dry B.C. Interior for treatment of a lung ailment. He trekked throughout the Okanagan Valley and Kootenays, then worked at the Hastings Sawmill in Vancouver in 1900. After returning to Scotland, he began publishing travel accounts in newspapers and magazines. His first novel, *The Lost Cabin Mine* (1908), was a forgettable potboiler set in the Canadian west. After marrying Mary Pauline Thorne-Quelch in 1911, he returned to western Canada on commissions as a freelance writer. Rejected for military service, Niven wrote for the British Ministry of Information during WWI. After three more novels, he was threatened with a serious heart ailment and moved to Willow Point, six miles outside of Nelson, B.C., in 1920.

Two of Niven's historical novels, *The Flying Years* (1935) and *Mine Inheritance* (1940), are set on the prairies, but most of his work is set in either Scotland or British Columbia. In his final novel, *The Transplanted* (1944), Niven depicts the rise of B.C.'s interior ranching, lumbering and mining industries and their effects on a broad range of characters. Two transplanted men from

THE
TRANSPLANTED
FREDERICK NIVEN

Cover art for The Transplanted *by Frederick Niven,
B.C.'s first full-time man of letters*

Glasgow, Robert Wallace and Jock Galbraith, maintain a strong bond despite difficulties. Robert Wallace is a shrewd visionary who becomes a builder of Canada, opening up the town of Elkhorn.

Historian and critic Charles Lillard's favourite Niven novel, *Wild Honey* (1927), is actually a fictionalized memoir, a work of hobo literature, a precursor to the sensibilities of B.C. writers such as Al Purdy, Patrick Lane and Jim Christy. The narrator meets two hobos, Slim and Hank, who work with him at a gravel pit near Savona. Niven writes, "Above the rasp of the shovels with which we worked astern of the big, rhythmically-coughing steamshovel, I would hear the murmur of the Thompson River lapsing past; and that murmur, somehow, was worth much weary labour to hear." The threesome cash their pay cheques at North Bend, then wander south to border towns below Kamloops. Long out of print, *Wild Honey* offers some splendid writing, akin to that of Jack London or George Orwell—directly based on Niven's own travels. Lillard named it one of the three best early B.C. novels, along with Hubert Evans' *Mist on the River* and Howard O'Hagan's *Tay John*.

Niven died of a heart attack in 1944. He remains an underrecognized as one of Canada's first "non-colonial" authors.

BERTRAND SINCLAIR

Poor Man's Rock (1920) by Bertrand Sinclair

Of the great B.C. writers most people have never heard of, Bertrand "Bill" Sinclair was one of the most successful. A cowboy, logger, fisherman, social activist, broadcaster and unionist poet, he wrote 15 novels, several of which became silent movies such as *North of '53* (1914) and *Big Timber: A Story of the Northwest* (1916). His main attempt at a "literary" novel, *The Inverted Pyramid* (1924), was inspired by the failure of the Dominion Trust Company. *North of '53* reputedly sold 340,000 copies but Sinclair considered *Poor Man's Rock* (1920) as his most successful work. According to critic and friend Lester Peterson, Sinclair showed a "general disgust for the mere entrepreneur, the man who manipulates but does not actually produce goods or services."

Born in Edinburgh, Scotland, in 1881, Sinclair immigrated to Canada with his mother in 1889, then ran away from home to become a cowboy in Montana at age 15. In 1905, he married novelist Bertha M. (Muzzy) Bower, who wrote more than 60 westerns under her first husband's surname, Bower. The protagonist of her best-known work, *Chip of the Flying U*, was based on Sinclair.

Dismayed by phony depictions of cowboys in romance novels, Sinclair turned his hand to fiction after he moved to San Francisco, starting with *Raw Gold* (1908) and *The Land of the Frozen Suns* (1909). After divorcing his first wife, Sinclair married her cousin Ruth and returned to Canada.

In B.C., Sinclair began to adapt his melodramatic, heroic stories to depict realistically the lives of loggers, fish-

Bertrand Sinclair was a successful novelist who wrote about working class men and women of B.C.

ermen and ranchers. Prior to writing *Big Timber* (1916), Sinclair observed logging operations at Harrison Lake for three years. For *Down the Dark Alley* (1936), which describes so-called rum-running during Prohibition, Sinclair accompanied a liquor shipment to the U.S.

Sinclair's Hardy-esque romance *Poor Man's Rock* (1920) is named for a place off Lasqueti Island, at Squitty Bay, where dense kelp and swirling currents prevented motorized fishing boats from approaching, restricting fishing to hand trollers. "Only a poor man trolled in a rowboat," Sinclair wrote. "Poor Man's Rock had given many a man a chance." The romance angle of this novel is secondary to Sinclair's superb depiction of how cannery operators—

the B.C. Packers Association—were unfairly controlling prices with price-fixing agreements, leading to poor working conditions. Jack MacRae, the hero, realizes how the Packers Association discourages competition by monopolizing cannery sites and licences. He concludes, "the wholesaler stood like a wall between the fishermen and those who ate fish." By offering fair prices to independent fishermen, MacRae scuttles his rival Horace Gower's control. When the hero ultimately marries Gower's daughter, Betty, the capitalist father-in-law confesses to MacRae that wealth never made him a happy man.

Bertrand Sinclair was also widely known for his VHF radio broadcasts to fishermen, "The Sinclair Hour," and his beloved 37-foot troller *Hoo Hoo* which was moored at Pender Harbour, where he first bought property in 1923. He didn't retire from fishing until age 83. After Sinclair died at age 91, in 1972, his ashes were scattered over Poor Man's Rock off Lasqueti Island. The *Hoo Hoo* was burned for an episode of *The Beachcombers* in 1985. Betty Keller wrote a biography of the author, *Pender Harbour Cowboy: The Many Lives of Bertrand Sinclair* (2000).

LILY ADAMS BECK

The most prolific female author of British Columbia in the 1920s, Lily Adams Beck, daughter of Royal Navy Captain John Moresby, wrote most of her 30-odd books in Victoria in less than ten years. It has been suggested she was the first female fantasy writer of Canada, having published *The Ninth Vibration and Other Stories* (1922), *The Key of Dreams* (1922) and *Dreams and Delights* (1926). Her real name was Elizabeth Louisa Moresby.

In her esoteric works, such as *The Splendor of Asia* (1926) and *The Story of Oriental Philosophy* (1928), she attempted to interpret the life and teachings of Buddha. Her romance entitled *The House*

Lily Adams Beck, the first widely read female novelist in B.C.

of Fulfillment: The Romance of a Soul (1927) incorporates some of the Hindu philosophy of the *Upanishads* to explain supernatural phenomena. *The Garden of Vision* (1929) is about an Englishwoman who forsakes materialism to seek wisdom and spirituality in Japan. "The publications of L.A. Beck and The Brother XII," wrote literary critic Charles Lillard in 1989, "must be considered the first serious religious writing done outside the established churches of Vancouver Island, and perhaps in British Columbia."

Having travelled in India, Tibet, China, Burma, Japan and Egypt, Beck was a staunch Buddhist. Arriving in Victoria in 1919, she surrounded herself with Oriental art and servants. A strict vegetarian with ascetic inclinations, she entertained fortnightly at her home on Mountjoy Avenue in Oak Bay.

Beck began her career by publishing stories in the *Atlantic Monthly* and other publications, which were gathered into a popular collection, *Dreams and Delights* (1926). Beck used various pen names such as Louis Moresby for non-fiction and E. Barrington for popular romances set in exotic locales, such as *The Way of Stars: A Romance of Reincarnation* (1925), *The Thunderer: A Romance of Napoleon and Josephine* (1927) and *The Laughing Queen: Romance of Cleopatra* (1929), set in ancient Egypt. She was also known as Elizabeth Louisa Beck, Eliza Louisa Moresby Beck and Lily Moresby Adams.

Beck's *The Divine Lady: A Romance of Nelson and Emma Hamilton* was made into a film in northern California in 1929. The script was credited to E. Barrington, Harry Carr, Forrest Halsey, Agnes Christine Johnston and Edwin Justus Mayer. The producers were Walter Morosco and Richard A. Rowland. It gained an Oscar for its director Frank Lloyd.

Associated with the rise of Theosophy, Lily Adams Beck continued to write her fantastical novels of faraway places from Victoria until her death in Kyoto, Japan, in 1931.

———≈∘∘∘≈———

B.A. MCKELVIE

Early History of the Province of British Columbia (1926)
by B.A. McKelvie

Before *B.C. BookWorld*, there was Charles Lillard. And before Charles Lillard, there was Alan Morley and Arthur Mayse. But before that, there was B.A. McKelvie. Bruce Alistair "Pinkie" McKelvie was an unabashedly middle-brow newspaperman who served as the first popularizer of B.C. history. According to McKelvie, he once saved the life of a drowning Sliammon girl and was made an honorary Coast Salish chief. Decades later, he was not averse to publishing *Tales of Conflict: Indian-White Murders and Massacres in Pioneer British Columbia* (1949). His best literary idea was an attempt to craft a popular biography of the Mowachaht chief who met Captain Cook in 1778, *Maquinna the Magnificent* (1946). In *Legends of Stanley Park* (1941), McKelvie recorded how Stanley Park was once home to Si'atmulth, the Rainmaker, who punished the first man, Kalana, by imposing a drought upon the world. McKelvie also wrote a teen adventure novel, *The Black Canyon: A Story of '58* (1927), and he is best remembered for his 118-page *Early History of the Province of British Columbia* (1926), published in the same year as his first novel, *Huldowget*, depicting the clash of values between encroaching Christianity and aboriginal spirituality.

The plot of *Huldowget: A Story of the North Pacific Coast* (1926) gives an indication of McKelvie's style. At a small mission up the coast called Fort Oliver, Father David, a didactic missionary with 40 years' experience, learns that a half-breed shaman named Thompson is practising heathen rites. Thompson wants to marry Father David's lovely missionary hospital assistant Mary

Cunningham, who in turn, loves the local police officer named John Collishaw. Mary falls temporarily under the spell of the "necromancer" Thompson. The Indians force Thompson and Collishaw to undergo "trial by mouse" whereby the tiny animal's movement towards one man or the other determines who is to be buried alive. Although McKelvie makes a sincere attempt to translate complex conflicts into a dramatic narrative, he mainly succeeds in his efforts "to picture some of the trials and tribulations and disappointments of a missioner and his wife."

Born in B.C. in 1889, McKelvie began working as a printer's apprentice at age ten. From 1913 onwards, he worked for more than 30 years in the Vancouver and Victoria newspaper trade, becoming managing editor of the *Victoria Colonist* in 1930. An ardent British Columbian, he launched a successful "Buy B.C. Products" campaign. He retired to Cobble Hill on Vancouver Island where he died in 1960. Mount McKelvie and McKelvie Creek are named in his honour.

A.M. STEPHEN

Few authors have contributed more to British Columbia society than Alexander Maitland Stephen, the first B.C. author to double prominently as a social reformer.

Born in Ontario in 1882, but raised in Victoria, "A.M.," as he was later known, abandoned law after one year to prospect for gold in the Klondike. Stephen punched cattle in Alberta, worked as a guide in the Rockies and taught school at Rock Creek, B.C., in 1906. He studied architecture at the University of Chicago until 1913 when he went to England and enlisted in 1914. Injured in France, he returned to Vancouver with a shattered right wrist, virtually penniless, and somehow opened a structural engineering firm in 1918.

Stephen believed that "in child welfare lay the welfare of all the world." His Child Welfare Association was instrumental in establishing the Mother's Pension Act, the Minimum Wage Act, divorce law amendments and improved social services for the destitute in B.C.

"Woman has rebelled," he wrote, "and rightly so, at the double standard, that she has been subjected to." Turning to teaching, Stephen agitated for more reforms, some of which were implemented after his dismissal for insubordination. "The central principle of our graded system," he claimed, "is that the child must fit the school and not the school must fit the child."

A. M. Stephen, prominent social reformer, poet and novelist

One of Stephen's radical beliefs was that sex education should form part of the school curriculum. In 1923, Stephen led the way for the creation of the Birth Control League of Canada, the first such organization in Canada, in keeping with the aims of Margaret Sanger's American Birth Control League. He criticized the "ignorance and inertia of those . . . still living in the dark ages of medieval priestcraft and superstition."

In the twenties, Stephen worked for the *Western Tribune*, a leftist weekly, and gained his reputation in poetry as "the Canadian Carl Sandburg." He also wrote an historical romance, *The Kingdom of the Sun* (1927), about a gentleman adventurer named Richard Anson who sailed aboard Sir Francis Drake's *Golden Hind*, only to be cast away amongst the Haida. Anson's love interest is a golden-haired princess, Auria, who must choose between her mystical duties and her earthly affection. The novel is drawn from evidence that fair-haired, blue-eyed Haida were encountered by explorers in the late 18th century.

In *The Gleaming Archway* (1929), Stephen's fictional prototype is journalist Craig Maitland, a dreamer in the twin realms of love and politics: Maitland takes his holidays in the Squamish Valley amongst "reds," aboriginals and expatriate English eccentrics. He befriends a Marxist publisher, a Russian revolutionary and a beautiful Englishwoman, who is married. Maitland returns to Vancouver to work for *The Beacon*, a socialist weekly headquartered on Pender Street. He forms a sentimental friendship with emancipated colleague, Madge, atop Grouse Mountain and in Capilano Canyon, but impulsively marries Shannon, a painted lady with a heart of gold whom he meets in a Chinatown gambling house.

The gleaming archways of Maitland's idealistic spirit come crashing down to earth until he accepts an invitation to leave on a treasure hunting expedition in the South Seas, unaware that friends have arranged for him to be reunited with his first true love, Jocelyn, whose husband has conveniently died.

Stephen launched the B.C. branch of the League Against War and Fascism and was narrowly defeated as a Co-operative Commonwealth Federation (CCF) candidate in the Alberni-Nanaimo riding. He was later expelled from the CCF for advocating a popular front with the Communists. He corresponded with Norman Bethune, raised funds for China and wrote pamphlets analyzing global politics. His radicalism was heightened by RCMP actions in Regina during the great trek of the unemployed to Ottawa in 1935. His son, Leslie, who was helping at his cousin's ranch for the summer in Saskatchewan, went into Regina to buy grain for seeding. Leslie Stephen was caught in the riot and so brutally beaten on the head by police that he became a lifelong invalid.

When A.M. Stephen succumbed to pneumonia in 1942, wreaths were sent by such diverse groups as the Chinese Benevolent Association and the Boilermakers and Iron Shipbuilders' Union. His wife arranged for publication of a collection of posthumous poetry, *Songs for a New Nation* (1963).

MARIUS BARBEAU

Marius Barbeau is considered the founder of folklore studies in Canada. After studying anthropology at Oxford as the first French-Canadian Rhodes scholar, he was hired as an ethnologist at the Museum Branch of the Geological Survey of Canada in Ottawa and first visited B.C. for ethnology research in 1914. As one of Canada's first two full-time professional anthropologists (the other was Edward Sapir), he conducted groundbreaking fieldwork among the Tsimshian of northern British Columbia and assisted William Beynon in his research in the Nass and Skeena River valleys in 1920s, leading to his 1928 novel *The Downfall of Temlaham* and *Totem Poles of the Gitksan, Upper Skeena River, British Columbia* (1929). Barbeau's two publications about totem poles in 1950 became extremely influential in spreading the word about Pacific Northwest totem poles around the world. These are *Totem Poles: Vol. I According to Crests and Topics* (1950) and *Totem Poles: Vol. II According to Location* (1950). As well, *Marius Barbeau's Photographic Collection: The Nass River* (1988), edited by Linda Riley, reproduces 294 photographs that were taken between 1927 and 1929, along the Nass River, of people, totem poles, grave monuments, masks and rituals, etc.

Although he incorrectly theorized that poles were only erected after contact with Europeans, Barbeau was one of the first ethnographers to document seriously the accomplishments of individual Haida artists, primarily in his book *Haida Carvers in Argillite 2* (1957), a follow-up to *Haida Myths: Illustrated Argillite Carvings* (1953). In the former he wrote, "The present *Haida Carvers* further sets forth the names and achievements of more than forty Skidegate and Masset artisans and illustrates their extraordinary progress within the memory of man. If one decides to learn at first hand about them, nothing will be out of focus, for neither would anonymity satisfy a French historian of the Barbizon school of painters concerning Millet, Rousseau and their impressionistic contemporaries. Likewise, in this book on Haida argillite work, we shall look into the recent lives and achievements of William Dixon, Tom Price, John Cross, Charlie Edenshaw, Isaac Chapman and others of the same school. All of them were contemporaries of our own Constable, Turner, Courbet, Millet, Gauguin and Cézanne."

A contemporary of Diamond Jenness, Barbeau became one of the first recipients of the Order of Canada. Born south of Quebec City in 1883, he died in Ottawa in 1969.

Marius Barbeau was the first widely read authority on totem poles.

For other authors pertaining to B.C. anthropology, see abcbookworld entries for Abbott, Donald; Adamson, Thelma; Allen, D.; Ames, Kenneth; Ames, Michael; Amoss, Pamela; Anderson, E.N.; Anderson, Margaret Seguin; Arima, E.Y.; Bancroft-Hunt, Norman; Barbeau, Marius; Barker, John; Barnett, Homer G.; Beck, Mary; Belshaw, Cyril; Bentley, Mary; Bentley, Ted; Bierwert, Crisca; Black, Martha; Blake, Michael; Bloch, Alexia; Bolanz, Maria; Bolin, Inge; Bouchard, Randy; Bringhurst, Robert; Brody, Hugh; Brown, Steven; Burridge, Kenelm; Castile, George; Chamberlain, Alexander Francis; Codere, Helen; Coe, Ralph; Cogo, Robert; Colson, Elizabeth; Crosby, Thomas; Cruikshank, Julie; Crumrine, N. Ross; Culhane, Dara; Cybulski, Jerome; Dauenhauer, Nora Marks; Davidson, Florence; Davis, Philip; Davis, Wade; Dawson, George M.; Dossa, Parin; Drew, Leslie; Drucker, Philip; Durlach, Theresa Mayer; Eijk, Jan van; Emmons, George Thornton; Ernst, Alice; Farrand, Livingston; Galloway, Brent; Galois, Robert; Garfield, Viola; Goddard, Pliney Earle; Goldman, Irving; Good, John Booth; Gunn, S.W.A.; Gunther, Erna; Gustafson, Paula; Halliday, W.M.; Halpin, Marjorie; Harkin, Michael; Harrison, Charles; Hayden, Brian; Hays, H.R.; Hilbert, Vi; Hill, Beth; Hill, Ray; Hill-Tout, Charles; Holm, Bill; Hoover, Allan; Hymes, Dell; Inverarity, R.B.; Jacobs, Melville; Jenness, Diamond; Jensen, Vickie; Jilek, Wolfgang G.; Jonaitis, Aldona; Jones, Joan Meagan; Kaiper, Dan; Keddie, Grant; Keithahn, Edward; Kew, Della; Kew, J.E. Michael; Keyser, J.D.; Krause, Aurel; Lopatin, Ivan Alexis; Lotz, Pat; MacDonald, George F.; Macnair, Peter; Malin, Edward; Matson, R.G.; Maud, Ralph; McCullagh, James B.; McFeat, Tom; McIlwraith, T.F.; McMillan, Alan; Meade, Edward; Miller, Bruce G.; Miller, Jay; Mills, Antonia; Muckle, Robert J.; Nankivell, Simon; Niblack, Albert; Oberg, Kalervo; Olson, Ronald; Phillips, W.S.; Pierce, William H.; Ravenhill, Alice; Reid, Martine; Ridington, Robin; Ritzenthaler, Robert; Robinson, Michael; Rohner, Ronald; Roquefeuil, Camille (de); Rosman, Abraham; Samuel, Cheryl; Sanger, David; Sendey, John; Stewart, Hilary; Strong-Boag, Veronica; Stuart, Wendy Bross; Suttles, Wayne; Swanton, John Alexander; Van den Brink, J.H.; van Deusen, Kira; Walens, Stanley; Wells, Oliver; Wherry, Joseph; Williams, Judith; Wright, Robin K.; Wyatt, Gary; Wyse, David; Zagoskin, Lavrentii Alekseevich.

GEORGE GODWIN

The Eternal Forest under Western Skies (1929) by George Godwin

George Godwin's *The Eternal Forest under Western Skies* (1929) is the great novel of the Fraser Valley. Through the thoughts and experiences of a central character called the Newcomer, *The Eternal Forest* (its 1994 republished title) vividly portrays homesteading, the prevailing racism of the times, the terrain of Pitt Meadows and Maple Ridge, the clash of socialist hopes versus capitalism's reality, and the emergence of Vancouver as a city. It remains a penetrating exploration of idealism as well as a revealing work of social analysis. The novel focuses on a couple who buys and clears property at Ferguson's Landing, a fictionalized version of Whonnock, approximately 25 miles upstream from New Westminster, but their poverty and WWI lead them to renounce pioneering in favour of a return to England.

George Godwin was born in London in 1889. His father died when he was four. He was partially educated in Germany where he learned German and admired the works of Wagner, Schumann and Goethe. Godwin formed an antipathy to the snobbery and pettiness of the English class system, making him curious about life in other places. His brother Dick had gone to Samoa to oversee a copra plantation and his brother Donald had settled in Coquitlam, B.C.

After his mother died in 1911, Godwin went to British Columbia, sent for his fiancée, the daughter of a Belfast physician, and they bought and cleared land at Whonnock. They soon spent most of their money, added a son to their family, and discovered they were unable to compete economically with Japanese, Chinese and American farmers during the recession of 1913.

Unimpressed by what the education system of B.C. could offer, and stirred by the outbreak of war, they admitted defeat and returned to England in the summer of 1916. Godwin was unable to join the English army due to his poor eyesight, so he memorized the eye chart and joined the Canadian infantry. With the help of his brother, Dick, he gained a commission from the Minis-

George Godwin's The Eternal Forest *under Western Skies was the first important novel set in the Fraser Valley.*

ter of Militia and joined Tobin's Tigers, the 29th Battalion from Vancouver. They fought in France where Godwin was unable to muster antipathy towards the Germans. He was also critical of the coercive use of religion in war.

Godwin was wounded by a gas attack and, like the protagonist in *The Eternal Forest*, contracted tuberculosis and spent a year in a sanitarium near the Arrow Lakes. Returning to England, Godwin passed the rest of the war in Dorset teaching tank warfare. In the 1920s, he was called to the bar as a lawyer but opted for a career as a writer. He proceeded to publish a remarkable array of more than 20 books on a variety of subjects, including a 320-page biography of Captain George Vancouver. He never returned to Canada.

Following a work called *Columbia, or The Future of Canada* (1928) and *The Eternal Forest*, Godwin provided a sequel, changing the name of his autobiographical protagonist from the Newcomer to Stephen Craig, and making him a B.C. fruit grower. The memoir novel, *Why Stay We Here?* (1930), describes Godwin's military experiences in 1916–1917. Godwin died at age 85 in 1974. Under an imprint called Godwin Books, Godwin's Vancouver-based grand-nephew, Robert Thomson, has set himself the task of reviving George Godwin's literary reputation. Thomson republished an expanded version of *The Eternal Forest* in 1994, and has since made other Godwin texts available via the internet.

ANDREW RODDAN

God in the Jungles: The Story of a Man Without a Home (1931)
by Andrew Roddan

Homelessness has been an issue in British Columbia since the Depression. As much as anyone, Andrew Roddan began the ongoing struggle against homelessness in Vancouver's Downtown Eastside during his 19 years at the First United Church, from 1929 until 1948. The Scottish-born clergyman became known as the Apostle to the Poor, locking horns with Mayor Gerry McGeer, lobbying for improved social welfare programs and providing an estimated 50,000 meals to the unemployed during the winter of 1930–1931.

Long before the term "homelessness" became *de rigueur* to explain poverty and mental illness, Roddan understood the plight of the unemployed. He shared his perspective in the first of his three books, *God in the Jungles: The Story of a Man Without a Home* (1931), modelled on Nels Anderson's Chicago-based study of tramps and transients during the early twenties, Roddan's book about western Canadian hobos in the early thirties was sociological as much as it was religious or political. The jungles he referred to were four makeshift encampments that sprang up within city limits by the summer of 1931, each housing hundreds of men.

Roddan put much of the blame for the situation on technology and noted the dangers of consuming "canned heat," a cooking fuel made from wax impregnated with alcohol. "It makes them blind, it makes them mad, and finally they take the count," he wrote.

Realizing transient workers had long been integral to the Canadian economy, Roddan also understood that the wanderlust of

Andrew Roddan (left) was the prime defender of the homeless and urban poor in B.C.

boxcar tourists during the Depression had precious little to do with sloth. "The Bohemian instincts find expression in the life of these men," he wrote, "free to come, free to go, to work or wander, sleep or wake, calling no man their master."

Like J.S. Woodsworth and Tommy Douglas, Andrew Roddan was a Bible thumper from the prairies who preached the social gospel. He felt morally obliged to translate his Christian sympathies into practical acts to improve the well-being of others. As managed by his church volunteers—most notably Jeannie MacDuff, "the Pin-Up Girl for the Hungry and the Homeless"—Roddan's First United soup kitchen at Gore and Hastings served 1,252 patrons in a single sitting in November of 1930. Roddan also became one of the first advocates of low rent housing projects for the Downtown Eastside.

The so-called jungles were destroyed in September of 1931, ostensibly due to a death attributed to typhoid. The death provided an excuse for Premier Simon Fraser Tolmie's government to relocate more than 1,000 men to labour camps outside the city. Hunger marches in 1932 and 1933 ensued. These culminated with the

On-to-Ottawa Trek led by Slim Evans in 1935 and the Post Office Sit-In and riot of 1938. Roddan never abandoned his social gospel principles, clearly expressed towards the end of his first book, "We must learn to take Jesus seriously and apply his teachings of His Gospel to every phase of life."

IRENE BAIRD

Waste Heritage (1939) by Irene Baird

Born Irene Todd in Carlisle, England, in 1901, Irene Baird moved to Victoria in 1937 and disguised herself as a nurse to visit the downtrodden and to write more effectively about their plight. Her novel *Waste Heritage* (1939) has been regarded as Canada's classic novel of the Depression. It is based upon the volatile aftermath of the 1938 occupation of the main Vancouver Post Office by unemployed "sit-downers" who were evicted by police with tear gas. This event sparked a protest trek to Victoria in which the two main characters in Baird's story participate. They are aptly named Matt Striker, a 23-year-old from Saskatchewan, and his simple-minded companion Eddy, who is obsessed with the idea of one day getting a new pair of shoes. Naive and reluctant to confront authority, they yearn for a fair deal after six years of drifting, looking for work. Matt is arrested, Eddy dies. Vancouver is fictionalized as Ascelon and Victoria as Garth. The dialogue is forced but the empathy for the unemployed is strong. A *Globe & Mail* reviewer claimed the novel was "the only piece of Canadian fiction on this topic which could be compared for quality with *Grapes of Wrath.*" George Woodcock praised the novel and Bruce Hutchison decreed, "I think it is one of the best books that has come out of Canada in our time." Baird herself said of the work, "I wasn't a journalist, just a writer, but the theme gripped me and it seemed as though journalists and writers both could share a rare opportunity with a story like this, and at the same time do a little something for Canada."

Baird's series of radio addresses in 1940 and 1941 on war were published in the pamphlet *The North American Tradition* (1941). She wrote a column for the *Vancouver Sun* in 1941 and joined the *Vancouver Province* in 1942. She moved to Ottawa to work for the National Film Board, serving as the NFB's representative in Washington and Mexico City. In 1947, she joined the Federal Department of Mines and Resources and the Department of Northern Affairs. She was appointed to work as senior information officer and then, as of 1962, as chief of Information Services. Baird became the first woman to head a federal information division. Her non-fiction books include *The Eskimos in Canada* (1971).

Irene Baird returned to Victoria in 1973 and died there in 1981. *Waste Heritage* was reissued both in 1974 and 2008 but the novel remains obscure.

A companion work to *Waste Heritage* is Earle Birney's equally overlooked novel, *Down the Long Table* (1955). Among the many B.C. authors concerned with civil rights, see abcbookworld entries for Barnholden, Michael; Baxter, Sheila; Berger, Tom; Cameron, Sandy; Culhane, Claire; Dickinson, Peter; Dixon, John; Fuller, Janine; Goldberg, Kim; Hannant, Larry; Hunter, Kendall; Krawczyk, Betty; Lambertson, Ross; McLaren, Jean; Mujica-Olea, Alejandro; Osborn, Bud; Rodriguez, Carmen Laura; Rule, Jane; Russell, John; Stanton, John; Swanson, Jean.

A policeman (left) beats the unemployed at the Vancouver Post Office sit-in of 1938. The occupation inspired Irene Baird's novel Waste Heritage, *a realistic look at labour.*

HOWARD O'HAGAN

Tay John (1939) by Howard O'Hagan

Set around the Yellowhead Pass in the early 1900s, Howard O'Hagan's *Tay John* (1939) mostly takes the form of a narrative by an Irish-born remittance man in Edmonton, Jack Denham, who tells stories about Tay John, a mixed-blood man of action—not words—who left his Secwepemc people to live as a trapper and guide. His blondish hair gave rise to the nickname Tête Jaune ("yellow head"), or Tay John, a name he preferred to Kumkleseem. The first quarter of the novel describes Tay John's fictional origins in the 1880s. (A "real life" Hudson's Bay Company guide in the early 1800s named Pierre Hastination was also nicknamed Tête Jaune due to his blonde hair. The town of Tête Jaune Cache is named for him, not for O'Hagan's fictional character.)

Born in his mother's grave, Tay John was welcomed as a messianic figure who would lead his people out of the Rocky Mountains for a reunion with the people of the coast. But he becomes estranged from his people and leads a solitary existence in league with nature. Denham's stories about Tay John's relations with whites begin with Denham witnessing Tay John kill a grizzly by wrestling with it and stabbing it in the heart. Tay John cuts off his own wrist with an axe to gain a horse after losing at poker. Hired as a guide for a British couple, he has sex with the young wife and she refuses to have him prosecuted. A final love affair with an exotic woman named Ardith Aeriola leads to tragedy in the snow.

Gary Geddes claims *Tay John* (1939) is "the most important work of fiction to come out of British Columbia before the Second World War" and "Canada's first serious work of metafiction." Geddes and Michael Ondaatje have suggested O'Hagan's mythic realism led the way for Western Canadian novelists that include Sheila Watson, Robert Harlow, Rudy Wiebe, Robert Kroetsch and Jack Hodgins.

Published during the onset of WWII, O'Hagan's writing superbly evokes the mystic power of the wilderness and mountains, but the novel went nowhere after its small British publisher went belly-up. O'Hagan would always complain he never received any royalties. It was reissued in the 1960s with minimal impact.

New Canadian Library, under Malcolm Ross, republished *Tay John* in 1974 and its reputation slowly grew, but by this time Malcolm Lowry's *Under the Volcano* was lionized as the great novel from B.C.

The "mountain man" of Canadian literature, Howard O'Hagan, was born in Lethbridge in 1902 and partially raised in the Canadian Rockies. He moved to Vancouver at age twelve, attended UBC and received a law degree in 1928 from McGill University.

O'Hagan reputedly practised law for only one day, preferring to return to his beloved Rockies where he worked as a tour guide in Jasper.

Howard O'Hagan wrote Tay John, *a groundbreaking "metafiction" about wilderness life in the Rocky Mountains.*

O'Hagan wrote for a variety of men's magazines in the 1940s and 1950s. He and his partner Margaret Peterson once lived in a house in Victoria that was previously owned by Emily Carr. They also lived in Sicily from 1963 to 1974, and returned to Victoria where he died in relative poverty in 1982. O'Hagan once arm-wrestled with Lowry at Deep Cove. "I put him down. It was a cinch," O'Hagan told Keith Maillard in 1979. "He's a great writer, but he is a miserable little bastard. First of all, he's not a Canadian anyway. So I don't see why he should be regarded as a Canadian writer. He's an English writer."

EMILY CARR

E mily Carr's reputation as a visual artist has somewhat over
shadowed her literary accomplishments, but in 1941, the same
year that Victoria-born poet Anne Marriott won a Governor General's Award for Poetry for her collection *Calling Adventurers!*, Emily
Carr received the Governor General's Award for her first non-fiction book, *Klee Wyck* (1941). They were the first two B.C. authors to win one of the country's top literary prizes, to be followed
soon thereafter by Earle Birney and Dorothy Livesay.

At age 69, having suffered a stroke, Emily Carr began writing 21
vignettes about wildflowers, partly as a tonic while she was bedridden. At age 70, Carr published non-fiction pieces based on her
visits to First Nations villages, called *Klee Wyck*. She confided in her
diary, "I tried to be plain, straight, simple and Indian. I wanted to
be true to the places as well as to the people. I put my whole soul
into them and tried to avoid sentimentality. I went down deep
into myself." Carr had enrolled in a short story writing correspondence course in 1926 and taken a similar course at Humber College
in 1934. She also benefited from the friendship of Garnett
Sedgewick, head of UBC's English Department, and Ira Dilworth,
regional head of the CBC, both of whom read her stories on the
radio. Dilworth was her editor and later served as her literary executor. Despite a 20-year-age difference—or perhaps because of
it—they were able to sign their many letters to one another "with
love." Carr confessed some of her most private feelings to him and
sometimes playfully referred to him as "My Beloved Guardian."

Encouraged by critical acclaim for *Klee Wyck*, Carr continued to
write memoirs and stories. Her other books include *The Book of
Small* (1942), *The House of All Sorts* (1944) and various posthumous
titles, such as *Growing Pains* (1946).

Emily Carr's paintings and eccentricity have overshadowed her writing career.

Although she preferred not to discuss her work, it is evident Carr was a more sophisticated writer than she cared to admit. She once commented, "I did not know book rules. I made two for myself. They were about the same as the principles I use in painting—get to the point as directly as you can; never use a big word if a little one will do." As a philosophical artist, Carr was very quotable on a variety of topics such as Canada, ageing and her own work. She once wrote, "It is wonderful to feel the grandness of Canada in the raw, not because she is Canada but because she's something sublime that you were born into, some great rugged power that you are a part of." As for ageing, she wrote, "It is not all bad, this getting old, ripening. After the fruit has got its growth it should juice up and mellow. God forbid I should live long enough to ferment and rot and fall to the ground in a squash."

Carr's dual adeptness at writing and painting once prompted George Woodcock to comment, "She would have made a good sister for William Blake."

CLELLAN S. FORD (WITH) CHARLES NOWELL

Smoke from Their Fires: The Life of a Kwakiutl Chief (1941)
by Clellan S. Ford

Written prior to an era when academics discussing aboriginals were self-censored by political correctness, *Smoke from Their Fires: The Life of a Kwakiutl Chief* (1941) is a refreshingly frank and classic account of the life and times of Kwakwaka'wakw Chief Charles James Nowell, mainly written by Clellan S. Ford, of Yale University, when Nowell was age seventy. Ford received some preliminary guidance for the project from Franz Boas. It is a landmark volume because it is the first full-length biography, presented in the form of an autobiography, about a B.C. aboriginal. Based on interviews conducted in 1940, *Smoke from Their Fires* includes a 40-page introduction to Kwakwaka'wakw culture and some very candid comments from Nowell about sexual behaviour and family customs such as child care. Drawings of a grizzly bear and a killer whale were contributed by Alfred Shaughnessy from Kingcome.

Born in 1870 at Fort Rupert, Nowell acquired the names Charles James from Reverend Hall while attending the Anglican school at Alert Bay. He married the daughter of Nimpkish Chief Lagius around 1895 and received the name Hamdzidagame ("you are the man that feeds other people").

In 1899, Nowell began assisting freelance museum collector Charles Frederick Newcombe by offering to collect skeletons for him. Despite some antagonism between the two men, Newcombe persuaded Nowell to be among a group of Kwakwaka'wakw and Nuu-chah-nulth who attended an exhibition held in St. Louis in 1904. Their entourage included Nowell's friend Bob Harris from Fort Rupert, the shaman Ateu (or Atlieu), his daughter Annie Ateu and others.

Nowell and his companions appeared in ceremonial regalia at the fairgrounds at Forest Park, five miles west of the Mississippi River, as were billed as representatives of the "singularly light-colored fisherfolk" of Vancouver Island. Afterwards Newcombe brought Nowell, Ateu and Harris to Chicago for a month where they proved themselves very useful by identifying and describing Kwakwaka'wakw materials that had been gathered by the museum.

Clellan S. Ford's name is better known around the world for co-writing *Patterns of Sexual Behavior*, published ten years later in 1951.

Charles Nowell is the subject of the first in-depth biography of a B.C. aboriginal.

EARLE BIRNEY

Earle Birney was British Columbia's central and most pivotal literary figure of the 20th century. "The history of the development of contemporary writing in Vancouver from 1946 to 1960," according to Earle Birney, "is pretty largely a one-man show, and that man was me." With Roy Daniells, he co-founded Canada's first accredited Creative Writing Department at UBC, and wrote one of the most-anthologized poems in Canadian literature, "David," about the death of a mountain climber. As a poet, novelist, editor, professor, dramatist, political activist, Chaucer scholar, womanizer and all-round galvanizer, Birney was peerless as a literary catalyst. Biographer Elspeth Cameron has alleged his skills as a self-promoter and organizer were the foundation of his success.

Reared on the Bible, John Bunyan's *Pilgrim's Progress* and the poetry of Robbie Burns, Birney had what he later called "a solitary and Wordsworthian childhood." Inadequate at sports but a social climber, the lanky, carrot-topped teen, "dazed with lust," rejected a banking career in Vernon, B.C., and headed for a brothel to be deflowered at 17. He enrolled in chemistry at UBC where Harvard-educated Garnett Sedgewick, "the man of all men who had stood nearest in the role of father to me," steered him towards English. With Sedgewick's help, Birney taught medieval literature at UBC from 1948 to 1965. In 1965, he became the first writer-in-residence at the University of Toronto.

Birney received Governor General's Awards for his poetry collections *David and Other Poems* (1942) and *Now Is Time* (1945). Ensconced at UBC, Birney increasingly turned his hand to experimental poetry and verse plays. Some of his most enduring works are *Trial of a City* (1952), *Near False Creek Mouth* (1964) and *The Damnation of Vancouver* (1977). While enthusiastic about a new generation of poets that included Leonard Cohen and bill bissett, Birney had severe reservations about the TISH movement engendered by American poetry professor Warren Tallman. "They introduced cultism in its extreme form," Birney once wrote. "Anything written unlike what they were writing was dubbed not just inferior, but Anti-poetry. How the Puritan mind is reborn in every new movement."

In 1933, Birney married fellow Trotskyite Sylvia Johnstone but their marriage was later annulled. He worked on a freighter to reach London where he completed his doctoral thesis on Chaucer and worked for the Independent Labour Party.

In 1936, he went to Norway to interview Leon Trotsky, his political hero. Having been an organizer for the Trotskyite branch of the Communist Party during the 1930s, Birney later wrote a Vancouver-based Depression novel, *Down the Long Table* (1955), at the end of which the reader is made aware that it is a

Earle Birney was B.C.'s most influential literary personality.

memoir prompted by the protagonist's appearance before a red-baiting hearing during the McCarthyite purges of the 1950s.

In Berlin, Birney met Esther Bull, born Esther Heiger, of Russian-Jewish descent, who served as his stenographer in England. The idealistic pair lived like gypsies in Dorset where Esther, recently divorced, helped him complete his lengthy thesis on Chaucer's irony.

Esther came to Canada where they had one child together. Birney was never a diligent father. "We got married for the sole purpose of giving the child legitimacy," Esther Birney later recalled. "We both thought that marriage was a bourgeois institution having to do with property and possessions. We had a Marxist beginning and set out to live according to the *Communist Manifesto*. We believed you don't possess people. For this reason, neither of us objected to affairs."

Birney had a prolific love life. Throughout his adult life he had affairs with countless women, as partially recorded in Elspeth Cameron's biography. Many of his lovers remained intimate friends. "I know full well that I brought genuine love to those women which is still with them and which they draw strength from to this day," he once wrote. As a professor, he encouraged gifted female students such as Phyllis Webb, Betty Lambert, Heather Spears, Marya Fiamengo and Rona Murray, and was not always able to limit his attentions to teaching. Birney linked his creativity with virility.

In 1973, after his heart attack at age 69, Birney began cohabiting with a 24-year-old Cantonese graduate student, Wailan (Lily) Low. This became his greatest love affair. After Birney suffered a near-fatal fall while climbing a tree in July of 1975—at age 71—Wailan lovingly nursed him back to health and revitalized his spirits and his writing. Earle Birney and Esther Birney finally divorced in 1977 on the grounds of adultery, ending an unusual 37-year marriage. Wailan Low remained at Birney's side after he suffered another near-fatal heart attack in 1987. She was steadfastly caring and protective when Birney was a long-term patient at Toronto's Queen Elizabeth Hospital with a disabling brain injury. Earle Birney died in Toronto in 1995. Wailan Low, now a judge in Ontario, has continued to manage his literary affairs.

Earle Birney developed literary relationships over the years with Lister Sinclair, E.J. Pratt, Louis Dudek, Lorne Pierce, Alan Crawley, Ralph Gustafson, Clyde Gilmour, Fred Cogswell, F.R. Scott, John Adaskin, Northrop Frye, Claude Bissell, Morley Callaghan, Robert Weaver, Jack Shadbolt, Anne Marriott, Roderick Haig-Brown, Bill McConnell, P.K. Page, Ethel Wilson, Paul Engle, Miriam Waddington, W. Kaye Lamb, Jack McClelland, Irving Layton, Stephen Vizinczey and Leonard Cohen, to name only a few. In Vancouver, Birney also befriended newcomers Malcolm Lowry and George Woodcock, and became a central personality in an unofficial writers' colony that existed on Bowen Island, hosted by Einer Neilson. Birney organized visits by Dylan Thomas, Theodore Roethke, Charles Olson and W.H. Auden, among others. He supported and encouraged countless writers and students such as Jack Hodgins, Tom Wayman, Daryl Duke, Norm Klenman, Heather Spears, George Bowering, Norman Newton, Frank Davey, George Johnston, Bill Galt, Lionel Kearns, Mary McAlpine, Daphne Marlatt, Ernie Perrault and Robert Harlow (who became Head of the Creative Writing Department). Earle Birney was also good at making enemies, including his fellow poet and leftist radical Dorothy Livesay who alleged that Birney's much-anthologized poem "David" had autobiographical origins.

ROBERT SWANSON

Robert Swanson, the "Bard of the Woods," travelled extensively in B.C. logging camps and also broadcast his poems via his weekly talk show on CJOR. Although his chapbooks were never accepted by the literary establishment, his books easily outsold the better-known poets of the 1940s, starting with *Rhymes of a Western Logger: A Book of Verse* (1942).

It was Robert Service who advised replicating his approach to writing poetry about the Yukon to B.C.'s logging industry. The extent of Swanson's popularity as a versifier for B.C.'s main industry is rarely appreciated today, but, in the late 1980s, B.C. forestry authority Ken Drushka once remarked that being on a reading tour with Robert Swanson was "like travelling with an octogenarian rock star."

Born in Reading, England, in 1905, Swanson worked as a logger, then gained his degree as a professional engineer. When new diesel locomotives created safety problems at highway crossings (because motorists could not recognize their monotone horns as an approaching train), Swanson invented a tuned hexatone airhorn that recreates the wail of a steam train whistle. It was adapted for use all over the world.

Swanson also invented a fail-safe braking system for logging trucks that was adopted as standard equipment all over North America. As the inspector for the Department of Transport, he devised runaway lanes on steep hills and insisted on better regulations for bridge designs. His expertise on steam trains and their whistles was central to the restoration of B.C.'s Royal Hudson excursion train. Air Chime, a company he founded in 1964, provided the "O Canada" air chimes for the Centennial train in 1967. In addition, Swanson engineered the horn that blasts the first four notes of "O Canada" from the roof of Canada Place every day at noon. Swanson's handiwork can also be seen and heard in Gastown's steam clock.

Swanson once represented Canada at the World Standards Organization. He was also the first president of the B.C. Truck Museum and helped his friend Gerry Wellburn establish the working locomotive at the B.C. Forest Museum. A Freemason for 64 years, B.C.'s bestselling poet was also one of the most ingenious of British Columbians. He died in 1994.

W.K. LAMB

Born in New Westminster in 1904, William Kaye Lamb, British Columbia's greatest librarian, is one of the most under-celebrated figures of British Columbia's literary history. A prodigious historian, editor and author, Lamb first published "Founding of Fort Victoria" (1943), in the *British Columbia Historical Quarterly*. "Any country worthy of a future," he maintained, "should be interested in its past."

Lamb's various works include a 256-page introduction to a four-volume edition of Captain George Vancouver's *A Voyage of Discovery to the North Pacific Ocean and Round the World, 1791–1795*. Lamb also edited essential reference works for the fur trade writings of

Brenda Guiled's portrait of scholar and historian W. K. Lamb, B.C.'s greatest librarian

Simon Fraser, Alexander Mackenzie, Daniel Harmon and Gabriel Franchère. Equally important, for many years Lamb was a fundamental force behind the *British Columbia Historical Quarterly*, the cornerstone of academically oriented research about the province.

Having attended UBC, the Sorbonne and the University of London, where he earned a Ph.D in 1933, Lamb was the provincial archivist and librarian of British Columbia (1934–1940), University Librarian of the University of British Columbia (1940–1948), dominion archivist of Canada (1948–1968) and national librarian of Canada (1953–1967).

He held ten honorary doctorates, received the Tyrrell Medal from the Royal Society of Canada and was an officer of the Order of Canada.

In a tribute delivered at W.K. Lamb's memorial service in 1999, UBC's Basil Stuart-Stubbs, University Librarian Emeritus, praised Lamb's capacious memory as "simply dazzling." Lamb, like his mentor F.W. Howay, was both a collector of knowledge and a builder of culture, keenly attuned to literature. As well, according to Stuart-

Stubbs, "He seemed to have an innate understanding of organizational behaviour and human nature. . . . Trust and delegation were to be the permanent hallmarks of his administrative style. Similarly, he seemed to have an instinctive knowledge of bureaucracies and how to work within them effectively."

Lamb cannot be overlooked. His incorporation here, as a literary builder of British Columbia, recognizes the integral role of B.C.'s librarians in fostering knowledge and education through literature.

ERIC NICOL

Under the pen name Jabez, the indefatigable Eric Nicol first co-published *Says We* (1943), a collection of *Vancouver News-Herald* columns with legendary Vancouver journalist Jack Scott. Some 67 years later, with his literary talents still in evidence even though he was suffering from Alzheimer's disease, the veteran newspaper columnist and playwright released another collection of whimsical musings, *Script Tease* (2010). Along the way, Nicol has received three Stephen Leacock Medals for Humour.

Nicol became the first living Canadian writer to be included in *The Oxford Book of Humorous Prose* and the first Vancouver playwright to have his work produced by the Vancouver Playhouse. In 1995, he received the first George Woodcock Lifetime Achievement Award for an exemplary literary career in British Columbia.

Born in 1919 in Kingston, Ontario, Eric Nicol "almost immediately persuaded his parents to flee a fierce winter in favour of a farmhouse on Kingsway." He later described B.C. as "a body of land surrounded by envy."

Nicol started his literary career with the *Ubyssey* newspaper, at the University of British Columbia, where he adopted his pen name of Jabez. Nicol served for three years with the Royal Canadian Air Force during WWII and returned to UBC for his M.A. in French Studies in 1948. He spent one year in doctoral studies at the Sorbonne, then moved to London, England, to write radio comedy for the BBC. He returned to Vancouver in 1951 to become a regular columnist with the *Province*, producing some 6,000 newspaper columns, several stage plays and numerous scripts for radio and television.

Nicol's best-known play, *Like Father, Like Fun*, first staged in 1966, concerns a crass lumber baron's attempt to contrive his son's initiation to sex. It was unsuccessfully staged on Broadway in 1967 under the title *A Minor Adjustment*. *The Fourth Monkey*, produced in 1968, is about a failed playwright who takes refuge on the Gulf Islands (where Nicol had a cottage).

For most of his life, Eric Nicol lived in the same house he purchased in 1957, near UBC. He liked to say he did not smoke, drink, play cards or run around with women—but he hoped to do so if royalties came pouring in. Terribly shy, he avoided parties. He was always afraid to take holidays in case he could not retain his job at the *Province*. After more than forty years of service, he was unceremoniously let go by Pacific Press.

An unstoppable punster, Nicol nonetheless did not wish to be pegged as simply a humorist. One of his *Province* columns against capital punishment resulted in a citation for contempt and a trial that attracted national interest.

Noteworthy titles among Nicol's 42 books include an excellent history, *Vancouver* (1970), *Dickens of the Mounted: The Astounding Long-Lost Letters of Inspector F. Dickens NWMP 1874–1886* (1989) and *Anything for a Laugh: Memoirs* (1998).

For other authors pertaining to humour, see abcbookworld entries for Adams, Victoria; Bartlett, Rex; Bierman, Bob; Black, Arthur; Boswell, David; Collins, Bob; Coyote, Ivan E.; Daacon, George; Duffie, John; Filbrandt, Rod; Freir, Pam; Gabereau, Vicki; Glave, James; Grayson, Steven; Gudgeon, Chris; Harrop, Graham; Hou, Charles; Hunter, Don; Juby, Susan; Julian, Terry; Kirkland, Gordon; Klunder, Barbara Wyn; Knighton, Ryan; Koshevoy, Himie; Krieger, Robert; Leiren-Young, Mark; Maartman, Ben; MacDonald, Kyle; McCardell, Mike; Mitchell, Howard; Morton, James; Mythen, John; O'Hara, Jane; Palmer, H.S.; Palmer, Hugh; Partridge, Colin; Peterson, Roy; Raeside, Adrian; Richardson, Bill; Rowe, Dwayne; Sager, Dorianne; Schroeder, Andreas; Shave, Barbara J.; Sisson, Hal; St. Ives, Dan; Struthers, Andrew; Thompson, Robert H.; Verchere, Ian; Whalen, Len; White, Howard.

BRUCE HUTCHISON

The Hollow Men (1944) by Bruce Hutchison

Published near the end of WWII, Bruce Hutchison's only novel, *The Hollow Men* (1944), is a rarely-mentioned portrait of a journalist named Leslie Duncan who is torn between his father's beloved Cariboo ranch and his political responsibilities in both Washington, D.C., and Ottawa ("the counterfeit little world on Parliament Hill") during WWII. Leslie Duncan yearns to be something more than another of the "hollow men" described in T.S. Eliot's famous poem. *The Hollow Men* is an unusually sophisticated portrayal of both the country life of ranchers and the limitations of politics. It evokes the plight of a B.C. intellectual who feels alienated from the centres of power: a timeless subject for anyone west of the Rockies.

Nauseated by the intrigue and interminable talk of Ottawa, Duncan is likewise disillusioned by the staged bravado and empty mythology of the United States. Life at his Cariboo ranch is the answer but, like the noble Cincinnatus who felt obliged to leave his family farm and serve in ancient Rome, Duncan repeatedly gets his hands dirty in politics to further the public good. His goal is to secure suitable irrigation for his district and, in order to do so, he compromises his relationship with his wife, losing his soul in a web of betrayals orchestrated by lesser men.

Bruce Hutchison became much better known as an influential fixture at the *Vancouver Sun*. He wrote 16 books, most notably *The Unknown Country: Canada and Her People* (1942), produced in about six weeks. "I didn't know anything about book writing," he told Trevor Lautens. He wrote the book only because he was asked to do so by an American when he was visiting New York, hence the title is from an American perspective. It received the Governor General's Award for Non-Fiction, as did *The Incredible Canadian: A Candid Portrait of Mackenzie King, His Works, His Times and His Nation* (1952) and *Canada: Tomorrow's Giant* (1957). Bruce Hutchison died in 1992, in Victoria.

The Hollow Men was not the first attempt to depict the Cariboo in fiction. Robert Allison Hood's melodramatic rancher-as-hero tale, *The Chivalry of Keith Leicester: A Romance of British Columbia* (1918) is an even more obscure novel. Ann Walsh's young adult novel *Your Time My Time* (1984) is a time-travel bestseller set in Barkerville. Ethel Wilson's *Hetty Dorval* (1947) deserves more attention than her better-known *Swamp Angel* (1954) or Sheila Watson's *The Double Hook* (1959) and *Deep Hollow Creek* (1992). Critic Robert Wiersema highly recommends *The Reckoning of Boston Jim* (2007) by Claire Mulligan, shortlisted for the Ethel Wilson Fiction Prize and longlisted for the Giller Prize in 2008. Touched by the kindness of Cowichan Valley settler Dora Hume, a lonesome trapper named Boston Jim decides to search for Dora's capricious husband in the gold rush town of Barkerville in 1863. For other fiction authors pertaining to the Cariboo-Chilcotin, see *Essentials* entries for Paul St. Pierre and Alan Fry. Also see abcbookworld entries for Gallaher, Bill; Krumm, Stan; Petersen, Christian.

DOROTHY LIVESAY

The annual B.C. Book Prize for poetry is named in honour of Dorothy Kathleen May Livesay, a social activist who lived in North Vancouver for much of her married years. Born in Winnipeg in 1909, daughter of one of the founders of Canadian Press, temperamental "Dee" Livesay was a lifelong agitator for women's rights who published her first poetry book as a Toronto university student in 1928. Her best-known poem is "The Unquiet Bed." In 1980, George Woodcock described her as "the best poet writing in Canada today, and for the past two decades as well."

Influenced by the Depression and by hearing lectures by anarchist Emma Goldman, Livesay first wrote Marxist poems for a short-lived Toronto communist newspaper and studied at the School of Social Work in Toronto (1932–1933). After moving to Vancouver in 1936, she married Duncan Cameron Macnair in 1937.

Dorothy Livesay was a two-time recipient of the Governor General's award for poetry.

Her involvement with the Progressive Arts Club led to her participation in founding *Contemporary Verse* with Alan Crawley, Anne Marriott and Floris Clark McLaren in 1941. It remained the main organ for new poetry west of Ontario throughout the forties.

Livesay received her first Governor General's Award for *Day and Night* (1944), followed by another for *Poems for People* (1947). In 1949, CBC aired her long poem about the internment of Japanese Canadians, "Call My People Home."

Livesay taught school in B.C. during the 1950s, lived in Northern Rhodesia during the early 1960s, and gained her M.Ed. from UBC in 1966.

Livesay was a co-founder, and for many years editor, of the literary quarterly *CVII* and a founding member of Amnesty International (Canada), the Committee for an Independent Canada, and the League of Canadian Poets. Her grandson Randal Macnair of Fernie now owns and operates Oolichan Books, a literary press founded by Ron Smith.

Feisty, opinionated and sometimes self-righteous, Dorothy Livesay lived briefly on Galiano Island before moving to Victoria where she died in 1996. In January of that year more than 200 people gathered at the Victoria Art Gallery to pay tribute to her spirit. Robert Kroetsch, who knew Livesay when she was writer-in-residence in Winnipeg, recalled that she once clinched an argument by pounding him on the chest with both fists. "She won that one," he said. Daphne Marlatt, who met Livesay in the early sixties, was astonished when Dee proceeded to instruct her on how she should and shouldn't read her own poetry. "For me she was courage and love," said Linda Rogers. "I loved the way Dorothy kicked ass," said Cathy Ford, B.C. representative for the League of Canadian Poets.

Mona Fertig, who was 18 when she first met Livesay, said, "I think of her as the grandmother of Canadian poetry."

RUDOLF VRBA

The most important memoir published by a British Columbian is Rudolf Vrba's co-authored the "Vrba-Wetzler Report," an eyewitness account in which Vrba estimated the scale of mass murder at Auschwitz-Birkenau and described the Nazis' methodology. It reached the governments of the Allies before the end of June, 1944, and alerted political and Jewish leaders about the true nature of the Nazi death camps.

The 32-page "Vrba-Wetzler Report" is one of the most important documents of the 20th century. Copies of the original "Vrba-Wetzler Report" are kept in the Franklin D. Roosevelt Library in New York, in the Vatican archives, and at the Yad Vashem memorial in Jerusalem. Vrba told his life story in *I Cannot Forgive* (1963).

Vrba was born as Walter Rosenberg in Topolcany, Czechoslovakia, in 1924. He was arrested by the Nazis at age 18, incarcerated at the Majdanek concentration camp, and in June of 1942 transferred to Auschwitz for slave labour. After his almost unprecedented successful escape—during which he and Alfred Wetzler hid inside a woodpile for several days while guards and dogs searched for them—he joined a partisan group, adopted the name Rudolf Vrba, and fought against the Nazis until the end of the war.

A Jew named Siegfried Lederer had successfully fled six days earlier, on April 5, 1944, in the company of one of the Nazi guards, a corporal named Viktor Pestek, who had fallen in love with a

Jewish woman in the camp. Pestek supplied Lederer with a Nazi uniform. Two other men escaped in May of 1944.

Vrba has been featured in numerous documentary films, most notably *Shoah* by Claude Lanzmann, and he has appeared as a witness for various investigations and trials, such as the Frankfurt Auschwitz trial in 1964.

In Canada, Vrba was called upon to provide testimony at the seven-week trial of Ontario's Ernst Zundel in 1985. Zundel was found guilty of misleading the public as a Holocaust denier. In 2001, the Czech Republic's annual One World International Human Rights Film Festival established a film award in his name.

Vrba graduated in chemistry and biochemistry from the Prague Technical University in 1951 and the Czechoslovak Academy of Sciences in 1956. He was later a member of the scientific staff of the British Medical Research Council from 1960 to 1967.

Vrba immigrated to Canada in 1967 to become associate of the Medical Research Council of Canada.

After two years (1973–1975) as research fellow at Harvard Medical School, Vrba joined the medical faculty at the University of British Columbia as associate professor of pharmacology, specializing in pharmacology pertaining to the brain.

Rudolf Vrba wrote the most important memoir by a British Columbian.

Although Vrba kept a low profile, he accepted an invitation to be a guest speaker at the 16th annual B.C. Book Prizes awards banquet in 2001.

Vrba lived in Vancouver from 1975 until his death in 2006.

"It is of evil to assent to evil actively or passively, as an instrument, as an observer, or as a victim," he concluded in his autobiography. "Under certain circumstances even ignorance is evil."

ELIZABETH SMART

By Grand Central Station I Sat Down and Wept (1945)
by Elizabeth Smart

Lonely, single, pregnant but above all fiercely in love—perhaps with love itself—Elizabeth Smart stepped off the steamer
Lady Cynthia at Irvine's Landing in Pender Harbour, B.C., in April
of 1941. The world was at war and she sought solitude. Eight months
later she left Pender Harbour, having produced her first born,
Georgina Barker, along with her rhapsodic lament entitled *By Grand
Central Station I Sat Down and Wept* (1945). Ever since, Smart's unusual upper class and bohemian lifestyle has both charmed and
appalled readers, who are astonished by her lifelong, masochistic
devotion to English poet George Barker, by whom she bore four
children without ever living with him.

Born to an affluent family in Ottawa in 1913, Smart was sent to
London to be educated. There she picked up a small book of
poetry by George Barker, a protegé of T.S. Eliot, and, as the story
goes, decided then and there, sight unseen, that she would marry
him and have his children. Along the way she met the likes of
Henry Miller and Picasso, and lost her virginity to the flamboyant
and arrogant painter Jean Varda in Cassis, France. In Mexico she
attended a birthday party of renowned Mexican muralist Diego
Rivera and had an affair with Alice Paalen. Varda showed up in
Mexico and he and Smart ended up living together in Big Sur,
California, in an artists' colony. In California, Smart wrote a no-
vella based on her lesbian experiences with Paalen entitled "Dig A
Grave and Let Us Bury Our Mother." It would appear in *In The
Meantime* (1984). Smart had previously been in touch with poet
George Barker, buying an original manuscript and exchanging

Elizabeth Smart wrote convincingly about love, longing and sex.

letters. Smart had sent some poems to Lawrence Durrell in 1938 and he had suggested Smart and Barker should meet—because Barker, who was teaching in Japan, was short of money. Barker approached Smart for funds to flee the country. Smart met him in Monterey and was taken aback to discover he had his wife with him. It is this scene which opens *By Grand Central Station I Sat Down and Wept*. Despite the presence of Mrs. Barker, the pair were soon having an intense affair which resulted in Smart's first pregnancy.

In Pender Harbour, Smart lived in one of three shacks near the mouth of the harbour and painted her door yellow, adding a line from William Blake's *The Marriage of Heaven and Hell* above it, "The cut worm forgives the plough." Barker visited briefly early in her pregnancy. She made a few friends, the most remarkable being Vienna-born Maximiliane Von Upani Southwell ("Maxie"), some 20 years her senior.

As Smart's pregnancy and manuscript came near completion, Maxie took her in, despite her own poverty, and assisted her. Elizabeth Smart, in return, dedicated *By Grand Central Station I Sat Down and Wept* to Maxie. When Barker tried to visit Smart a second time during the pregnancy, Smart's mother used their Ottawa connections to keep him out of Canada. Barker was stopped at the border. Their child was born in August and Smart left Canada on December 7, 1941—the day Japan attacked Pearl Harbor—leaving the infant with Maxie in order to meet up with Barker. He failed to meet her at Grand Central Station.

Elizabeth Smart left Canada for England in 1984 and died there at age 72 two years later. Smart once said, "It's a natural feeling to want to have a baby when you're really in love. Every woman feels it and I think men do, too, when they're really involved. A woman is a man with a womb, that's what the word means. It's not a man without something, it's a man with something and that something is a womb. I wanted these female experiences."

MALCOLM LOWRY

Under the Volcano (1947) by Malcolm Lowry

For most of the twentieth century the most famous book ever written mainly in British Columbia was *Under the Volcano* (1947) by Malcolm Lowry, ranked eleventh by the editors of Modern Library in their list of the best 100 novels written in English in the 20th century. Set in Mexico on the Day of the Dead, but including a reference to British Columbia as a "genteel Siberia," *Under the Volcano* was continuously revised during many of Lowry's 14 years of intermittent residence in Vancouver and North Vancouver, primarily at two squatter's shacks at Dollarton, near Deep Cove. A sign saying Malcolm Lowry Walk, located at the beginning of a waterfront trail at the eastern end of Cates Park in North Vancouver, provides some modest recognition for his infamously alcoholic, self-tortured literary life. According to Lowry's first wife, Jan Gabriel, "he would drink anything."

Malcolm Lowry at Dollarton, North Vancouver, 1946, where he wrote most of Under the Volcano

Lowry first took occupancy of his beloved "little lonely hermitage" without plumbing or electricity in 1940 following his marriage to Margerie Bonner. In June of 1944 his shack burned, destroying some of the manuscript. Lowry rebuilt the shack. According to Bonner, the fourth and final draft of *Under the Volcano* was completed at Dollarton on Christmas Eve, 1944. He habitually despised Vancouver, referring to it in his fictions as Enochvilleport, meaning "city of the son of Cain." Conversely, he referred to the tiny gathering of squatter's shacks on the fore-shore of Burrard Inlet as Eridanus, a name drawn from the river in Virgil's *Aeneid* that waters the Elysian Fields of the Earthly Para-dise.

Writing about Lowry is an industry unto itself. His literary ar-chives are kept at UBC. Sherrill Grace of Vancouver has become one of the world's foremost authorities on his life and works.

ETHEL WILSON

The top fiction award in B.C., the Ethel Wilson Prize, com-memorates the author of six books and the subject of two biographies and one critical study. Wilson's first and arguably best novel, *Hetty Dorval* (1947), was supposedly written in three weeks while her husband was away. It's a post-WWII parable, narrated by an innocent girl in the B.C. Interior who recalls her unusual friend-ship with a visiting city woman named Hetty Dorval, who is sophis-ticated, charming and selfish. Wilson's most celebrated novel, *Swamp Angel* (1954), concerns the escape of Maggie Vardoe from an unpleasant second marriage in Vancouver to a new life at a remote interior B.C. lake. In *Love and Salt Water* (1956), she wrote that "the formidable power of geography determines the charac-ter and performance of a people." Hence Wilson was highly at-tuned to what she called "the genius of place." Wilson's phrase was used by one of her biographers, David Stouck, for the title of a non-fiction anthology of B.C. writing, co-edited with Myler Wilkinson. "No other writer," George Woodcock declared, "has more successfully evoked British Columbia as a place or its inhab-itants as a strange and unique people than Ethel Wilson."

Born in 1888 in South Africa, Ethel Wilson was the daughter of a Wesleyan Methodist minister. She went to live in Pembroke, Wales, in 1890 after her mother died. Her father died when she was nine. At age ten she was taken to live with her maternal grandmother in Vancouver, she was remembered as "the school beauty." She taught in Vancouver elementary schools, dutifully but without pleasure, until 1920. In 1921, she found lasting security and happiness when she married Dr. Wallace Wilson, a much-respected president of the Canadian Medical Association and professor of medical ethics at UBC. The couple lived in relative luxury in their spacious Kensington

Ethel Wilson, circa 1921, before she became a novelist

Place apartment overlooking English Bay, surrounded by Oriental rugs, books, a photo of a sketch of Winston Churchill, an original Burne-Jones pencil drawing and the same housekeeper for 22 years. Ethel Wilson's presence was fundamental to the careers of both Alice Munro and Margaret Laurence, who have acknowledged their appreciation.

Margaret Laurence wrote to her friend Adele Wiseman: "She is so terrific. I don't know how to describe her. She not only writes like an angel (in my opinion) but is, herself, a truly great lady— again, that probably sounds corny, but I don't know how else to express it. Her husband is a doctor (retired) and they live in an apartment overlooking English Bay. She is very badly crippled with arthritis, but she never mentions her health. She is poised in the true way—she never makes other people feel gauche. And she is absolutely straight in her speech—she has no pretensions, nor does she say anything she doesn't mean, and yet she has a kind of sympathetic tact."

After Dr. Wilson died in 1966, Ethel Wilson moved to an apartment on Point Grey Road, suffered a stroke and no longer wrote. She lived for nearly eight years in the Arbutus Private Hospital until her death in 1980.

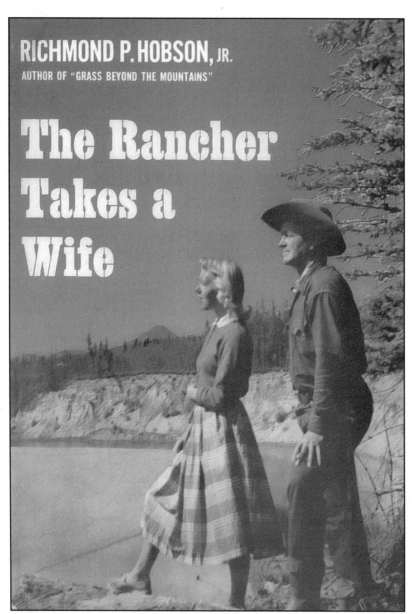

Book jacket for Richmond P. Hobson, Jr.'s The Rancher Takes a Wife

IV

1950s

RODERICK HAIG-BROWN

Measure of the Year (1950) by Roderick Haig-Brown

The Roderick Haig-Brown Regional Prize for best book contributing to the understanding and appreciation of British Columbia is named in honour of the Campbell River angler and essayist. His name will also endure for his foresight as a conservationist long before the word "environment" became common. In 1982, he wrote, "Can man make a rational response to his knowledge of the environment? Can he become sensitive, generous, and considerate to his world and the other creatures that share it with him, or is his nature immutably rooted in blood, sex and darkness?"

To favour any one of the 26 Haig-Brown titles between *Silver: The Life Story of an Atlantic Salmon* (1931) to *The Salmon* (1974), one might well agree with the editors of the anthology *Genius of Place* (2000) and select his meditations on life and nature near the midway point of his career, *Measure of the Year* (1950). In an excerpt entitled "Let Them Eat Sawdust," he writes: "I think there has never been, in any state, a conservationist government, because there has never been a people with sufficient humility to take conservation seriously. . . . Conservation means fair and honest dealing with the future, usually at some cost to the immediate present." A juvenile novel, *Starbuck Valley Winter* (1943), has been cited as Haig-Brown's bestselling title. An angling classic, *A River Never Sleeps* (1946), guides the reader through the course of a fictional fishing year, visiting different rivers month by month. Adult novels *Timber* (1942) and *On the Highest Hill* (1949) concern life in the logging camps.

Roderick Haig-Brown was born in 1908 in Sussex, England. His

Roderick Haig-Brown, a pioneer conservationist,
with his children Valerie, Mary, Alan and Celia

mother was from a wealthy family in the brewery business. As a teenager, Haig-Brown met Thomas Hardy. A family friend, Major Greenhill, inspired his refined appreciation for hunting and fishing. Expelled from Charterhouse School for drinking and unsanctioned absenteeism, he persuaded his mother to send him to Seattle to visit his uncle, promising to return when he was of an age to apply for entry into the civil service. After working in a lumber camp in Washington State, he came north to avoid visa problems, spending three years in the Nimpkish Lake area of Vancouver Island, variously employed as a logger, guide and fisherman. In Seattle he had met his future wife Ann Elmore, also born in 1908. They married in 1934 and took up residence on the banks of the Campbell River where they lived until their deaths: Roderick in 1976 and Ann in 1990. Their "Above Tide" residence is preserved as a heritage site. Valerie Haig-Brown edited some of her father's books; Alan and Celia Haig-Brown are significant authors.

The pipe-smoker with a hyphenated name never attended university, but Haig-Brown served ably as a lay magistrate for northern Vancouver Island from 1941 until 1974. He also served as Chancellor of the University of Victoria from 1970 to 1973. E. Bennett Metcalfe published a controversial but intriguing biography called *A Man of Some Importance* (1985) "to rescue Haig-Brown from the myth-makers." It was loathed and fiercely repressed by Haig-Brown's widow. Anthony Robertson, Valerie Haig-Brown and Robert Cave have produced more laudatory books.

RICHMOND P. HOBSON, JR.

Richmond P. Hobson, Jr. wrote two non-fiction ranching classics, *Grass Beyond the Mountains* (1951) and *Nothing Too Good for a Cowboy* (1955). Born in Washington, D.C., in 1907, Hobson, Jr. was the son of American war hero Rear Admiral Richmond P. Hobson who, in turn, was named for Lt. Richmond Pearson who fought in the American Revolution. After attending Stanford University, "Rich" Hobson worked to save money to buy a cattle ranch. When he lost his savings with the 1929 crash of the stock market, he went west to Wyoming and teamed up with Pan Phillips, also known as Panhandle Phillips. They came north to explore B.C. in the early 1930s. Phillips and Hobson, Jr. formed the Frontier Cattle Company and created the Home Ranch in the Chilcotin, north of Anahim Lake.

Grass Beyond the Mountains: Discovering the Last Great Cattle Frontier on the North American Continent recalls the early days of a fledgling enterprise on thousands of acres of land, culminating in a successful test cattle drive in 1937 known as the Starvation Drive. This tale of hardship and perseverance was initially serialized by *Maclean's* magazine during a period when Ralph Allen and Pierre Berton were editors. *Nothing Too Good for a Cowboy* is a follow-up volume in which Hobson, Jr. recalls his struggles with Phillips to maintain their four-million-acre spread with a shortage of men and supplies due to the outbreak of WWII. The ranchers endure frozen faces, marauding wolf packs and blood poisoning mixed with the romance of starry skies and sweet mountain air. To break the solitude, Hobson has a recurring vision of a beautiful blonde woman. This true story of ranch life on the 52nd parallel reputedly sold more than 100,000 copies.

Hobson's partnership with Phillips dissolved in the 1940s. Hobson resumed ranching in the Vanderhoof area with his wife, Gloria, leading to his third and final book, *The Rancher Takes a Wife* (1961). Hobson died suddenly at his River Ranch, 50 miles south of Vanderhoof, in 1966. His stories were the basis for a CBC television series entitled *Nothing Too Good for a Cowboy*, filmed in British Columbia.

For other authors pertaining to ranching, see abcbookworld entries for Adams, Ramon F.; Affleck, Edward L.; Alsager, Dale; Alsager, Judy; Bliss, Irene; Brown, Jack; Bulman, T. Alex; Carroll, Campbell; Cohen, Bill; Conkin, Jake; Cox, Doug; Duncan, Eric; Freeman, Richard; Hobson Jr., Richmond; Kind, Chris; Knight, Rolf; Lavington, Dude; Lee, Norman; Lee, Todd; Loggins, Olive Spencer; MacDonald, Ervin Austin; Mann, Elizabeth; Marriott, Harry; Mather, Ken; McCredie, Andrew; McLean, Alastair; McLean, Stan; Picard, Ed; Piffko, Karen; Place, Hilary; Resford, Eliza; Roger, Gertrude Minor; Shoroplava, Nina; Simmons, Clarence; Stangoe, Irene; Tepper, Leslie; Wuest, Donna.

WILSON DUFF

The mystical extent to which Wilson Duff devoted himself to his work as the first anthropologist to be fully employed by the provincial government of B.C., and as the curator of anthropology at the provincial museum in Victoria from 1950 to 1965, is legendary among those who knew him, but otherwise unknown to the general public.

Born in Vancouver in 1925, Wilson Duff committed suicide in 1976, in Vancouver, hoping to be reincarnated as an aboriginal from Haida Gwaii or the Tsimshian First Nation. Bill Reid had given Duff a silver medallion with a Haida design, with an inscription on the back saying "survivor, first class," for his 50th birthday. Duff was wearing the medallion when he shot himself. Claude Lévi-Strauss wrote, "I wonder if it was not, after all, this desperate quest for infinite mysteries—perhaps because they were above all an exigency of his mind—that killed this unaffected, charming, altruistic and kind man, who was also a great scholar."

Five years later, Donald N. Abbott and others edited *The World Is as Sharp as a Knife: An Anthology in Honour of Wilson Duff* (1981). The title was drawn from a poem by Wilson Duff of the same name. "There are no laws, / which you can trust to work. / There are just rules, / which you must make to work. / In the one hand, / you are holding the mirror. / On the other hand, / you are the mask. / Put on the mask and look in the mirror. What you see / (the mirror does not lie) / is that which is common to both, / the truth you can believe."

Based on his fieldwork with six main informants in the summers of 1949 and 1950, Duff provided the first modern ethnographic study of the Cowichan group in 1952. He was involved with Mungo Martin in the reclamation of totem poles, and he chaired the Archaeological Sites Advisory Board from 1960 to 1966. Having served as a consultant for the Kitwancool in northern B.C., Duff served as an expert witness for both the Calder Case and the ensuing Nisga'a land claims case before the B.C. Supreme Court. According to "Wilson Duff's Dystopia" published in 2010 by Maureen Flynn-Burhoe, "Duff published a guide to Victoria's Thunderbird Park and he made an important contribution towards identifying personal art styles among aboriginal artists, particularly Charles Edenshaw. This work led others, such as Bill Reid, to believe that most of the finest carving on Haida Gwaii was accomplished by relatively few gifted artists."

Following his preparation of the 191-page *Arts of the Raven* catalogue for a Vancouver Art Gallery exhibit in 1967, Wilson became obsessed with the notion of bringing together the only two stone masks known to exist from the Northwest Coast: one Tsimshian mask with closed eyes was kept in Ottawa and the other with open eyes was kept in Paris. In 1975 he and art gallery director Richard Simmins obtained permission from France to transport their priceless mask to British Columbia for a one-year period. Wilson Duff retrieved the twin mask from the Musée de l'Homme, bringing it to Vancouver; Hilary Stewart transported the mask from Vancouver to the Victoria Art Gallery where it was reunited with the mask from Ottawa.

"The sightless mask was lifted carefully and placed over the face of its seeing twin," Stewart recalled. "...the two nested together in a close, snug fit. It was a deeply moving moment as the two masks came together again for the first time in a hundred years or more." The mask from Ottawa had been collected by I.W. Powell at the Tsimshian village of Kitkatla in 1879; the "open-eye" mask was donated to the French Museum of Man by Alphonse Pinart. It was said to have been collected at Metlakatla or on the Nass River. After consulting with Musqueam Della Kew, Duff brought the stone masks together, one cradled by the other, each an equal part of a whole. He later wrote, "Life is a pair of twin stone masks which are the very same but have opposite eyes." The masks represented the "living paradoxes in myth and life" that he believed were near the source of Northwest Coast aboriginal art.

At least two of Wilson Duff's books, *The Indian History of British Columbia: The Impact of the White Man* (1964) and *Images: Stone: B.C.: Thirty Centuries of Northwest Coast Indian Sculpture* (1975), are cornerstones of B.C. ethnology. Other books by Wilson Duff include *The Upper Stalo Indians of the Fraser Valley, British Columbia* (1952), *Histories, Territories and Laws of the Kitwancool* (1959), *Arts of the Raven: Masterworks by the Northwest Coast Indian. An Exhibition in Honour of the One Hundredth Anniversary of Canadian Confederation* (1967) and *Bird of Paradox: The Unpublished Writings of Wilson Duff* (1996).

GILEAN DOUGLAS

Gilean Douglas, author of *River for My Sidewalk* (1953), was a female Thoreau of Canada. A loner from a well-to-do family, she retreated to wilderness cabins and became an environmentalist before the word existed, leaving four marriages behind her.

Gilean Douglas, born in Toronto in 1900, was orphaned at age 16 and soon became a reporter. She travelled extensively prior to her arrival in B.C. in 1938 where she first lived in a cabin on the Coquihalla River. She then moved to an abandoned miner's shack on the Teal River near Duncan, B.C. "It was the great moment of my life when I waded the Teal River," she wrote, "with my packboard on my back and stood at last on my own ground. I can never describe the feeling that surged up inside me then. . . . I felt kinship in everything around me, and the long city years of noise and faces were just fading photographs." Subsisting mainly on produce from her garden, Douglas began to write about her adventures but could not find acceptance as a woman writing about outdoor life. Adopting the male pseudonym Grant Madison did the trick—and she published *River For My Sidewalk*, her best-known book.

Gilean Douglas continued to use her male name until 1983 when she revealed herself in a *Vancouver Sun* interview. Douglas next moved to Cortes Island, near Campbell River. "I have spoken many times of "my land" and "my property," but how foolish it would be of me to believe that I possessed something which cannot be possessed," she once wrote. Along with seven poetry books, she produced two more meditative memoirs, *Silence is My Homeland: Life on Teal River* (1978) and *The Protected Place* (1979). The latter describes life on her 140-acre homestead on Cortes Island where she was employed as an Environment Canada weather observer and a Search and Rescue agent. Her cottage was situated at Channel Rock on Uganda Pass. For nine years she served as the Cortes representative on the Comox-Strathcona Regional Board. Gilean Douglas also contributed a nature column called "Nature Rambles" to the *Victoria Daily Colonist* (which became the *Times Colonist* in 1980) for 31 years, from 1961 to 1992, a longevity for a B.C. columnist that places in her in the company of Eric Nicol and Arthur Mayse. She died on Cortes Island in 1993.

Douglas was preceded into print by Pennsylania-born Theodora Stanwell-Fletcher, whose memoir of homesteading at Takla Landing, near Babine Lake, *Driftwood Valley: A Woman Naturalist in the Northern Wilderness* (1946), was reprinted 17 times in the 1940s and early 1950s. For other memoirs by women about the wilderness, see abcbookworld entries for Daisy Elizabeth Callison, Chris Czajkowski, Tor Forsberg, Deanna Kawatski, Monica Storrs and Sunny Wright.

HUBERT EVANS

Mist on the River (1954) by Hubert Evans

The Quaker outdoorsman Hubert Reginald Evans was a professional writer in British Columbia for seven decades. Revered by his pen pal Margaret Laurence as "the Elder of our Tribe," Evans was born in Vankleek Hill, Ontario, in 1892, and started building a waterfront cabin at Roberts Creek, B.C., in 1926.

In response to the horrors he witnessed in the trenches as a soldier in WWI, Evans wrote an autobiographical novel, *The New Front Line* (1927), about a soldier named Hugh Henderson who migrates from older societies to the "new front line" of idealism in the wilds of B.C.

In 1927, his first year as a fulltime writer, he earned $97 less postage.

Evans is best remembered for his second novel, *Mist on the River* (1954), the first Canadian novel to portray aboriginals realistically as complex, central characters. This classic arose after Evans and his wife received a visit from aboriginal activist Guy Williams of Kitimaat (separate from present-day Kitimat) towards the end of WWII, requesting Ann Evans move to Kitimaat to teach his children. She had taught Williams in a residential school near the Evanses' floathouse at Cultus Lake in the early 1920s.

Williams told the Evanses that some aboriginal children in Kitimaat hadn't had a teacher for five years and they had forgotten how to speak English. "I had quite a number of chums in the army who were Indians," Evans later recalled, "but it was really my wife's Quaker concern over Indians that took us north in the first place."

Upon their arrival in Kitimaat in January of 1945, the Evanses were greeted by the entire village. They stayed for two and a half years. "We were the only white people around," Evans recalled. "It was 140 miles to a hospital at Bella Bella, in a gas boat mostly. Sometimes in bad weather you couldn't get there. The Indian agent handed me the little black bag that the nurse who'd been there years before had had. He said, 'You're the dispenser.' And so I coped."

The Evanses' experiences resulted in a short story "Let My People Go" that appeared in *Maclean's* in 1947. It concerns a Gitksan schoolteacher named Cy who struggles to assimilate his stubbornly backward father-in-law, Old Paul. This led to a second *Maclean's* story about the same characters, "Young Cedars Must Have Roots" in 1948.

Both stories were excerpted and serialized in the *Native Voice* newspaper. By the late 1940s the Evanses had moved to a less isolated mission school near Hazelton so their son could attend a one-room school.

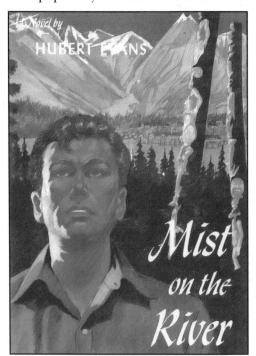

Hubert Evans' Mist on the River,
the first Canadian novel realistically to portray aboriginals as complex, central characters

Mist on the River follows the struggles of Cy Pitt, an 18-year-old Gitksan, destined to be chief, who leaves his village to work in a Prince Rupert fish cannery.

Dot, a relative who has turned to prostitution, warns him, "If staying a stick Indian suits you, fine. But be sure you stay one. Don't try playing it both ways." Throughout the novel Cy Pitt must find an original and honourable path between conflicting white and aboriginal cultures. He loves Old Paul's orphaned granddaughter Miriam, and eventually he returns to his village where Old Paul invites him to carve one more canoe.

Meanwhile Dot's halfbreed son Steve contracts spinal tuberculosis. The boy dies after Cy reluctantly respects the village's superstitious fears of sending the boy to Prince Rupert for medical treatment. This incident was derived from Evans' memory of reading the burial service over the body of a young aboriginal boy who might have survived if hospitalization had been attempted. Cy and Miriam marry, "Indian fashion," and live together in Old Paul's house, but Cy must return to Prince Rupert to find work.

The novel culminates in a violent confrontation between Cy and a trio of drunken aboriginals, but there is never any overt confrontation between Cy Pitt and Old Paul. The white characters in the story are peripheral throughout.

Evans later said he was absolutely determined not to falsify anything for dramatic effect: "I could have written about the injustices Indians faced. You know, like *The Ecstasy of Rita Joe*. I've seen all that. I know all that. But I had commercial-fished and trapped and built canoes with these people. I could roll a cigarette and sit on my heels and talk with them. I was one of them. I wanted to show how they were really just like us.

"This is what I wanted to do with *Mist on the River*. Just show them as people. Basically I was just being a reporter. . . . I knew the people. I felt for them. I was there. Not like an Indian agent or somebody like that. I was one of the guys. They cried on my shoulder. I straightened out the family problems. The rows and the boozing and that sort of thing. People say to me, 'Do you like Indians?' Well, I like some Indians and there are some Indians I don't like. The same with white people."

While nearly blind in his late eighties, hardly able to type, Hubert Evans wrote *O Time in Your Flight* (1979), a memoir novel of growing up in Ontario in the year 1900.

The Hubert Evans Non-Fiction Prize was first presented in 1985. The "Old Journeyman" died the following year.

LELAND STOWE

Crusoe of Lonesome Lake (1957) by Leland Stowe

In February of 1956, Ralph Edwards and his wife Ethel received an unusual guest at their remote home on Lonesome Lake in the Atnarko Valley: Pulitzer Prize–winning journalist Leland Stowe. He arrived by ski plane at 22-below to write about the couple and their remarkable devotion to trumpeter swans. Stowe expanded his research for a *Reader's Digest* article into a bestseller called *Crusoe of Lonesome Lake* (1957) in which the backwoods couple were credited with having done more to save trumpeter swans from extinction than anyone else.

With the release of *Crusoe of Lonesome Lake* from New York, Ralph Edwards was invited to Hollywood where he was duped into appearing as a genuinely surprised guest on a popular TV show called "This Is Your Life," hosted by a man also named Ralph Edwards. As a gift, the show's producers wanted to fly a new cabin into Lonesome Lake. The hermit demurred. "I didn't bother to explain," he later wrote, "I could build a log cabin in less time than it would take to ship one."

Raised as a Seventh Day Adventist, the son of missionary parents in India, Ralph Edwards lived at Lonesome Lake, 60 miles east of Bella Coola, from 1912 to 1966. Despite poor vision and lack of education, he managed to see action during WWII. Afterwards Edwards raised three children at his "tiny kingdom scratched foot by foot out of the Canadian wilderness." At age 65 he taught himself to fly a plane. At 70 he took up commercial fishing.

Edwards' conservation work was spurred by a 1926 meeting at Ootsa Lake with an American bear hunter named John P. Holman, also a member of the Audubon Society. Later asked to keep a log of swan flights, Edwards was appointed assistant migratory bird warden for $10 a month. This money was used to buy a typewriter for reports. In the harsh winter of 1932–1933, Edwards was given authority to purchase $25 worth of barley for feed. Eight 100-pound sacks were delivered by horseback to the end of the nearest road, 13 miles from a storage depot on Lonesome Lake. Having decided better access to feed was required, Edwards wanted to learn to fly. He subscribed to aviation magazines and started to build his own plane. Parts were sent from Winnipeg to Bella Coola, then hauled to the lake with horses. "The engine was the most difficult part to transport," he said. "It weighed 180 pounds. An Indian-style travois seemed to be the best way to carry it." After Queen Charlotte Airlines pilot Johnny Hatch suggested they might purchase a used plane, it was decided to send Edwards' daughter Trudy to get her pilot's licence. The family bought a Taylorcraft float plane for $2500 and built their own hangar. In 1954, Ralph made his first visit to Vancouver since 1919. He obtained a pilot's licence. "If God had given me a choice," Edwards once said, "I probably would have chosen to have been born a bird." He died in 1977 prior to the release of Ed Gould's "as-told-to" book, *Ralph Edwards of Lonesome Lake* (1979).

R.E. WATTERS

British Columbia: A Centennial Anthology (1958)
edited by R.E. Watters

Reginald Eyre Watters edited the first major showcase of British Columbia writing, *British Columbia: A Centennial Anthology* (1958), with noteworthy assistance from Gordon Elliott, who became the only B.C.-born English professor at Simon Fraser University when it opened.

R.E. *Watters edited* British Columbia: A Centennial Anthology *(1958).*

Watters can be viewed in retrospect as an unsung hero of Canadian literature. In 1959, he also compiled *A Checklist of Canadian Literature and Background Materials, 1628–1960* (1959), a volume that marked the emergence of Canadian literature as a subject worthy of study.

In that same year, George Woodcock began editing the new, critical journal *Canadian Literature* from UBC, a rare national publication from Vancouver. He and editor W.H. New steered its course for more than than 35 years.

In *British Columbia: A Centennial Anthology* (1958), Watters wrote, "British Columbia is such a vast province that our centres of habitation may still seem like little more than a glimmering of campfires in an almost empty land. But within the glow of our lamps, whether the glow be that of an isolated cabin or a city of half a million, British Columbians are shown dreaming and striving, hating and loving, growing up and growing old in the universal cycle of existence."

Watters' anthology encompassed natural history, photography, geography, contemporary visual art, agriculture, humour, coastal First Nations art and architecture. Published by McClelland & Stewart from Toronto, it is seldom cited as the beginning of B.C. literary self-consciousness.

In the wake of Watters' landmark text, there have been several sophisticated literary anthologies, particularly *Skookum Wawa* (1975) edited by Gary Geddes, as well as important works shepherded by Carole Gerson, David Stouck, Ron Smith and Keith Harrison, to name a few.

ERIC COLLIER

Three Against the Wilderness (1959) by Eric Collier

E ric Collier's hugely successful and only book, *Three Against the Wilderness* (1959), is rarely cited in major guides to Canadian literature, but if there was ever a "top-ten" of classic B.C. titles, Collier's Chilcotin memoir might make the grade.

Born in England in 1903, Collier, the son of an iron foundry owner, was sent to the wilds of Canada to work as a "mud pup" on his uncle's property near Clinton, B.C., in 1920. That uncle was Harry Marriott, author of *Cariboo Cowboy*. Collier worked at the Riske Creek store for Fred Becher, at the Gang Ranch, at Cotton Ranch, and married Lillian Ross in 1928 at Riske Creek. A few years later, in spite of his wife's hip deformity due to a childhood accident, the couple took a wagon, three horses and their 18-month-old son Veasy, along with a tent, some provisions and $33, and reached the Stack Valley where they lived in an abandoned cabin built by trapper Tom Evans. In a few years they relocated to Meldrum Creek, ten miles away. Collier and his wife Lillian had promised her 97-year-old First Nations grandmother, LaLa, to bring the beavers back to the area that she knew as a child before the white man came. Collier imported several pairs of beaver, and raised the area's water table sufficiently to reinstate the beaver population.

In 1946, Collier became the first president of the B.C. Registered Trappers Association, an organization he co-founded with Ed Bobbs. With the second guiding licence issued for the Chilcotin, Collier supplemented his meagre income from trapping and hunting. He also accepted speaking engagements and sometimes took adversarial positions in talks with the B.C. Game and Forests Department. To encourage more humane trapping methods, Collier undertook field tests for the Conibear trap invented by Frank Conibear and turned his hand to writing for *Northwest Digest* in Quesnel, the *Williams Lake Tribune* and *Outdoor Life* in the U.S. In 1949, he became the first non-American to win *Outdoor Life*'s Conservation Award. Written in longhand and transcribed onto his Remington typewriter, Collier's recollections of "roughing it in the bush" for *Three Against the Wilderness* were condensed by *Reader's Digest* and translated into seven languages.

Soft-spoken and usually unassuming, Eric Collier moved his family to Riske Creek in 1960. He sold his 38-mile trapline to Orville Stowell and Val Coulthard in 1964 for $2,500 and died at Riske Creek in 1966.

The Meldrum Creek homesite where Collier lived in isolation for 26 years was restored by Canadian Army engineers in 1994, but Collier's homesteading masterpiece has been gradually slipping into obscurity, as B.C. society becomes increasingly urbanized. A rough road leads off Highway 20, west of Williams Lake, to the Collier's four-room log home erected in 1946, one of the few historical sites that have been preserved for writers in British Columbia. Others are the former residences of Roderick Haig-Brown (Campbell River), George Ryga (Summerland) and Joy Kogawa (Vancouver).

LOUISE JILEK-AALL

In 1954, as a medical student in Oslo, Louise Aall was deeply impressed by Albert Schweitzer's visit to Scandinavia to receive his Nobel Peace Prize. She studied tropical medicine in Zurich, worked as a bush doctor in Tanganyika and received the Henri Dunant Medal from the Red Cross for distinguished service with U.N. forces during the Congo civil war in 1960. In 1961, when she arrived unannounced at Schweitzer's jungle hospital in Lambaréné,

Louise Jilek-Aall with her husband Wolfgang Jilek, both trans-cultural psychiatrists

Gabon, Schweitzer asked her, "And what do you want to learn from me?" She nervously blurted out, "I want to learn to extract teeth." Some 30 years later she recalled her apprenticeship in *Working with Dr. Schweitzer: Sharing his Reverence for Life* (1990). "In my work as a psychiatrist," she writes, "I am keenly interested in people who are role models and who serve as ego-ideals, especially for the young; but only a very few appear to be worthwhile models."

After working with Schweitzer, she discovered outcasts in the Mahenge Mountains who suffered from a severe form of epilepsy. She founded the still-functioning Mahenge Epilepsy Clinic to treat patients and educate their families. Since her arrival in Mahenge, sufferers are no longer stigmatized or forced to live as outcasts. She has continuously supported the Mahenge Clinic and initiated research into epilepsy with a team of specialists from Austria, Germany and Tanzania. They have scientifically confirmed the existence of a unique form of epilepsy, "head nodding syndrome," first described by Dr. Jilek-Aall in Mahenge, in the 1960s. She now works to confirm its likely source is a parasite found in many tropical regions, Filaria worm *(Onchocerca volvulus)*.

Also a trans-cultural psychiatrist and anthropologist, Jilek-Aall has been a member of the UBC Faculty of Medicine since 1975. She speaks Norwegian, English, German, French, Spanish, Swedish, Danish and Swahili. Her remarkable bush doctor experiences were first recalled in *Call Mama Doctor* (1979), covering the years from 1959 to 1979. Redesigned and enlarged with new chapters, drawings and photos, *Call Mama Doctor: Notes from Africa* (2009) covers the years 1959 to 2009. She lives in Tsawwassen with Dr. Wolfgang G. Jilek, also a trans-cultural psychiatrist and anthropologist. They married in 1963.

Although *Working with Dr. Schweitzer* has been published in China, Japan and Hungary, Louise Jilek-Aall's books are almost unknown in North America. They are fascinating and inspiring nonetheless. Jilek-Aall has been too busy and self-effacing to describe her life in heroic terms, or to pursue sophisticated marketing, but she epitomizes the best human qualities. Such role models are essential—whether they are famous or not.

Books about and by medical practitioners include the harrowing Chinese memoirs of Li Qunying in *The Doctor Who Was Followed by Ghosts* (2007) and R.E. McKechnie's *Strong Medicine: History of Healing on the Northwest Coast* (1972), an attempt to cover material spanning four centuries. For other authors pertaining to medicine, see abcbookworld entries for Appleton, Paul; Beattie, B. Lynn; Billington, Keith; Blair, Geoffrey K.; Coldman, Andrew J.; Dale, John; Down, Sister Mary; Duncan, Allan; Flynn, Bethine; Frobb, Mark; Gibson, Morris; Hadley, Michael; Hannant, Larry; Haynes, Sterling; Helmcken, John Sebastian; Hister, Art; Jackson, Stewart M.; Jilek, Wolfgang G.; Kalla, Dan; Khorana, Har Gobind; Large, Richard Geddes; Lee, Eldon; Lu, Henry; Mackenzie, Roderic; Magnussen, Hazel Joan; McKechnie, R.E.; McNeill, John H.; Millar, Thomas P.; Miyazaki, M.; Monro, A.S.; Muller, Nestor; Murphy, Herbert; Newcombe, C.F.: Patterson, Frank Porter; Patterson, Kevin; Perrin, Dave; Qayumi, A.K.; Rachman, Stanley Jack; Robinson, Geoffrey; Rose, T.F.; Russell, James A.; Samwell, David; Scouler, John; Shah, Amil; Steele, Peter; Taylor, Patrick; Taylor, Steven; Tolmie, William Fraser; Tomlinson, Robert; Weisenburger, Earle; Willoughby, Charles; Zhu, Hong Zhen.

V

1960s

⥈⥈⥈

NORMAN LEE

Klondike Cattle Drive: The Journal of Norman Lee (1960)
by Norman Lee

Born in 1862 in England, Norman Lee received a classical education and trained to be an architect, but sailed from Liverpool in 1882, lured by tales of the Cariboo gold rush. After learning the rudiments of ranching at Redstone, near the confluence of the Chilanko and Chilcotin rivers, he survived by operating the only store between the Fraser River and Bella Coola, trading in furs and raising cattle. He had purchased a "chicken coop" cabin and store from a Finlander, Dan "Ole" Nordberg, 40 miles east of Redstone at Hanceville, in 1894.

Hoping to raise enough money to finance a return to England, Lee decided to take 200 cattle on a 1500-mile journey north to the new Klondike gold fields in 1898. The obstacles were immense. After five months, winter forced him to butcher the herd. He loaded the meat onto scows but the entire shipment was lost on Teslin Lake, 500 miles short of his destination of Dawson Creek.

Only one companion, Lee's driver and scow captain William "Bill" Copeland, remained with him. They barely made it to Wrangel, Alaska, from which they took steamers south, to Nanaimo and Victoria respectively.

"As funds were getting short again; and as my clothes were in rags," Lee wrote, "I did not care to look up any of my aristocratic friends in Victoria."

Lee made it to Vancouver with a roll of blankets, a dog and one dollar. Undaunted, he returned to his "Chicken Ranch" in the Chilcotin and became a successful cattle rancher.

In 1902, Lee returned to England, witnessed the coronation of

Edward VII, and married his second cousin Agnes "Nessie" Lee. The newlyweds arrived in Halifax in 1903 and returned to the Chilcotin where Lee devised an ambitious irrigation scheme to bring water from Big Creek, across the Chilcotin River by flume. The flume ultimately collapsed and the project was discontinued.

At age 52, indomitable Norman Lee joined the Gordon Highlanders but he was not allowed to go overseas to fight in WWI due to his age.

Norman Lee remained a fixture in the Cariboo, living at Hanceville on the Chilcotin Plateau, until his death at age 77 in 1939. Lee left behind a self-illustrated manuscript, completed around the turn of the century, about his doomed cattle drive.

Eileen Laurie of CBC Radio interviewed Lee's widow, in 1954, in conjunction with a province-wide program that broadcast authentic stories by B.C. pioneers. The following summer Laurie and her husband visited the Lees' log house and store where she read Norman Lee's journal. Laurie received permission from Lee's widow to read excerpts on her CBC program *Party Line* and agreed to serve as her agent.

The wife of Vancouver book designer Robert R. Reid heard Eileen Laurie read excerpts of Lee's journal on the CBC, whereupon Reid approached Howard Mitchell of Mitchell Press with a proposal to co-publish *Klondike Cattle Drive* with an introduction by SFU English professor Gordon R. Elliott, who grew up in Williams Lake and had visited the Lees' ranch in the summers. And so a B.C. literary classic appeared in 1960; since republished in 1991 and 2005.

For other independent authors printed by Mitchell Press, see abcbookworld entries for Audain, James; Baity, Earl S.; Barr, James; Bissley, Paul; Broadfoot, Anne; Burris, H.L.; Carroll, Campbell; Cherrington, John; Cramond, Mike; Cronin, Kay; Dawson, Will; Fennelly, John F.; Hamilton, Bea; Hamilton, W.R.; Huçulak, M.; Johnson, F. Henry; Kennedy, Warnett; Kopas, Cliff; Ladner, Leon Johnson; Large, Richard Geddes; Lee, Norman; Logan, Harry T.; Ludditt, Fred; Lyons, Cicely; MacPherson, Ian; Marshall, J. Stirrat; Matches, Alex; McGregor, D.A.; McPhee, Harry; Mitchell, Dorothea; Mitchell, Howard; Morley, Alan; Owen, Margaret; Patterson, Helen; Peake, Frank A.; Peterson, Lester; Pethick, Derek; Ramsey, Bruce; Read, Stanley E.; Reekie, Isabel; Rothenburger, Mel; Scott, David; Sinclair, James; Stavrakov, Marion; Thornton, Mildred Valley; Tolmie, William Fraser; Turnbull, Elsie Grant; Walker, Russell Robert; Wild, Roland.

M. WYLIE BLANCHET

The Curve of Time (1961) by M. Wylie Blanchet

The most enduring bestseller about sailing and cruising along the Pacific coast of Canada is undoubtedly *The Curve of Time* (1961) by M. Wylie Blanchet. Originally published in Scotland when the author was 70 years old, this unlikely classic recalls Blanchet's 15 summers with her five home-schooled children aboard a 25-foot by 6.5-foot cedar launch named *Caprice*. As captain of *Caprice*, Blanchet gained her nickname "Capi." With advice from Hubert Evans, she condensed her family's June–to–October adventures during the 1930s and 1940s into a series of sketches, as if all events were one extended voyage.

Born as Muriel Liffiton in 1891 in Lachine, Quebec, Blanchet grew up in a well-to-do, high Anglican family as a tomboy. At age 18, she married Geoffrey Blanchet from Ottawa. Theirs was not a marriage made in heaven. After he fell ill in his early 40s and retired from his job as bank manager, the couple and their four children drove west in a Willys-Knight touring car, serendipitously discovering and buying a cottage at Curteis Point on Vancouver Island, near Sidney, B.C., in 1922.

This strange and abandoned house, which they dubbed Little House, had been designed by Samuel Maclure. It hadn't been occupied since 1914.

In 1923 the family bought their 25-foot gas boat, *Caprice*, for $600, after it had been sunk at anchor by ice dislodged by the Brentwood ferry.

The boat was only one year old but its engine had to be overhauled after it was raised to the surface. Blanchet's affinity for mechanics and boats was born of necessity. The engine would remain in use for 20 years until 1942. One more child was born, then Geoffrey Blanchet disappeared, under very mysterious circumstances in 1927, after he embarked on the *Caprice* and stopped at nearby Knapp Island. The boat was found by a Chinese gardener on the island. Blanchet's husband might have drowned while going for a swim. The mystery of his disappearance remains unsolved.

Each summer thereafter for 15 years, Blanchet rented her house to a family from Washington State and sought freedom along the coasts of Vancouver Island, taking her children whether they liked it or not. Their adventures were retrospectively recorded in *The Curve of Time*. The unusual title is derived from some writing she had on board by Maurice Maeterlinck (1862–1949), in which the Belgian Nobel Prize winner considered time as a curve.

The Curve of Time was first published by Blackwoods, the company for which Blanchet had written freelance articles. Few copies reached the West Coast of Canada.

The *Caprice* was sold for $700 after WWII. The ivy-covered home known as Little House was torn down in 1948, beset by dry rot, and replaced by a new building.

Capi Blanchet lived alone at Curteis Point, resisting her doctor's advice to move. To combat emphysema and the damp climate, she sat with her head inside her oil stove for 20 minutes each day. In 1961, she was found dead at her typewriter, having suffered a heart attack. Cathy Converse's *Following the Curve of Time* (2008) focuses on where Blanchet travelled and her family background.

Gray Campbell of Sidney released the first Canadian edition of *The Curve of Time* in 1968. It sold for $1.95. Campbell is often described as B.C.'s first professional trade publisher of the modern era. The other seminal trade publisher of that era was Art Downs who gave rise to Heritage House. Gray's Publishing Ltd. of Sidney published 61 titles between 1962 and 1982. These included Harry Marriott's *Cariboo Cowboy* (1966), R.M. Patterson's *Dangerous River* (1966), George Clutesi's *Son of Raven, Son of Deer* (1967), Hugh McKervill's *The Salmon People* (1967), S.W. Jackman's *Portraits of the Premiers* (1969), William Rodney's *Kootenai Brown* (1969), Cliff Kopas' *Packhorses to the Pacific* (1976), Beth Hill's *The Remarkable World of Frances Barkley* (1978) and Gilean Douglas' *The Protected Place* (1979). The Gray Campbell Distinguished Service Award for outstanding service to the publishing and writing community of B.C. was established in 2000.

WARREN TALLMAN

Writing about writing, sometimes called literary criticism, as opposed to literary appreciation, is not exactly a popular field, and yet writing about the alcoholic genius of Malcolm Lowry has emerged as a mini-industry unto itself. Meanwhile, biographers of other B.C. writers include Sandra Djwa (Roy Daniells), Elspeth Cameron (Earle Birney), George Fetherling (George Woodcock), David Stouck (Ethel Wilson), Alan Twigg (Hubert Evans), Ben Metcalfe (Roderick Haig-Brown), James Hoffman (George Ryga), Anthony Robertson (Roderick Haig-Brown) and Betty Keller (Bertrand Sinclair).

Few English professors have been more influential in B.C., in terms of fostering writers and books, than mentor and impresario Warren Tallman. He and his wife Ellen Tallman were chiefly responsible for inviting an influx of American poets to Vancouver, giving rise to the *TISH* poetry newsletter which was published from 1961 to 1969. "The journal started by George Bowering, Frank Davey, David Dawson, Jamie Reid and Fred Wah," wrote George Fetherling in 2001, "is probably the most influential literary magazine ever produced in Canada, of greater significance than even *Preview* or *First Statement*, the two that brought poetic modernism to the country in the 1940s."

Born in Seattle in 1921, Warren Tallman was raised in Tumwater, Washington. He went to college on the G.I. Bill, writing dissertations on Henry James and Joseph Conrad. At Berkeley he met Ellen King, whom he married in 1951. They came to teach at the UBC English department in 1956.

The Tallmans' house became a literary community centre, hosting friends such as Charles Olson, Robert Duncan, Gary Snyder, Robert Creeley and Allen Ginsberg, all of whom came to Vancouver for literary events and parties. Most importantly, Tallman organized a poetry conference in Vancouver in 1963 that featured Denise Levertov, Charles Olson, Allen Ginsberg, Robert Duncan, Margaret Avison and Philip Whalen. A similar conference was held in Berkeley in 1965.

The poetic links with southern California for many years made Vancouver appear to serve as a branch plant for a distinctly American approach to writing.

Tallman was also a strong defender of bill bissett, and an influence on writerly publishers such as Stan Persky, Howard White and Richard Olafson—to name a few. He was co-editor with Donald Allen of *New American Poetics,* a widely-used textbook. His main books were *Godawful Streets of Man* (1978) and *In the Midst* (1992). He once rented the Vancouver East Cultural Centre to deliver a diatribe against Canadian nationalist Robin Matthews who has consistently viewed Tallman as a negative influence on Canadian culture. Warren Tallman smoked incessantly, drank Black Label beer chronically and died in 1994.

Warren Tallman, one of B.C.'s most influential professors of English

For other authors pertaining to literary criticism, see abcbookworld entries for Abbey, Lloyd; Asals, Frederick; Bowering, George; Breton, Rob; Brook, Susan; Budra, Paul; Buitenhuis, Peter; Burnham, Clint; Candelaria, Fred; Clews, Hetty; Comeau, Paul; Cook, Meira; Cooperman, Stanley; Crawford, Julie; Daniells, Roy; Danielson, Dennis; Davey, Frank; Davis, Leith; Delany, Paul; Delany, Sheila; Derksen, Jeff; Doyle, Charles; Dunham, Robert; Gerson, Carole; Gillies, Mary Ann; Goldfarb, Sheldon; Gomez-Moriana, Antonio; Good, Graham; Grieve, Tom; Guy-Bray, Stephen; Hardwick, Joan; Hatch, Ronald; Hekkanen, Ernest; Howard, Lloyd; Hulcoope, John; Kroller, Eva-Marie; Lane, Richard J.; Macey, Samuel; Markson, David; Matthews, Robin; Maud, Ralph; Merivale, Patricia; Messenger, William; Morra, Linda; Moss , Laura; Murphy, P.J.; Nadel, Ira; New, William; Novik, Mary; Petro, Peter; Potter, Tiffany; Quartermain, Peter; Ricou, Laurie; Saltman, Judith; Schellenberg, Betty; Schmidt, Jerry; Schraner, Margrith; Scobie, Stephen; Serafin, Bruce; Stephens, Don; Stevenson, Warren; Stewart, Jack F.; Struthers, J.R.; Summerfield, Henry; Thompson, Dawn; Warland, Betsy; Warner, Janet; Wisenthal, Jonathan; Woodcock, George.

bill bissett

ill bissett took off in British Columbia where Earle Birney left off. The "man-child mystic" is proof of William Blake's adage that "the spirit of sweet delight can never be defiled." He has written more than 60 books of poetry, all identifiable by the incorporation of his artwork and his consistently phonetic (funetik) spelling. His idealistic and ecstatic stances frequently obscure his critical-mindedness, humour and craftmanship.

Born in Halifax in 1939, bissett spent many of his teen years in hospital for treatment of an abdominal condition, peritonitis. During this period he became deeply immersed in movies, to the consternation of his father, a judge who hoped his son would follow in his footsteps and become a lawyer. His mother died in 1953. While attending Dalhousie University in 1956, bissett ran away with a preacher's son to join the circus, ending up in Vancouver "in either 1958 or '59".

bill bissett

While the TISH poetry movement was forming at UBC, bissett, according to his Talonbooks publisher Karl Siegler, was "universally recognized as one of the grooviest, stonedest, weird freaks—one of the great Olympians of the Kitsilano hippie scene." The first issue of his *blewointment* poetry magazine appeared in 1962. "in th beginning," he writes, "othr magazeens n publishrs wud not publish us as we wer the downtown poets n mostlee

142

vizual non linear n not cumming from aneewhere n mostlee left wing politikalee."

From 1963 to 1965, bissett attended the University of British Columbia and met poetry professor Warren Tallman. In 1968, bissett was busted while taking marijuana to a Powell River commune. He spent several weeks at the Oakalla prison farm, plus some time in jail in Powell River, Vancouver and Burnaby. He was fined $500. Federal authorities vowed to appeal the ruling, wanting a stiffer sentence.

The major disaster—or turning point—in bissett's life occurred at a Kitsilano house party in 1969. He fell through a folding door that was supposed to be latched shut. Stairs had been removed. He plummeted 20 feet to the concrete floor in the basement, severely injuring his head. bissett was paralyzed and catatonic, about to be sent to Riverview for electric shot treatments, when an interning neurologist rescued him by correctly diagnosing his inter-cerebral bleeding. After an emergency operation, bissett couldn't communicate and he suffered from edema and aphasia (memory loss). "So I was like a write-off," he has said. The neurologist was the only person who believed he might recuperate.

Stirred by visits from poetry comrades such as Tallman and Gerry Gilbert, bissett confounded the physicians by relearning body movements and speech with the aid of the young neurologist who brought him balls to squeeze, taught him the alphabet and insisted he try to paint again. Gradually his combination of aphasia, edema, paralysis and epilepsy abated—and bissett was able to see and paint auras. When federal authorities arrived at the hospital to serve notice of appeal within a prescribed 30-day period, the head nurse advised them bissett would be dead within a week, so the case was dropped.

bissett's poetry was the subject of a six-month brouhaha in Parliament in 1977–1978 over the fact that taxpayers were subsidizing allegedly profane poetry. Tallman and Talonbooks organized benefits with poets that included Allen Ginsberg and Margaret Atwood. Since the 1990s, bissett has mostly divided his time between the West Coast and London, Ontario ("Centralia"), where he was the vocalist for a rock group, The Luddites. As much a painter as a poet, bissett has largely supported himself since the 1960s by selling his paintings and reading poetry. The Vancouver Art Gallery hosted an extensive one-man show of bissett's art, curated by Scott Watson, in 1984, called *fires in th tempul*. After 45 years as a writer and publisher, bissett received the George Woodcock Lifetime Achievement Award in 2007.

GEORGE NICHOLSON

Vancouver Island's West Coast, 1762–1962 (1962)
by George Nicholson

Some of the province's most integral book publishing imprints arose from self-publishing and many of the best books continue to be self-published. The "classic" title of this genre has to be George Nicholson's *Vancouver Island's West Coast, 1762–1962* (1962), reprinted by Morriss Printing at least twelve times. "George Nicholson was not only a West Coast pioneer," says B.C. historian T.W. Paterson, "but a publishing pioneer."

New Zealand–born George Salier Willis Nicholson travelled to Australia as a boy where he worked on Australian sheep stations and banana trading boats, visiting Fiji, Tonga and Samoa, before arriving in Victoria in 1911 where he found a job as secretary of the Camosun Club. During WWI, he joined the 67th Western Scots, a Victoria unit, and was awarded the Military Cross after fighting at Vimy Ridge. Between the wars, Nicholson worked on a 50-foot boat, the *Miowera*, when it was involved in fishing, freighting and rum-running. He rejoined the army during WWII, but was invalided home.

Nicholson went through jobs running hotels in Port Renfrew, Clayoquot and Sooke. At Zeballos he had a sign outside his Deputy

Mining Recorder's Office listing his adjunct professions: "George Nicholson, Postmaster; Justice of the Peace; Registrar of Births, Deaths and Marriages; Marriage Commissioner; Air Harbour Licensee and Wharfinger; Agent for Standard Oil and Zeballos Trading Co. Ltd." In those days, there were no commercial book publishing houses, so he went ahead on his own steam, producing *Vancouver Island's West Coast*, largely a compilation of his freelance contributions to the *Islander* magazine. When Nicholson died at age 92 at James Bay Lodge in Victoria in 1980, Alec Merriman in the *Colonist* described him as "the authority on anything pertaining to Vancouver Island's West Coast." He's forgotten now. But he started B.C.'s self-publishing tradition of the modern era, leading to the likes of fiction author and editor Ernest Hekkanen in Nelson, and the Blackfoot historian and train expert Adolf Hungry Wolf of Skookumchuck—and at least a thousand others.

JANE RULE

Of the great B.C. writers easily described as great people, Jane Rule ranks near the top. For six decades Jane "Jinx" Rule was one of the most mature, humorous and responsible voices in Canadian letters, befriended and admired by the likes of Kate Millet and Margaret Atwood. Rightfully revered for her groundbreaking novel *Desert of the Heart* (1964), in which two women fall in love in Reno, Nevada, Rule became known throughout the world as an articulate spokeswoman on issues pertaining to personal liberty and social responsibility, but she never clamoured for the limelight. "Politics really are to clean up the house," she said. "You have to do it every week. I don't find it interesting, just as I don't find sweeping the floor every week interesting. I prefer to work wherever there's a possibility of changing things. I really believe through the counter-movements in society change

Margaret Atwood with Jane Rule, on Galiano Island, 2000

can be made. We're living witnesses of it.'"

Jane Rule's influential testimony in the Supreme Court of B.C. on behalf of Little Sister's Book and Art Emporium in 1994, during a constitutional challenge to Canada Customs' practice of seizing materials destined specifically for a gay and lesbian bookstore, was published as *Detained at Customs: Jane Rule Testifies at the Little Sister's Trial* (1995). Specifically, Rule was responding to the absurd seizure by Canada Customs of her non-erotic novels *The Young in One Another's Arms* (1977) and *Contract with the World* (1980), as well as the movie version of *Desert of the Heart*—a 1985 feature film called *Desert Hearts.*

Born in New Jersey in 1931, Rule lived in B.C. with her partner Helen Sonthoff, a UBC English instructor, from the late 1950s until Sonthoff's death in 2000. Jane Rule also taught some classes at UBC. The couple's relocation to Galiano Island from Vancouver in 1976, coincidental with Rule's first attack of chronic and crippling arthritis in her spine, was hugely significant to her life and work. As a senior member of a closely-knit community, Rule became an integral and supportive figure for many of her fellow islanders, lending them money, providing guidance and gaining the nickname "the bank of Galiano."

A resolve to forge community and group connections was reflected in her novels *Memory Board* (1987) and *After the Fire* (1989), both of which explore community bonds and incorporate the elderly as central characters. *The Young in One Another's Arms* and *Contract with the World* are similarly concerned with mutual compassion and love born of strength, not weakness, as characters struggle to generate unconventional solutions. The latter concerns the difficulties faced by a variety of artists as they approach middle age without having gained much outward success.

Renowned for her generosity, Jane Rule offered her final collection of short essays, *Loving the Difficult* (2008) to Hedgerow Press, a Sidney-based imprint of neophyte publisher Joan Coldwell. This little book is arguably her best because it captures her provocative wisdom as an inspirational progressive thinker. In it Rule reasserts her view of marriage as problematic because individuals should not require permission from the state in order to cohabit. Rule consequently looked askance at the eagerness of gay colleagues to gain the legal right to marry. A heavy smoker and avid drinker, Jane Rule died with her typical strength and dignity in 2007.

CHRISTIE HARRIS

Raven's Cry (1966) by Christie Harris

Children's literature in British Columbia languished for about half a century, from the time Martha Douglas Harris published Cree and Cowichan stories in 1901 until a second Harris— Christie—became the first writer successfully to relate aboriginal myths and stories to young readers in *Raven's Cry* (1966).

Born Christie Irwin in New Jersey in 1907, Harris was brought to Fernie, B.C., by her family of Irish immigrants in 1908, then to the Shuswap area, then to the Fraser Valley. She moved to Prince

George to be in the vicinity of Thomas Arthur Harris, an RCMP constable she had known from a neighbouring farm in Surrey, leading to their marriage in 1932.

Harris wrote primarily for the CBC and the *Province*'s women's page until she adapted her radio work for her first book, *Cariboo Trail* (1957).

When Harris' husband's work as an immigration officer temporarily took the family to Prince Rupert in 1958, she agreed to undertake a series of school broadcast scripts on Coastal First Nations cultures. "I discovered that clearly the artistic genius of the North West Coast had been Charles Edenshaw, Haida Eagle Chief Edinsa," she wrote.

Harris' prolific output might be largely overlooked today were it not for *Raven's Cry*, an historical novel that traces the Edenshaw lineage.

"Everyone except Bill [Reid] warned me that Edenshaw relatives would never tell their family stories to a white woman, a stranger," Harris recalled. "I was actually afraid to let them know I was coming. What if they said, 'Don't bother!'? My husband and I arrived in Masset and Edenshaw's daughter Florence Davidson was pointed out to me on the street. I rather anxiously introduced myself. And she said, 'We've been expecting you. We were going to have a reception for you tonight at my house, but there's been a small fire. So we're gathering at my son's house.'"

Raven's Cry was the first book to be illustrated by Bill Reid. Harris' many other books are less memorable.

Christie Harris died in 2002. A B.C. Book Prize for best illustrated children's book was inaugurated in her honour in 2003.

There are approximately 400 B.C. authors of children's books included on the abcbookworld reference site. With his series of 23 books for reluctant readers, Eric Wilson has been touted as Canada's bestselling author for juveniles. Julie Lawson has published 26 books over a 20-year period. Most extraordinary are John Wilson's 23 titles since 1995, many of which are well-researched historical works. Other notables include Sue Ann Alderson, Ann Blades, Alan Bradley, Norma Charles, Sarah Ellis, Dennis Foon, Nan Gregory, James Heneghan, Constance Horne, Polly Horvath, Shelly Hrdlitschka, Nancy Hundal, Carrie Mac, Ainslie Manson, Barbara Nickel, Cynthia Nugent, Sylvia Olsen, Kit Pearson, Mary Razzell, Don Sawyer, Andrea Spalding, Nikki Tate, Meg Tilly, Diane Tullson, Maggie de Vries, Anne Walsh, Betty Waterton, Irene N. Watts, Joan Weir, Paul Yee. To name only a few.

PAUL ST. PIERRE

Breaking Smith's Quarter Horse (1966) by Paul St. Pierre

Paul St. Pierre is one of the few B.C. writers—probably the only one—who has had his photograph on a Canada Post stamp. A wry comic writer, sometimes compared to Mark Twain, he refers to writing as indoor work with no heavy lifting. St. Pierre has been especially adept at depicting aboriginals and ranchers in the Cariboo-Chilcotin. His stories from that region showcase the humour and stubborn independence of hardy people who instinctually resent government.

In the 1960s, he wrote more than 20 scripts as the basis for a popular and award-winning CBC TV series, *Cariboo Country*, that launched the acting career of Chief Dan George as Ol' Antoine. Dan George later gained stardom in George Ryga's *The Ecstasy of Rita Joe* and an Academy Award nomination for his appearance opposite Dustin Hoffman in the movie *Little Big Man. Cariboo Country* was the first significant portrayal of non-urban B.C. culture on television that percolated beyond British Columbia.

Paul St. Pierre's best-known book, *Breaking Smith's Quarter Horse* (1966), began as a television episode called *How to Break a Quarter Horse.* Both became the basis for a 1969 Disney feature film entitled *Smith!* starring Glenn Ford with Keenan Wynn, Dean Jagger and Warren Oates. Known only by his surname Smith, the tenacious rancher enlists the help of an aboriginal, Ol' Antoine, to help him break a horse that he believes will be an ideal cutting horse, but the story is more about Smith's character than the horse. Smith feels he is someone who likes to mind his own business, and he is fond of sarcasm, but his strong aversion to injustice, and his instinctual need to help others, gets him into trouble and lands him before the judge. The comedy shows a serious side when Smith helps out a fugitive First Nations boy. *Breaking Smith's Quarter Horse* has never been out of print since its publication.

Born in Chicago in 1923, Paul St. Pierre grew up in Nova Scotia, served in the RCAF and began his journalism career in B.C. with stints at the *Columbian* in New Westminster and the *News Herald* in the late 1940s. He wrote for the *Vancouver Sun* from 1947 to 1968, and again from 1972 to 1979. He served as the Liberal MP for the Coast Chilcotin riding from 1968 to 1972 and he chaired the B.C. Liberal caucus for two years. He was a police commissioner for B.C. from 1979 to 1983. His play *How to Run the Country* was produced by the Vancouver Playhouse in 1967. Other early books by St. Pierre include *Boss of the Namko Drive* (1965); *Chilcotin Holiday* (1970), a collection of newspaper columns; and *Smith and Other Events* (1983), one story from which made him the first Canadian winner of the Western Writers of America Spur Award for fiction.

GEORGE CLUTESI

Son of Raven, Son of Deer: Fables of the Tse-shaht People (1967)
by George Clutesi

A painter, actor, author, and First Nations spokesman, George Clutesi was the first abo-riginal artist to gain widespread recognition in B.C. after Pauline Johnson. Clutesi's benchmark volume, *Son of Raven, Son of Deer: Fables of the Tse-shaht People* (1967), was published 54 years after Johnson's death. Although they had known one another only a short time before she died in Victoria in 1945, Emily Carr bequeathed her brushes, oils and blank canvasses to Clutesi in her will.

Born in Port Alberni in 1905, George Clutesi endured residential school, worked as a pile driver, labourer and fisherman for 20

George Clutesi

years, and took up painting and writing after he was injured at work as a piledriver. While receiving treatments in Vancouver, Clutesi met Ira Dilworth, Vancouver's chief executive at the CBC, who encouraged Clutesi to refine his writing for a series of CBC Radio broadcasts. By 1947, Clutesi, a father of five, was broadcasting aboriginal stories for young listeners on the CBC, province-wide. In 1947, Clutesi also began contributing inspirational essays on aboriginal culture to *Native Voice*. The newly formed aboriginal newspaper published transcriptions of Clutesi's "folk lore of the Seshaht tribe which have been handed down from father to son for generations." By 1949, Clutesi was sufficiently self-confident to hitchhike from Port Alberni to Victoria to address the Rt. Hon. Vincent Massey, chairman of the Royal Commission on National Development in the Arts, Letters and Sciences, during the Commission's two-day meetings at the Legislative Buildings.

The pubication of Clutesi's Son of Raven, Son of Deer as an intriguing history. According to Gray Campbell of Sidney, when he heard about Clutesi, he went to the Port Alberni Indian Reserve and found Clutesi atop his house, fixing his roof. Understandably wary of white men in the wake of his experiences in the Port Alberni residential school, Clutesi would not come down off the roof. Campbell climbed up the ladder and they had a long talk. Almost a year later, Clutesi telephoned from the Vancouver Airport. He said he was thinking over what Campbell had said up on the roof. And so, with the assistance of a freelance editor, Clutesi's *Son of Raven, Son of Deer* became a cornerstone of aboriginal literature in B.C., published as a Centennial Project with Morriss Printing. Including 18 original illustrations, Clutesi's collection of 12 fables soon became commercially successful, leading the way for aboriginal writers in the second half of the 20th century.

George Clutesi created a large mural for the Indian Pavilion at Expo '67 in Montreal, followed by a second book, *Potlatch* (1969). In his introduction to *Potlatch*, Clutesi claims the word "potlatch" was derived from the Nuu-chah-nulth verb "Pa-chitle," to give, in association with the noun "Pa-chuk," in reference to an article to be given. It's one of various interpretations of the term.

Clutesi appeared as an actor in three movies: *Dreamspeaker* (1977) directed by Claude Jutra; *Nightwing* (1979) directed by Arthur Hiller; and *Prophecy* (1979) directed by John Frankenheimer. Clutesi received the Order of Canada along with other awards and citations prior to his death in Victoria in 1988. A non-fiction book, *Stand Tall, My Son* (1990), appeared posthumously.

George Clutesi's benchmark volume preceded two bestselling collections of oratory, *My Heart Soars* (1974) and *My Spirit Soars* (1982), by Chief Dan George of the Burrard Indian Band. His granddaughter Lee Maracle, a novelist, maintains Dan George directly narrated the words that appeared in print. Dan George's friend and biographer, Hilda Mortimer, has credited Catholic priest Father Herbert "Bert" Francis Dunlop as Dan George's ghostwriter. Either way, a text credited to Chief Dan George was read aloud to the world during the opening ceremonies of the 2010 Olympic Games to represent the literary voice of B.C.'s First Nations.

MARGARET CRAVEN

I Heard the Owl Call My Name (1967) by Margaret Craven

Set in the remote Kwakwaka'wakw community of Kingcome Inlet, located about 500 kilometres north of Vancouver, and five kilometres up a shallow fjord, Margaret Craven's bestseller *I Heard the Owl Call My Name* (1967) prompted a 1973 movie starring Tom Courtenay and Dean Jagger, directed by Daryl Duke.

I Heard the Owl Call My Name was inspired by the life of Anglican missionary Eric Powell. In the novel, Mark Brian, a missionary with three years to live, absorbs the wisdom and language of the Kwakwaka'wakw and learns they are "none of the things one has been led to believe. They are not simple, or emotional, they are not primitive." While dying, Brian witnesses the disintegration of

Kwakwa̱ka'wakw society due mainly to liquor and residential schools. To complicate matters, an English anthropologist arrives with limited understanding of the Kwakwa̱ka'wakw. At the same time, the government prohibits traditional polatch ceremonies. When the missionary hears the owl call his name, he knows he must soon die. His bishop arrives, promising to replace him, but Mark Brian decides to stay and die at Kingcome Village. Although the novel received praise as a sympathetic rendering of aboriginal dilemmas in the 1960s, the protagonist is white and Craven's knowledge of Kwakwaka'wakw culture borders on superficial. The movie version nonetheless constituted a cultural breakthrough as an attempt to tell a realistic story within the context of a contemporary First Nations community of British Columbia.

Other books and stories by B.C. authors that were the basis for movies include Bertrand Sinclair's *Shotgun Jones* (1912), *Whiskey Runners* (1912), *North of 53* (1914), *Big Timber* (1916); Guy Morton's *The Black Robe* (1927); Lily Adams Beck's *Divine Lady* (1924); Rohan O'Grady's *Let's Kill Uncle* (1963); Jane Rule's *Desert of the Heart* (1964); Paul St. Pierre's *Breaking Smith's Quarterhorse* (1966); William Gibson's *The New Rose Hotel* (story, 1981), *Johnny Mnemonic* (story, 1981); W.P. Kinsella's *Shoeless Joe* (1982); Edith Iglauer's *Fishing with John* (1988); Evelyn Lau's *Runaway: Diary of a Street Kid* (1989); and Michael Turner's *Hard Core Logo* (1993). Anne Cameron's script *Dreamspeaker* (1977) was a movie that became a book in 1978.

SHEILA A. EGOFF

With her motto, "the right book, for the right child, at the right time," scholar and critic Sheila Agnes Egoff raised the stature and critical awareness of children's literature in Canada more than any children's librarian in the country. Consequently the B.C. Book Prize for Children's Literature was named after her in 1987.

Born in Maine in 1918 and raised in Galt, Ontario, Egoff started working at the Galt Public Library at age 15, for 25 cents an hour. In 1964, Egoff was commissioned by the Children's Recreational

Sheila A. Egoff (centre) surrounded by B.C. children's authors and illustrators, 2000

Reading Council of Ontario to write *The Republic of Childhood* (1967), the first major critical survey of Canadian children's literature. It was updated and co-authored with Judith Saltman for a third edition as *The New Republic of Childhood* (1990). As Canada's pre-eminent promoter of children's literature, Egoff wrote two other major critical works, *Thursday's Child* (1981) and *Worlds Within: Children's Fantasy from the Middle Ages to Today* (1988).

Egoff taught for many years in the Faculty of Education at UBC, until 1983. In 1994, she became the first children's literature professor to receive the Order of Canada and she was honoured by a reception at the BC Book Prizes gala in 2000. "I am very happy to be here tonight," she told the gathering. "Mind you, at age 82, I am happy to be anywhere. . . . I know things aren't as good as they should be, but every time I pick up a Canadian children's book, I can see they're acknowledging help from the Canada Council, the Ontario Arts Council or the B.C. Arts Council. It's like our social security network. We know it isn't perfect, but, my gosh, it's sure better than it used to be."

Sheila A. Egoff (she insisted on including the middle initial) died in Vancouver in 2005. Her memoir *Once Upon a Time: My Life with Children's Books* (2005), appeared posthumously, compiled with the partnership of Wendy Sutton. Her students included award-winning writers of children's books, Kit Pearson and Sarah Ellis. Egoff once told her protégé, Judith Saltman, "Writing is the only thing that lasts." Saltman has followed in her mentor's footsteps in 2010, co-authoring with Gail Edwards the first comprehensive guide to illustrated Canadian children's books.

AUDREY THOMAS

Audrey Thomas is not a household name, and yet she has long operated in the upper echelon of Canadian literature. She has received the Writers' Trust of Canada Matt Cohen Award, the W.O. Mitchell Prize, the Canada-Australia Literary Prize and the Marian Engel Award. She is also the only three-time recipient of B.C.'s top fiction award, the Ethel Wilson Fiction Prize, for *Intertidal Life* (1984), *The Wild Blue Yonder* (1990) and *Coming Down from Wa* (1995).

Since 1967, Thomas has written 16 books of fiction and more than 20 plays. Often concerned with gender politics, secrets, language and identity, her stories concern the struggles of women—oppressed, or bitter with disappointment—with few happy endings. "Page for page," Margaret Atwood has decreed, "she is one of the country's best writers." Her other close literary associates have included Jane Rule, George Bowering and Alice Munro.

Born in New York State in 1935, Thomas came to the West Coast to teach English 100 at UBC in 1959. From 1964 to 1966 she lived in Ghana where she wrote her first published story, "If One Green Bottle. . ." It concerns the author's confinement and miscarriage in a Ghana hospital and won her an award for debut fiction from *Atlantic Monthly*.

Thomas' first collection of short stories, *Ten Green Bottles* (1967), was followed by her first novel, *Mrs. Blood* (1970), which harkens back to her Ghanaian experiences.

As the second novel she published, but the first novel she wrote, *Songs My Mother Taught Me* (1973) recalls growing up in New York State. Thomas has also lived in Greece, France, England and Scotland, but she has maintained a home at the north end of Galiano Island since 1969. She became a Canadian citizen in 1979. An excellent special issue of *Room of One's Own* in 1986 highlighted her work and life.

The female protagonist in Thomas' novel *Isobel Gunn* (1999) is based on an historical figure from the Orkney Islands who disguised herself as a man in 1806 and signed on with the Hudson's Bay Company to work in Rupert's Land, concealing her identity for a year and a half.

Thomas next picked a character from Charles Dickens' household for *Tattycoram* (2005), about a relatively powerless woman struggling with her identity as Dickens interacts with his own characters.

The Audrey Thomas Issue

Volume 10, Numbers 3 & 4 $5.50

Thomas' early books were mainly published by Talonbooks of Vancouver; then with Ontario imprints from 1981 onwards. She continues to write fiction by longhand, avoiding computers.

Thomas received the George Woodcock Lifetime Achievement Award and the Order of Canada in 2009.

Audrey Thomas in 1963, featured on the cover of Room of One's Own (1986). She is the only three-time recipient of the Ethel Wilson Fiction Prize.

PAT LOWTHER

In medieval times, villages banished independent women who knew too much, or those who enacted their own sexual destinies. Sometimes these women were burned as witches. In our global village, they are still often beaten and raped. Or husbands kill them. Nary a week goes by when some ghastly story about violence against women is not in the news. The germ of violence against women is so deeply imbedded in the male psyche that the only medicine society can prescribe seems to be widespread denial. But this not true with poet Pat Lowther, who was murdered

Pat Lowther

by her husband with a hammer in 1975, and people are still asking about her.

Pat Lowther was born Patricia Louise Tinmuth in 1935. She grew up in North Vancouver in a working class environment and left school at 16. At 18 she married Bill Domphousse, a fellow worker at the North Vancouver Shipbuilding Company. They had two children and subsequently divorced. In 1963, she married Roy Armstrong Lowther, a public school teacher, an aspiring writer and a left-wing political activist. He was eventually dismissed from his teaching job due to his radical politics. Encouraged by other writers such as Pat Lane and Dorothy Livesay, Pat Lowther published her first collection of poems in 1968. Six years and two more books later, she was teaching at UBC and had been elected co-chair of the Canadian League of Poets. One prominent critic declared, "She was on the edge of whatever fame and success Canadian poetry had to offer."

On October 15, 1975, Pat Lowther's body was discovered five

kilometres south of Britannia Beach at Furry Creek, badly decomposed. Police discovered 117 bloodspots on the walls of Pat and Roy Lowther's bedroom. Crown prosecutor John Hall argued that Roy Lowther, also a poet, was jealous of his wife's success and angered by an extra-marital liaison. He killed her with blows from a hammer. The hammer in question and the couple's mattress were taken by Roy Lowther to Mayne Island, where the mattress had been washed on both sides. Reddish stains remained. He suggested they could be menstrual blood. Roy Lowther was convicted of the crime.

bill bissett co-published Pat Lowther's first book, *This Difficult Flowring* (1968). Allan Safarik published her *The Age of the Bird* (1972). Lowther's life and death is also the focus for her daughter Christine Lowther's first poetry collection, *New Power* (1999) and the subject for Keith Harrison's *Furry Creek: A True-Life Novel* (1999). Toby Brooks of Ottawa published *Pat Lowther's Continent: Her Life and Work* (2000). Christine Wiesenthal published *The Half-Lives of Pat Lowther* (2005). Every year the Pat Lowther Memorial Award is presented for the best book by a female poet in Canada. She does not go away.

ALICE MUNRO

Many would argue Alice Munro is the finest writer Canada has produced. It is impossible to select one collection of her short stories as being superior to the rest.

Winner of the 2009 Man Booker International Prize, twice winner of the Giller Prize, three times the recipient of the Governor General's Award for Fiction, Alice Munro is peerless. Her work has gained her the distinction, accorded by the *New York Times*, of being "the only living writer in the English language to have made a major career out of short fiction alone." In 2005, she became the 11th recipient of the George Woodcock Lifetime Achievement

Alice Munro, circa 1978

Award for an Outstanding Literary Career in British Columbia, but most readers assume she is an Ontario writer.

Born as Alice Laidlaw in Ontario in 1931, she married fellow student Jim Munro in 1951 and moved to Vancouver, where her two eldest daughters were born. While writing in West Vancouver, she befriended Margaret Laurence and was encouraged by Ethel Wilson. Another daughter was born in Victoria, where she and her husband opened Munro's Books in 1963, still considered one of the finest independent bookstores in Canada. She gave birth to her youngest daughter in 1966. In all, she lived in Vancouver and Victoria for 22 years before her first marriage ended and she moved back to Ontario. After her divorce, Alice Munro married former university friend, Gerald Fremlin, a geographer, in 1976. She has since maintained two residences: one in Clinton, Ontario, and the other in Comox, on Vancouver Island.

"I like the West Coast attitudes," she said in 2004. "Winters [in B.C.] to me are sort of like a holiday. People are thinking about themselves. The way I grew up, people were thinking about duty."

Alice Munro made her critically acclaimed debut with *Dance of the Happy Shades* (1968). Her second book, *Lives of Girls and Women* (1971), was the basis for a Canadian movie. In addition, Sarah Polley adapted the story "The Bear Came Over the Mountain" for the film *Away from Her* (2006), starring Julie Christie and Gordon Pinsent.

With her mother's encouragement and consent, Sheila Munro of Powell River has published an astute study of their family dynamics and her mother's books, *Lives of Mothers and Daughters* (2001).

GEORGE WOODCOCK

The Doukhobors (1968) by George Woodcock & Ivan Avakumovic

Of the approximately 150 books written or edited by George Woodcock, the most vital for B.C. was his collaboration with co-author Ivan Avakumovic for *The Doukhobors* (1968). The work's sobriety and perceptivity undercut the sensationalism of Simma Holt's cynically packaged *Terror in the Name of God* (1964), the cover of which featured a large, naked woman outside a burning building and omitted its interior subtitle *The Story of the Sons of Freedom Doukhobors.* This omission enhanced the misconception that all Doukhobors were unruly nudists and troublemakers. The agrarian, pacifist sect was so relieved to have their story finally told with some depth of understanding that Woodcock was offered a permanent place of residence in the Kootenays if he wished to live among them. He declined.

Born in Winnipeg in 1912, George Woodcock once wrote, "I began even as a boy to realize how wide the world can be for a man of free intelligence." True to his word, he operated as a man of free intelligence, living underground during WWII in London and later fracturing relations with the University of British Columbia, where he had been the first editor of *Canadian Literature*, in order to assert his independence. Woodcock commonly published several new books per year, on a wide variety of subjects, until his death in 1995.

During his lifetime, Woodcock was variously described as "quite possibly the most civilized man in Canada," "by far Canada's most prolific writer," "Canada's Tolstoy," "a regional, national and international treasure," and "a kind of John Stuart Mill of dedication to intellectual excellence and the cause of human liberty." Woodcock's oft-reprinted *Anarchism: A History of Libertarian Ideas and Movements* (1962) demystifies anarchism and views it as a constructive philosophy. A biography of his dear but difficult friend George Orwell, *The Crystal Spirit* (1966), will also long remain in print.

The George Woodcock Lifetime Achievement Award for British Columbia is fittingly named for the anarchist philosopher whose unrivalled productivity was achieved in concert with consistent ideals and humanitarian actions ever since he and Ingeborg Woodcock arrived from London, England, and built a rough cabin at Sooke in 1949. The Woodcocks remained close friends with the Dalai Lama after they first visited him in Dharamsala, India, in 1961. As the generators of two still-functioning, non-profit organizations, Trans-Himalayan Aid Society (TRAS) and Canada India Village Age (CIVA), the Woodcocks quietly and constructively influenced millions of lives, but never had children of their own and avoided the public spotlight. In addition, they bequeathed a $2.3 million endowment fund, as of 2009, to benefit Canadian writers in distress, administered by The Writers' Trust.

George Woodcock

George Woodcock once described himself as a British Columbian first, and a Canadian second. His books pertaining to B.C. include *Ravens and Prophets*

(1952), *The Doukhobors* (1968), *Victoria* (1971), *Amor De Cosmos: Journalist and Reformer* (1975), *Peoples of the Coast: The Indians of the Pacific Northwest* (1977), *A Picture History of British Columbia* (1980), *British Columbia: A Celebration* (1983), *The University of British Columbia: A Souvenir* (1986) and *British Columbia: A History of the Province* (1990).

For other authors pertaining to Doukhobors, see abcbookworld entries for Bell, Archie; Bonch-Bruevitch, Vladimir; Cran, Gregory J.; Elkington, Joseph; Ewashen, L.A.; Friesen, John W.; Greig, Hugh; Horvath, Maria; Janzen, William; Kalmakoff, Jonathan J.; Mealing, F.M.; Novitski, Orest; O'Neail, Hazel; Plotnikoff, Vi; Popoff, Eli; Rak, Julie; Snesarev, V.; Sorokin, Stefan; Stenson, Bill; Stoochnoff, John Philip; Sulerjitski, Leo; Tarasoff, Koozma; Zonailo, Carolyn; Zubek, John P.

G.P.V. AKRIGG & HELEN AKRIGG

1001 British Columbia Place Names (1969) by the Akriggs

Everyone knows the town of Spuzzum, but what about the Houdini Needles? Or Miniskirt? Or a place called Elephant Crossing? They are three of the thousand-plus names for towns, rivers, mountains and lakes explained by George Philip Vernon and Helen Akrigg in *1001 British Columbia Place Names,* a landmark volume based on more than 40 years of collaborative research.

Houdini Needles, located in the Adamant Mountains, northeast of Revelstoke, is "so named because only a contortionist like Houdini could ascend these peaks." Miniskirt, northwest of Victoria, is near Skirt Mountain. The derivation of Elephant Crossing, near the Canadian Armed Forces base at Holberg, west of Port Hardy, is more complex. When a logging truck is unloaded, the trailer portion is hoisted up behind the driver's cab and carried piggyback for the return journey, with the "reach" (the long connecting bar) jutting out above the cab. Upon seeing this strange sight at a roadway crossing, a warrant officer, newly arrived from

Helen and G.P.V. Akrigg

Ontario, remarked that the empty trucks looked like elephants holding up their trunks. This intersection on Vancouver Island was recorded in the *Gazetteer of Canada* as Elephant Crossing.

The Akriggs were self-publishing pioneers when they released *1001 B.C. Place Names* under their Discovery Press imprint in 1969 (updated in 1997). Another classic in this field is Walbran's *British Columbia Coast Names*. Remembered as the namesake for the Walbran Valley, Walbran Creek, Walbran Rock and Walbran Point, Captain John T. Walbran produced his seminal work derived from his hobby of investigating place names. For much of the 20th century it was said that any captain worth his salt on the B.C. coast had to travel with a well-thumbed copy of Walbran's 546-page *British Columbia Coast Names, 1592–1906, To Which Are Added a Few Names in Adjacent United States Territory; Their Origin and History. With Map and Illustrations* (1909), reprinted in 1971.

Exactly 100 years after Walbran's omnibus appeared, former *Western Living* editor (1980–1987) and longtime *Georgia Straight* travel columnist Andrew Scott produced his 650-page lighthouse of a book, *The Encyclopedia of Raincoast Place Names: A Complete*

Reference to Coastal British Columbia (2009), that supplies the origins and meanings of more than 5,200 names, with photos and maps.

The Akriggs also produced a valuable two-volume history about the origins of the province, *British Columbia Chronicle, 1778–1846: Adventures by Sea and Land* (1975) and *British Columbia Chronicle, 1847–1871: Gold & Colonists* (1977).

For other authors pertaining to place names, see abcbookworld entries for Aitken, Neil; Allen, Richard Edward; Balf, Edward; Bell, Aula Agnes Louise; Brown, Harrison; Ford, Helen; Havinga, Marlene; Little, C.H.; Manning, Helen Brown; Middleton, Evelyn Maude; Nelson, Denys; Parizeau, Paul; Rozen, David Lewis; Snyders, Tom; Speare, Jean E.; Swanson, James L.; Vancouver, George; Walker, Elizabeth; White, James.

RAYMOND HULL & LAURENCE J. PETER

The Peter Principle (1969) by Raymond Hull & Laurence J. Peter

One of the most famous non-fiction books written in British Columbia, *The Peter Principle* (1969), was co-authored by Raymond Hull and Laurence J. Peter after the pair met as strangers while attending an amateur production at the Metro Theatre in south Vancouver. In the lobby, during intermission, after Hull mentioned the production was a failure, Laurence J. Peter, an instructor of English at UBC, suggested to Hull that people invariably rise to their level of incompetence.

This was the grist for their bestseller *The Peter Principle,* now translated into more than 20 languages. Peter has described the theme of their collaboration as "hierarchiology," a term now commonly used when analyzing systems in human society. Hull has described the content as, "the tragi-comic truth about incompetence, its causes and its cure." The principle involved was named after Peter mainly for purposes of alliteration. Hull happily conceded the title had sexual connotations. With the runaway success of the book, Laurence Peter moved to southern California to pursue a career as a novelist. "We did no more collaborations," said Hull, "because the way we worked involved sitting down, face to face, and talking over each point in detail. Obviously this could not be done by correspondence."

Peter reached his level of incompetence as a novelist, but turned out various Peter books such as *The Peter Prescription: How To Make Things Go Right* (1972), *The Peter Plan: A Proposal for Survival* (1976), *Peter's Quotations: Ideas for Our Times* (1977) and *Peter's People and Their Marvelous Ideas* (1979). He died in 1990.

Born in Shaftesbury, England, in 1919, Raymond Hull was a public servant prior to his arrival in Vancouver in 1947. In 1949, he responded to an advertisement for a summer creative writing course at UBC and soon discovered his aptitude for writing. He sold radio plays to the CBC, wrote stage plays and formed the Gastown Players, a semi-professional company specializing in melo-dramas. Hull wrote plays for the troupe that included *The Drunk-ard, Son of the Drunkard* (now known as *The Drunkard's Revenge*) and *Wedded to a Villain.* Hull wrote and published his 50-minute play about Sweeney Todd long before the character became the subject of a successful Broadway musical.

Co-authored with Helmut J. Ruebsaat, M.D., Hull's *The Male Climacteric* (1975) was based on the supposition that men undergo a male "change of life" or mid-life crisis that can frequently ruin their sex lives, destroy marriages, change temperaments and upset careers. Examples provided included Shakespeare, Tolstoy, Dickens, Napoleon and Mussolini. Hull died in 1985, bequeathing royalties from six plays and 18 books to the Canadian Authors Association, and most of the rest of his estate, approximately $100,000, to the Vancouver Public Library.

VI
1970s

ALAN FRY

How a People Die (1970) by Alan Fry

The importance of Federal Indian Agent Alan Fry's novel *How a People Die* (1970) has gradually been glossed over. Whistleblowers are seldom cited as heroes, but when it was published, Alan Fry's first-hand reportage on social decay in Indian reserves in the form of a novel, along with Cree leader Harold Cardinal's *The Unjust Society* (1969), ushered in a new era of realistic writing about Canada's First Nations.

How a People Die concerns the death of an infant named Annette Joseph on the fictitious Kwatsi Reserve, a collection of shabby houses strewn with empty bottles. Examining the unsanitary conditions surrounding the death, RCMP Corporal Thompson, a veteran of 15 years on the force, takes the controversial measure of charging the infant's parents with criminal neglect. The question soon arises among the characters of the story as to who should be held blameworthy for the tragedy. "Tell us how a people die," says one of the aboriginal characters, "and we can tell you how a people live."

Fry's hard-hitting novel, in the aftermath of George Ryga's *The Ecstasy of Rita Joe* at the Vancouver Playhouse, forced British Columbians to wake up to the plight of marginalized aboriginals, but Fry was branded a racist for his assertion that "alcoholism is an inheritable disease and Indian people inherit it to a greater extent than do non-Indians." After more than 20 years working in northern and central B.C., including 15 years as an Indian agent, and three more realistic novels about life in the B.C. Interior, Fry quit working for the Department of Indian Affairs out of frustration and settled in the Yukon in 1974.

Cover art for How a People Die *(1970)*

Alan Fry was born in 1931 and raised on a family ranch near Lac La Hache, B.C. His introduction to a reissued edition of *How a People Die* contains an amalgam of statistical evidence of violence and familial dysfunction among First Nations. "It is my firm conviction that the succession of increasingly destructive lifestyles [on Indian reserves] can be traced back to the end of liquor prohibition to status Indians in the decade following the Second World War," he writes. Fry divulges he was himself an alcoholic and also relates an incident from his boyhood when an aboriginal male teenager tried to cajole him into a sexual encounter in the woods.

To further his contention that dependency on alcohol can be overcome, he cites the example of the Alkali Lake Band in the Chilcotin, southwest of Williams Lake, that managed successfully to prohibit alcohol in its midst, as initiated largely by Phyllis and Andy Chelsea and recorded in the community-produced film *The Honour of All: The Story of Alkali Lake.*

Fry objects to "the brutal treatment of so many women and children by their men. . . . Indian self-government must not be so structured that women and children living under such a government have less protection than is afforded to other Canadian citizens by other levels of government."

For more B.C. authors who have written about alcohol, see abcbookworld entries for Allen, Harold; Anderson, Frank; Audain, James; Campbell, Robert A.; Cutler, Ron; Dawe, Alan; Dawson, Kimberley Rose; Hamilton, Douglas; Givton, Albert; Gough, Lyn; Graefe, Sara; Hagelund, William A.; Hodgson, Kenji; Lemert, E.M.; Miles, Fraser; Milton, Lorraine; Mooy, Lyn; Newsome, Eric; Parker, Marion; Patrick, Carmen; Ruskin, Olga; Sager, Ed; Schreiner, John; Seyd, Jane; Stone, Jim; Strachan, J. George; Tod, John; Townsin, Troy; Wenzel, Jan-Udo.

SUSAN MUSGRAVE

Born in 1951, Susan Musgrave has been one of the most prolific, hard-working and written-about writers of British Columbia. She is a fourth-generation Vancouver Islander who has spent extended periods living in Ireland, England, Haida Gwaii, Panama and Colombia—always outside the mainstream. In one of her brilliant and amusing personal essays, she writes, "In our culture, these days, there is no core, no authenticity to our lives; we have become dangerously preoccupied with safety; have dedicated ourselves to ease. We live without risk, hence without adventure, without discovery of ourselves or others. The moral measure of man is: for what will he risk all, risk his life?"

Susan Musgrave has taken risks. While married to Victoria lawyer Jeff Green, she became involved with one of his clients, an accused drug trader. She later married Stephen Reid, a convicted bank robber, in 1986, and they had two daughters. After she rescued Reid from prison and gave him a literary life, he reoffended and was incarcerated again. Their story was front page news.

Unfortunately this public side of Musgrave's risk-taking threatens to obscure her record of excellence as an irresistibly thoughtful, clever and entertaining author of more than 30 titles. It does not help that no particular Musgrave poetry collection or novel stands out as superior to her other works and she is yet to win a major prize.

Musgrave is now increasingly at home on the Sangan River, ten miles from Masset, on Haida Gwaii, where she lives in a seven-sided house built of logs obtained by a local beachcomber. Although Musgrave is largely out of the public eye, her remarkable range and wit as a poet, editor, novelist, critic, essayist and humorist must be acknowledged for its influence during the seventies,

Susan Musgrave, circa 1970s

eighties and nineties. Along with the experimentalist bill bissett
and logging poet Peter Trower, Musgrave has been the embodi-
ment of the maverick, unclassifiable, non-university-coddled B.C.
literary tradition that is far more attuned to Haight-Ashbury than
Yonge & Bloor. Like Anne Cameron in Tahsis, Musgrave has veered
away from urbanity, away from anything "safe." Meanwhile her
novels *The Charcoal Burners* (1980), *The Dancing Chicken* (1987) and
Cargo of Orchids (2000) and her noteworthy poetry collections,
such as *Songs of the Sea-Witch* (1970), *Grave-Dirt and Selected Strawberries* (1973) and *A Man to Marry, a Man to Bury* (1979), will likely be
anthologized for many years to come.

GEORGE RYGA

The Ecstasy of Rita Joe (1970) by George Ryga

George Ryga is British Columbia's greatest playwright. "More than any other writer," said theatre director John Juliani, "George Ryga was responsible for first bringing the contemporary age to the Canadian stage." The published version of Ryga's most famous play, *The Ecstasy of Rita Joe* (1970), helped Talonbooks grow into the country's leading publishing house for drama.

The play dramatizes the story of a young aboriginal woman named Rita Joe who comes to the city only to die on skid row. Commissioned as a work for Canada's centennial celebrations, *The Ecstasy of Rita Joe* has a circular structure with the Brechtian use of a singer outside of the action. Ultimately the integrity of its central character demands self-destruction. "In a perverted way," noted critic R.B. Parker, "her [Rita Joe's] rape and death are the ecstasy of a martyr."

The Ecstasy of Rita Joe premiered in 1967 at the Vancouver Playhouse starring Frances Hyland as Rita Joe, Chief Dan George as her father, Ann Mortifee as the singer, Robert Clothier as the priest and August Schellenberg as Jaimie Paul. It was the first play in English to be presented in the National Arts Centre Theatre in Ottawa in 1969.

Ryga's *Grass & Wild Strawberries*, its follow-up at the Vancouver Playhouse, was a greater commercial success in B.C. with original music from The Collectors (who later became Chilliwack). The Vancouver Playhouse then commissioned another play from Ryga slated for presentation in February of 1971. Ryga's political drama *Captives of a Faceless Drummer* closely paralleled the events of the October Crisis in 1970, dramatizing conflicting ideologies. The

Playhouse board of directors reversed their decision to produce the play. Neil Simon's *Plaza Suite* was produced instead. Although this led to the outright dismissal of artistic director David Gardner, it also caused Ryga to be regarded as being "too radical." The repercussions for Ryga were devastating. "The potentially greatest playwright in this country was blacklisted," theatre director Richard Ouzounian has claimed, "as carefully and as thoroughly as any one of the Hollywood Ten were under McCarthy."

George Ryga was born in Deep Creek, Alberta, in 1931. He was raised by poor immigrant Ukrainian parents on a farm in northern Alberta. After seven years in a one-room school, he left to work at a variety of occupations. Despite success writing for television and radio, money was always scarce. Ryga persevered with a series of hard-edged and increasingly political novels published by Talonbooks. Ryga died in 1987 at age 55. James Hoffman produced a comprehensive biography in 1995. In 2003, John Lent of Okanagan College, theatre director Ken Smedley and Alan Twigg conceived an annual George Ryga Prize for the best book by a B.C. author that exemplifies George Ryga's passion for social issues. His house in Summerland has been preserved as the George Ryga Centre, mainly through the efforts of Ken Smedley.

For other authors pertaining to theatre, see abcbookworld entries for Aguirre, Carmen; Angel, Leonard; Armstrong, Gordon; Armstrong, Michael; Atkey, Mel; Austen-Leigh, Joan; Blackley, Stuart; Bossin, Bob; Botting, Gary; Brennan, Kit; Brinkman, Baba; Bruyere, Christian; Bushkowsky, Aaron; Carlson, Tim; Carson, Linda; Chai, Camyar; Clark, Sally; Clarke, Denise; Clements, Marie; Cone, Tom; Conlon, Christopher; Cowan, John; Crossland, Jackie; Dawe, T.J.; Diamond, David; Dumaresq, William; Evans, Chad; Fairbairn, A.M.D.; Frangione, Lucia; Gale, Lorena; Garrard, Jim; Grace, Sherrill; Gray, John MacLachlan; Gregg, Kevin; Highway, Tomson; Hoffman, James; Hollingsworth, Margaret; Hoogland, Cornelia; Hull, Raymond; Irani, Anosh; Irvine, Andrew; Kalsey, Surjeet; Kaplan, Beth; Kerr, Kevin; Lambert, Betty; Langley, Rod; Leiren-Young, Mark; Lill, Wendy; Loring, Kevin; Lowe, Lisa; Loyie, Larry; MacLean, David; MacLeod, Joan; Manuel, Vera; McNicoll, Susan; Mercer, Michael; Moore, Mavor; Murphy, John; Page, Malcolm; Panych, Morris; Parkin, Andrew; Payton, Brian; Quan, Betty; Ratsoy, Ginny; Rhys, Captain Horton; Richmond, Jacob; Ringwood, Gwen; Roberts, Kevin; Roberts, Sheila; Russell, Chester; Russell, Lawrence; Seelig, Adam; Seng, Goh Poh; Shiomi, Rick; Simons, Beverley; Skinner, Constance Lindsay; Snukal, Sherman; Stearn, Sharon; Sumter-Freitag, Addena; Szanto, George; Thomas, Colin; Tidler, Charles; Verdecchia, Guillermo; Wade, Bryan; Walmsley, Tom; Warre, Henry James; Wasserman, Jerry; Weiss, Peter Elliot; Williams, Tennessee; Wilson, Sheri-D; Wyatt, Rachel; Yates, J. Michael; Youssef, Marcus.

BARRY GOUGH

B arry Gough, B.C.'s most integral maritime historian, wrote the first book ever published by UBC Press, *The Royal Navy and the Northwest Coast of North America, 1810–1914* (1971). Now UBC Press publishes more than 50 new books annually and has a backlist of 700 titles. Along the way, Gough has become "the foremost expositor of B.C. nautical history."

As a former high school teacher who was born in Victoria in 1938, Gough gradually climbed the academic history ladder, becoming founding director of Canadian Studies at Wilfrid Laurier University, then a fellow of the Royal Historical Society, fellow of Kings College, London, and life member of the Association for Canadian Studies and of the Champlain Society. He has been archives fellow of Churchill College, Cambridge, and a member of the board of academic advisors of the Churchill Center, Washington, DC. He has won the Lieutenant Governor of British Columbia's Medal and the Clio Award of the Canadian Historical Association. And so on.

Barry Gough in the 1970s

But it is the books that count. Fourteen of them so far, including *Fortune's a River* (2007), a cumulative work that integrates Gough's knowledge of the Spanish, Russian, French, American and British influences on the development of the Pacific coast of North America "with particular emphasis on Canadian traders' influences on and responses to the Lewis and Clark expedition."

At 400-plus pages, *Fortune's a River* is not for beginners. It needs to be digested slowly, so only time will tell if it becomes the primary overview for pre-Confederation history for the Pacific Northwest, standing alongside Robin Inglis' wide-ranging who's who, *Historical Dictionary of the Discovery and Exploration of the Northwest Coast of America* (2008). The art of concision is seldom rewarded, or even mentioned, so few readers will appreciate that Inglis' 428-page labour of love, is an artful as it is indispensable for anyone with an abiding interest in B.C. maritime history.

Other Barry Gough titles include *Distant Dominion: Britain and the Northwest Coast of North America, 1579–1809* (1980), *Gunboat Frontier: British Maritime Authority and Northwest Coast Indians, 1846–1890* (1984) and *Across the Continent: Sir Alexander Mackenzie* (1997).

JACK JAMES

Divorce Guide for B.C. (1971) by Jack James

The unplanned meeting that gave rise to Self-Counsel Press, the pioneer publishing house for self-help law titles in North America, occurred in New Westminster, between the Dairy Queen and the library, at a bookstore called Select Books. That's where Diana Douglas was working when UBC articling law student Jack James entered with his newly self-published book, *Divorce Guide for B.C.* (1971). This was the world's first self-help divorce guide.

Although she was the daughter of Jim Douglas, founder of J.J. Douglas, soon to be Western Canada's best-known publishing house, Diana Douglas was not doing it Dad's way. She had just left behind a one-year stint milking cows on 120 acres near Duncan, and ended up selling her Select Books to join James in his new business venture. As partners in business, then in life, Douglas and James had the right book when they wanted to untie the knot.

Douglas secured full ownership of Self-Counsel Press in 1984 and, as a single mother with three children, she built a plethora of how-to titles into an empire of sorts—International Self-Counsel Press Ltd.—often considered the most consistently successful publishing enterprise in the province. *Divorce Guide for B.C.* represents a hugely important category—books that mainly impart useful information—and it was not only the basis for one of the country's most durable publishing enterprises, but also the start of a new genre: self-help law books.

There are hundreds of guidebooks, how-to books, or advice books from B.C. They seldom get reviewed, and they are ineligible for grants, but they are vital literature. Betty Pratt-Johnson's guide to scuba and skin diving in B.C. and Washington, *141 Dives* (1976), went through eleven printings until it was updated and expanded to become two companion volumes in 1994, then revised again as *151 Dives* (2007). Mary and David Macaree co-wrote *103 Hikes in Southwestern B.C.* (1973) a classic regional title that has reputedly sold more than 100,000 copies and been reprinted six times. The Orca Books imprint in Victoria arose after its founder, Bob Tyrrell, an English teacher, self-published *Island Pubbing* (1984). Book distributor Nancy Wise of Kelowna and Marion Crook did everyone a favour by co-writing *How to Self Publish and Make Money* (1987).

For books of advice and guidance, see abcbookworld entries for Abramson, Arnold M.; Aiken, Sean; Aitken, Neil; Alei, Ariole; Anderson, Suzanne; Argent, Judith; Ashford, Mary-Wynne; Austen, Stephen; Bakas, Tania; Barlas, Aqlim; Batchelor, Bruce; Bell, Sarah; Belshaw, Cyril; Bendall, Pamela; Bennett, Guy; Bewsey, Susan; Bosworth, Brian; Brazier, Brendan; Brooke, Paula; Bruckner, Virginia; Buente, Gail; Burgess, Ann Carroll; Burich, Helen; Burnett, Bruce Ian; Cameron, Nancy J.; Cardinal, Maurice; Chang, Ginger; Charleson, Mary; Christian, Jean; Cochrane, Don; Cohee, Allison; Connelly, Dolly; Coombs, Ann; Copeland, Andy; Copeland, Kathy; Corbel, Eve; Corrigan, Boyd; Cottam, Kevin J.; Couper, Jim; Cramp, Beverly; Dalian, Eliza Mada; Davis, Akeela; Davis, Barry; Derbitsky, Harold; Diamond, Ruby; Dixon, Norma; Dobson, Charles; Donnelly, Louise Miki; DuMoulin, Barbara; Eaton, Diane; Eker, T. Harv; Ferguson, Julie H.; Ford, Collene L.; Foster-Walker, Mardi; Franklin, Jill (a.k.a. Satya Bharti); Frobb, Mark; Gannon, Lorraine; Garber, Anne; Giannone, Kelly; Gibson, Katherine; Goheen, Duncan; Goodwin, Margaret; Gordon, Donald; Gosse, Bonnie; Gothe, Jurgen; Gottberg, John; Green, Valerie; Greenwood, Michael; Griffiths, David; Gross, Jessica Berger; Gysi, Werner M.; Hall, Daryl; Hall, Scott; Harmon, Tanya; Heinrich, Linda; Helliwell, Tanis;

Hempstead, Andrew; Hesse, Jurgen; Hickling, Meg; Hiebert, Bruce; Hister, Art; Holmes, Douglas; Horak, Wence; Hudson, Rick; Ince, John; Jamal, Azim; James, Dawn; James, Jesai; Jane, Kaycee; Janson, JoAnn; Jayhmes, Jasai; Jennings, Lynn; Johnson, Eileen Rickards; Jones, Vincent; Kaellis, Eugene; Keating, Kathleen; Keator, Glenn; Kenyon, Janice; Kimura, Manami; Kootnekoff, Jon-Lee; Kramer, Pat; Kuntz, Ted; Kyra, Suzanne; Lake, Kathrin; Latremouille, Louise; Lautsch, Brenda; Lawrence, Iain; Lee-Son, Jacqueline; Legault, Stephen; Leggo, Carl; Lewis, Jim; Lightfoot, Marge; Lim, Sylvia; Losier, Michael; Lydon, Christine; Malet-Veale, Decima; Mallard, Colin; Mapleton, David H.; Matthews, Carol; Mavrow, Cecilia; McArthur, Dannie; McBeath, Charleen; McCurdy, Diane; McFetridge, Grant; McGaw, Darry; McGuckin, Frances; McPhee, Harry; Meikle, Marg; Melina, Vesanto; Messier, René L.; Miller, Saul; Milton, Lorraine; Mina, Eli; Moshansky, Tim; Moskovitch, Deborah; Moulton, June Fuller; Mucalov, Janice; Munro, Deborah; Naiman, Linda; Nault, Kelly; O'Hara, Bruce; Obee, Bruce; Ogden, Frank; Ogden, Reg; Osing, Ray; Patterson-Sterling, Catherine; Pattison, Kenneth Manning; Paul, Kevin; Peterson, Lois J.; Petrie, Anne; Plant, Albert; Pocock, Christopher L.; Poteryko, Derek; Powell, Elinor D.U.; Rains, Elizabeth; Reeves, Nancy; Reid, Judith; Reigh, Maggie; Richardson, Pamela; Richardson, Ron; Rickwood, Lisa; Robbins, Emma Mae; Rosenbluth, Vera; Ryan, Liz Mitten; Sandborn, Calvin; Santiago, Geraldine; Schendlinger, Mary; Setter, Doug; Seyd, Jane; Shaw, Matthew; Sikundar, Sylvia; Skinner, David; Slade, Robert M.; Sosnowsky, Cathy; Stephens, Richard; Stewart, Gordon; Stewart, John Thomas; Strong, Kenneth V.; Sutherland, Jessie; Syberg-Olsen, Ebbe; Tait, Stephanie; Taylor, Debra; Thompson, Peggy; Thomson, Robert S.; Tillotson, Betty; Tully, Brock; Vesey, Maureen; Vincent, K. Louise; Wagar, Samuel; Walsh, Brian; Walter, Ryan; Welbanks, Douglas P.; Werschler, Terri; Wheatley, Tim; Williams, Nicole; Wilson, Colleen; Wilson, Tony; Woollam, Ray; Yap, James; Yu, Mei; Zimmerman, Lillian.

CHARLES LILLARD

After twenty books, bibliophile Charles Lillard is remembered for his passionate devotion to B.C. literature in general. "He was one of the people who wrote about the Northwest Coast in a way that gave it a mythology," said Susan Musgrave, "and in that way he'll last." Howard White once observed that Lillard's literary column in the *Times Colonist*, "dominates the field like a leafy oasis in mid-Sahara." Doug Beardsley referred to him as "a beacon on this coast."

Born in California in 1944, Charles "Red" Lillard was raised in Alaska and spent much of his childhood on his parents' fish scow.

He preferred to view the Inside Passage as a river running from Skagway to Seattle. He worked at forestry jobs as a faller, rigger, and boom man, drove a truck and taught at Ocean Falls, before entering the UBC Creative Writing Department. He published his first poetry collection, *Cultus Coulee* (1971), and became a Canadian citizen the following year. In 1977, he met his partner and fellow poet Rhonda Batchelor.

Important Lillard titles include his history of Vancouver Island, *Seven Shillings a Year* (1986), which received the Lieutenant Governor's Medal for Historical Writing; *Circling North* (1988), which won the first Dorothy Livesay Poetry Prize; and *Just East of Sundown* (1995), his history of Haida Gwaii. *Shadow Weather* (1996) was nominated for a Governor General's Award. With Michael Gregson he compiled a coffee table book on post-war B.C. icons, *Land of Destiny* (1991); and with Ron MacIsaac and Don Clark he co-wrote a study of the 1920s religious cult leader Edward Arthur Wilson, *The Brother XII, B.C. Magus* (1989). Lillard's enthusiasm for B.C. and Alaskan literature resulted in the reprinting of several West Coast classics. He also edited the *Malahat Review* and some *Sound Heritage* titles. In addition, he co-founded Reference West and he edited a gathering of writings about Haida Gwaii, *The Ghostland People* (1989), to "allow the actors in our history to give their own speeches."

Lillard could be somewhat erratic in his writing, selective in his scholarship and highly opinionated in his judgments, but his enduring enthusiasm for Pacific Northwest literary culture made his presence necessary and constructive. After Charles Lillard died in 1997, a memorial service was held at the home of Robin and Sylvia Skelton. "Perhaps people in this country think of him mainly as a poet—which he was, of course, a fine poet," said Marlyn Horsdal, one of Lillard's publishers, "but he was also an extraordinary repository of information on the literature of the coast and coastal history; he loved collecting it and talking about it." Charles Lillard also had a deeply melancholy streak. "History is endless in this country. It is boundless," he wrote in a personal letter to Alan Twigg, "but no one really cares deeply."

Ulli Steltzer portrait of Bill Reid

BILL REID

Among the dozens of B.C. artists who have published books, irascible Bill Reid is surely the most culturally significant. Reid's mother Sophie was a Haida from Skidegate and his father Billy Reid was a naturalized Canadian of Scottish and German ancestry. They were married in 1919 but soon estranged. Born in 1920, Reid grew up in Victoria, where he and his sister Peggy were raised by their mother. He also spent some time in the Alaska border town of Hyder where his father owned and operated several hotels. Reid never saw his father after age thirteen. In 1943, Reid visited his mother's hometown of Skidegate where he watched his maternal grandfather, Charles Gladstone, using silver and argillite to produce traditional Haida motifs. Gladstone had learned his craftsmanship from his uncle Charles Edenshaw.

Having moved to Toronto in 1948 to work for CBC Radio as a scriptwriter, Reid noticed an advertisement for classes in making jewelry at the Ryerson Institute of Technology. His subsequent training in making silver and gold jewelry and engraving led him to a greater interest in Haida art.

Reid returned to Vancouver in 1951 and opened a small jewelry workshop in a basement. His sideline career as an artist received a boost in 1957 when B.C. Provincial Museum curator Wilson Duff introduced him to carver Mungo Martin who, in turn, introduced him to wood carving. Under Martin's direction, Bill Reid carved his first totem pole in 1957, but Reid later claimed Martin was not his mentor.

Bill Reid quit the CBC and worked with Kwakwaka'wakw carver Doug Cranmer (who had been staying at Mungo Martin's house in Victoria) from 1958 to 1962, helping to construct a portion of a Haida village at UBC, at the invitation of Harry Hawthorn, and also repairing totem poles in Stanley Park. He later trained at the Central School of Art and Design in London and accepted a commission for Expo '67 in Montreal. He carved a 78-foot red cedar totem for the Skidegate Band office in 1978. His best-known works include his jade sculpture, *Spirit of Haida Gwaii*, a pair of 19-foot canoes, one at the Vancouver International Airport and the other at the Canadian Embassy in Washington, D.C.; *Lord of the Under Sea*, a killer whale at the Vancouver Public Aquarium; *Raven and the First Men*, a 4.5-ton yellow cedar sculpture at UBC's Museum of Anthropology; and *Lootaas*, the Haida-style canoe that was commissioned for Expo '86. In 1995, he was paid $3 million by the Vancouver International Airport Authority for his second version of the *Spirit of Haida Gwaii*. Reid received honorary degrees from six universities and lived mainly in cities. He once remarked, ascerbically, "The Haida live their lives, I live mine."

As an author, Reid collaborated with Bill Holm for *Indian Art of the Northwest Coast: A Dialogue on Craftsmanship and Aesthetics* (1975) and with Robert Bringhurst for *Raven Steals the Light* (1984). Other Reid titles are *Out of the Silence* (1971) and *All the Gallant Beasts and Monsters* (1992). *Solitary Raven: Selected Writings of Bill Reid* (2001) reveals he was a refined social, artistic and spiritual commentator. He died in 1998 after a 30-year struggle with Parkinson's disease. An eight-hour memorial gathering at UBC's Museum of Anthropology attracted approximately one thousand people. At Reid's request, his ashes were interred at T'annu, a deserted village near Skidegate, where his grandmother was born.

In 2004, the Bank of Canada issued 25 million new $20 bank notes that feature four works by Reid, including *Raven and the First Men*.

Some of the other B.C. artists who have published books include Allister, William; Amos, Robert; Bantock, Nick; Bateman, Robert; Caetani, Sveva; Chow, Raymond; Croft, Philip; Davidson, Robert; Douglas, Stan; Evans, Carol; Falk, Gathie; Griffiths, Bus; Harrison, Ted; Hirnschall, Helmut; Holmes, Rand; Hughes, E.J.; Jungen, Brian; Kane, Paul; Kluckner, Michael; Koerner, John; Lukacs, Attila Richard; Odjig, Daphne; Onley, Toni; Pavelic, Myfanwy; Plaskett, Joe; Point, Susan; Regehr, Duncan; Sandwyk, Charles van; Seaweed, Willie; Shadbolt, Jack; Tanabe, Tak; Tetrault, Richard; Thornton, Mildred Valley; Varley, F.H.; Vickers, Roy Henry; Wall, Jeff; Wallace, Ian; Yu, Mei.

RICK ANTONSON et al

In Search of a Legend, Slumach's Gold: The Search for the Slumach-Lost Creek Gold Mine (1972) by R. Antonson, B. Antonson, M. Trainer

Resource exploitation is at the heart of British Columbia. First they came for sea otter pelts, then gold, fish and forests. Of the countless B.C. books about man's insatiable desire to find gold, one of the most enduring has been *In Search of a Legend, Slumach's Gold: The Search for the Slumach-Lost Creek Gold Mine* (1972) by Rick Antonson, Brian Antonson and Mary Trainer, repackaged in 2007 as *Slumach's Gold: In Search of a Legend*.

Based on both local hearsay and fact, it recounts the story of an aboriginal named Slumach who reputedly found gold in the Fraser Valley, near Pitt Lake, about 35 miles from Vancouver. He placed a curse on anyone who tried to find it just before he was hanged for murder in 1891, having shot and killed a Métis man, Louis Boulier, also known as Louis Bee, at Lillooet Slough near the Pitt River, in 1890. Slumach was already disliked by whites in the area because he reputedly came to New Westminster with large gold nuggets and used them to consort with white women in the local "sporting houses."

In the early 1900s, an American miner named Jackson reportedly found Slumach's mine but he died soon afterwards. Leaving behind an intriguing letter that provided hints as to the site of the mine in a remote part of what is now Garibaldi Provincial Park, he became the first victim of the mine's curse. Many have since ventured into dangerous terrain to seek Slumach's mysterious motherlode. The *Vancouver Province* once estimated that some thirty people had died.

There are more than 11,000 references for Slumach on the internet, and Fred Braches of Whonnock maintains a web site on the subject.

There are only imaginary images of Slumach and verification that he really had access to gold nuggets from a hidden mine does not exist, but the story endures and Slumach's reputation has gone global.

One of the earliest books about gold in B.C. was *Handbook to the New Gold Fields: A Full Account of the Richness and Extent of the Fraser River and Thompson River Gold Mines* (1858) by Robert Michael Ballantyne, a Scot who was dubbed "Ballantyne the Brave" by Robert Louis Stevenson. For other authors pertaining to gold, see abcbookworld entries for Anderson, Doris; Baird, Andrew; Banon, Edward Magowly; Barlee, N.L.; Basque, Garnet; Beeson, Edith; Boissery, Beverley; Brown, Robert; Caldwell, Francis E.; Claudet, F.G.; Dickinson, Christine Frances; Domer, John; Douglas, David; Dower, John; Elliott, Marie Anne; Fetherling, George; Ficken, Robert E.; Fitzgeorge-Parker, Ann; Forsythe, Mark; Futcher, Winnifred; Gates, Michael; Green, Lewis; Hall, Ralph; Harris, Lorraine; Hauka, Donald J.; Hawkins, Elizabeth; Hayman, John; Hazlitt, William Carew; Ingersoll, Ernest; Johnson, F. Henry; Johnson, Peter; Krumm, Stan; Langston, Laura; Laut, Agnes; Lazeo, Laurence; Lindley, Jo; Ludditt, Fred; McNaughton, Margaret; Miller, Naomi; Minter, Roy; Morrell, W.P.; Murphy, Claire Rudolph; Patenaude, Branwen; Paterson, T.W.; Phillipps-Wolley, Clive; Porsild, Charlene; Ramsey, Bruce; Reinhart, Herman Francis; Service, Robert; Sheepshanks, John; Sinclair, James; Smedley-L'Heureux, Audrey; Smith, Robin Percival; Sterne, Netta; Swindle, Lewis J.; Trueman, Allan Stanley; Verne, Jules; Villiers, Edward; Waddington, Alfred; Wade, Mark Sweeten; Wright, Richard; Wright, Rochelle.

DAVID WATMOUGH

Homosexuals in British Columbia can now express themselves openly in print; and for that they owe a debt to David Watmough. The Cornishman has been a mainstay of the West Coast fiction scene ever since he accepted Canadian citizenship in 1963. As the first male homosexual writer out of the closet in British Columbia, Watmough is the senior gay male fiction writer in Canada, active for five decades, with 20 books. Long concerned with the cultural climate of B.C. as a whole, Watmough was also the first president of the Federation of B.C. Writers.

With a bravura prose style, Watmough's short stories and novels have chiefly explored the life of his fictional protagonist Davey Bryant. He once noted his ambition was to create "a fictional autobiography of Davey Bryant, a 20th-century man who happens to be an author, an immigrant and a homosexual." All volumes of Watmough's Davey Bryant series of fiction were written in Kitsilano, where Watmough lived for more than forty years with opera critic and university professor Floyd St. Clair. Playwright and screenwriter Michael Mercer once observed, "For David and Floyd, a closet was a place to hang their guests' coats. They were never secretive, and never ghettoized, either."

David Watmough (right) met Floyd St. Clair in 1951 at a Wednesday night social at St. George's Anglican Church in Paris. This photo was taken in Paris.

Born of Cornish ancestry near Epping Forest on the eastern edge of London in 1926, David Watmough grew up mainly in Cornwall. His first published book, *A Church Renascent* (1951), concerns the worker-priest movement and arose from his studies in theology at King's College. He first visited Vancouver in 1959 and returned in 1961 to produce a series of reports on the Vancouver Festival for CBC. His partner Floyd St. Clair subsequently sent his CV to the head of the UBC French department and secured a job teaching French at the university.

In 2004, Watmough and St. Clair purchased a new residence in the Boundary Bay area of Tsawwassen (a home they named Kernow; Celtic for Cornwall). After St. Clair died in 2009, Watmough returned to live in Vancouver. Poet and critic Trevor Carolan wrote in 2007, "David Watmough rewrote the rules on what fiction could discuss in this country. He's still at it, writing as a wise, compassionate elder with Vancouver in his bones and the Cornish muse in his DNA—changing the way we think about the human condition in this city he's called home for nearly fifty years."

BARRY BROADFOOT

Ten Lost Years, 1929–1939 (1973) by Barry Broadfoot

Studs Terkel is generally credited as the pioneer of oral history in the United States; his equivalent in Canada is Barry Broadfoot, whose best-known history remains *Ten Lost Years, 1929–1939* (1973), a collection of stories from survivors of the Great Depression. "It flew off the shelves," recalls editor Douglas Gibson, "to an extent that its success provoked articles wondering how on earth a book by an unknown author, about the Great Depression, for God's sake, could have such a success. I have an answer. Many of the stories are so good you will never forget them. The book is still in print forty years after it appeared. The hardcover edition sold more than 200,000 copies, and the paperback has sold much more than that."

Born in 1926 in Winnipeg, Barry Broadfoot worked for a year on the *Winnipeg Tribune* before serving in the infantry for 1944–1945. After graduating from the University of Manitoba in 1949, he worked primarily as a journalist with the *Vancouver Sun* for 29 years. He said he originally came to the West Coast as the result of "wanderlust and the refusal to endure another bloody winter."

While at the *Vancouver Sun* he published *Stanley Park, An Island in the City* (1972), with photos by *Vancouver Sun* photographer Ralph Bower. "He seemed to me straight out of *The Front Page*," recalls Gibson, who first met Broadfoot in the late 1960s, "a feet-up-on-the-desk, yell-across-the-noisy-newsroom sort of guy who almost certainly had a bottle stashed away within easy reach. He belonged to that generation of men who had made it through the war and, what the hell, were going to smoke and drink and swear at the boss and have fun."

Broadfoot once described himself as the world's greatest listener. "Although oral history has been my financial rod and staff for twenty years," he wrote in 1991, "I have never been comfortable with the phrase. I prefer the term living memories, used by historian Peter Stursberg."

Broadfoot's gruff style seemed anachronistic by the 1990s. Along with the likes of white male literary pioneers such as Eric Nicol, Robert Harlow, Norman Newton and Paul St. Pierre, he was cast adrift in a new age of B.C. literature in which new authors, comfortable with self-marketing and the internet, expect the world to take serious notice of their first books. Broadfoot did it the long, hard way, talking to people and reflecting their deepest concerns.

Like most other B.C. authors, Broadfoot lacks his own entry in the *Oxford Companion to Canadian Literature* and the *Encyclopedia of Literature in Canada*. He once said, "The academic historians resent what I do because they say it isn't history and somehow I'm taking away from the pool of money that might go toward history books. But the people I talk to have no vested interests, beyond the desire to tell their stories as honestly as they could. Precious memories are our heritage."

Barry Broadfoot is also remembered for *Years of Sorrow, Years of Shame* (1977) about the internment of Japanese Canadians. Broadfoot's other works are *Six War Years* (1975), *The Pioneer Years* (1976), *The Veterans' Years* (1985), *The Immigrant Years* (1986), *Next Year Country* (1988) and *Ordinary Russians* (1989). "History is the lies you believe," he once told the *Globe & Mail.* "It's being rewritten all the time because generals, industrialists and academic historians all serve different interests."

LEWIS J. CLARK

Wild Flowers of British Columbia (1973) by Lewis J. Clark

Lewis J. Clark (1907–1974) was head of the Department of Chemistry at the University of Victoria and held degrees from the University of British Columbia, the University of Washington and Oregon State University.

A renowned scholar, Clark became one of the leading naturalists and nature photographers of his day. Following publication of his encyclopedic classic, *Wild Flowers of British Columbia* (1973), with 573 colour plates and information on 792 species and subspecies, Clark broke his masterwork down into compact field guides that collectively sold more than 200,000 copies. These have included *Wild Flowers of Field and Slope* (2002), *Wild Flowers of Forest & Woodland in the Pacific Northwest* (2003), *Wild Flowers of the Mountains in the Pacific Northwest* (2003) and *Wild Flowers of the Sea Coast in the Pacific Northwest* (2004).

For other authors pertaining to plants and gardening, see abcbookworld entries for Adolph, Val; Allen, Christine; Anderson, James R.; Bradbury, Elspeth; Brayshaw, T. Christopher; Cadwaladr, Margaret; Dooling, Peter J.; Elmhirst, Janice; Fawcett, Brian; Field, Dorothy; Gillard,

Spring; Gordon, Quinton; Grant, John A.; Griffith, B.G.; Havard, David; Hermary, Heide; Hobbs, Thomas; Horn, Elizabeth; Horsfield, Margaret; Jason, Dan; Jonsson, Roy; Kennedy, Des; Kruckenberg, Arthur; Lascelle, Michael K.; Lyons, C.P.; MacDonald, Bruce; McClement, Donna; MacKinnon, Andy; Merilees, Bill; Milnes, Lynne; Moore, Bernard; Newton, Judy; Norris, John; Parish, R.; Pettinger, April; Pojar, Jim; Preston, Dave; Resh, Howard M.; Reynolds, James I.; Richardson, Noel; Rubin, Carole; Stainsby, Donald; Stevens, Elaine; Straley, Gerald; Tapson-Jones, Mary; Tarrant, David; Trelawny, John; Turner, Nancy; Vander Zalm, Bill; Varner, Collin; Wales, Paddy; Wheeler, Robin; Whysall, Steve.

HERSCHEL HARDIN

In the 1960s, the likes of Ben Metcalfe and Robert Hunter could have their views regularly incorporated into the B.C. media. A half-century later, the two major Vancouver newspapers have been jointly owned, from outside B.C., for decades, and seldom threaten the status quo. The Fraser Institute has successfully infiltrated their editorial pages, preaching free enterprise. CKNW newscaster Bill Good sets the mainstream tone. An ex-sportscaster from Ontario handles the CBC Radio morning show for current affairs. Nobody rocks the boat. Nobody cares about heavy thinkers.

Herschel Hardin is a heavy thinker. Born in 1936 and raised in Vegreville, Alberta, Hardin studied philosophy and politics at Queen's University and ran for the leadership of the federal NDP in the early 1990s—but his seriousness and brain power were next-to-ludicrous in an era of sound bites and photo-ops. A self-described "western-Canadian patriot" and polemicist, Hardin wrote *Esker Mike and His Wife, Agiluk* (1973), a theatrical satire about Inuit life and white society, and *The Great Wave of Civilization* (1976), a musical with composer John Gray that reveals how the Blackfoot Confederacy was destroyed. His best-known work, *A Nation Unaware: The Canadian Economic Culture* (1974), examines 200 years of Canadian economics. *A Nation Unaware* was described by Allan Fotheringham as "the most under-rated book published in Canada in this decade."

Hardin's *Closed Circuits: The Sellout of Canadian Television* (1985) argues on behalf of public broadcasting and reveals how the Canadian Radio-television and Telecommunications Commission has failed Canadians in its mandate to ensure broadcasting in Canada is "predominantly Canadian in character and ownership." *The New Bureaucracy: Waste and Folly in the Private Sector* (1992) shows that the private sector is not necessarily more efficient than the public sector—contrary to propaganda that is strewn throughout modern media. Hardin catalogues countless corporate excesses and heaps scorn on the advertising industry. "We have to demythologize the private sector," he says. *The New Bureaucracy* is a populist version of Hardin's *The Privatization Putsch* (1989) for the Institute for Research on Public Policy. With *Working Dollars: The VanCity Story* (1996), Hardin tried to reinvigorate the soul of an initially progressive financial institution that has increasingly veered towards conventional corporate behaviour.

VIC MARKS

Cloudburst: A Handbook of Rural Skills and Technology (1973)
by Vic Marks

To paraphrase Joni Mitchell, "We were stardust, we were golden. And we had to get ourselves back to the garden." And so a young Mayne Islander named Vic Marks, with his press headquarters in Brackendale, produced a practical hippie bible for rural living, *Cloudburst: A Handbook of Rural Skills and Technology* (1973). A former editor of *B.C. Access Catalogue*, Marks provided a no-nonsense guide for city dwellers who might wish to try remote, back-to-the-land living.

According to a 1975 book review in the *Village Voice*, "It is a charming encyclopedia that tells you how to build a 16-foot personal dome, a compost shredder, a chicken house, a juice press, a sauna, a root cellar . . . and how to cure and smoke fish, build beehives, split shakes, and on and on." *Cloudburst* has reputedly sold more than 100,000 copies. Revised versions led to Marks editing *Cloudburst 1 & 2: Handbook of Rural Skills and Technology* (1977), from Cloudburst Press in Seattle. Again, there were detailed illustrations for building a loom, a solar roof, a wood-fired kiln, an insulated chimney, a hand-operated washing machine, a treadle-operated wood lathe, sod housing, a sunpit greenhouse, a composter toilet, a fruit dryer, a sod barn, a rock stove, a honey extractor, a carding machine, a hay and leaf baler, a scroll saw, a spinning wheel and more.

Marks' Cloudburst imprint followed up with a natural foods cookbook and two small-format illustrated food guides, *Foraging for Edible Wild Mushrooms* and *Poisonous and Hallucinogenic Mushrooms*. Back-to-the-lander Marks has long since moved back to the city where he operated Hartley & Marks, a Vancouver publishing company that evolved into an editorial service based in Kitsilano. He now specializes in beautifully bound "blank books." A 25th-anniversary edition of *Cloudburst* was released by Hartley & Marks.

J.I. PACKER

Knowing God (1973) by J.I. Packer

There is nothing trendy about J.I. Packer's *Knowing God* (1973), a Christian classic that has reputedly sold more than one million copies worldwide. Packer appreciates Martin Luther King's dictum that three forms of activity and experience make the theologian: sustained prayer, meditation and fidelity to truth.

Born in England in 1926, James Innell Packer is an unabashed Calvinist who studied classics and theology at Oxford, receiving his Ph.D. in 1954. He came to Vancouver and was appointed professor of Systematic and Historical Theology at Regent College in 1979. In 1989, he became the first Sangwoo Youtong Chee Professor of Theology.

Packer has also been senior editor and visiting scholar for *Christianity Today*. Considered one of the most influential evangelicals in North America, Packer remains active on Regent College's board of governors.

B.C. is rife with authors and books pertaining to religion and spirituality. The notorious Brother XII [see John Oliphant entry] left behind several works of spiritual nonsense, and Finnish utopian leader Matti Kurikka published works of visionary idealism. Books by New Age guru Eckhart Tolle (*The Power of Now, A New Earth*) have generated impressive sales worldwide while some view his prose as bafflegab for the needy and gullible. More ennobling is sufi teacher Murat Yagan's spiritual autobiography, *I Come from Behind Kaf Mountain*. Journalist Douglas Todd continues to write about contemporary religion and ethics with dignity and clarity.

For other religious and spiritual-oriented authors, see abcbookworld entries for Adams, Neale; Anderson, Charles; Anderson, Mark; Arctander, John William; Atkinson, Ron; Baker, J.C.; Beanlands, Arthur J.; Beavon, Chester; Benjamin, Verna; Bergsma, William; Best, Marion; Botting, Gary; Bowman, Phylis; Brabant, Augustin Joseph; Bramham, Daphne; Brown, Brian; Browne, Don; Browne, Donald Elgin; Burkinshaw, Robert Kenneth; Burrows, Bob; Carmichael, William; Celis, Luisa Maria; Coggins, James; Cohen, Martin S.; Colebrook Peace, Barbara; Cronin, Kay; Crosby, Thomas; Curtis, Eileen; Das, Jagessar; Davis, E.A.; De Roo, Remi; Down, Edith E.; Downs, Barry; Dubois, Veronica; Dunn, Alexander; Durgananda, Swami; Ehman, Daniel; Ferguson, Julie H.; Forsee, David; Foster, Chris; Franklin, Jill; Gerard, Bernice; Glavin, Terry; Good, Linnea; Gowen, Hubert H.; Gresko, Jacqueline; Grove, Lyndon; Guyatt, Nicholas; Hadley, Michael; Hamilton, Rosemary; Hayden, Brian; Henderson, R.W.; Hills, George; Horsfield, Margaret; Iredale, Jennifer; Jamieson, Patrick; John Paul, Pope; Kokai-Kuun, Zoltan; Lascelles, Thomas A.; LeClair, Marcia; Lunny, William; Mackay, Ellen; Mackey, Lloyd; Maltwood, Katharine; Manji, Irshad; McCullagh, James B.; McGrath, Alister; McKervill, Hugh; Milton, Ralph; Montgomery, Charles; Mornin, Lorna; Nayar, Kamala; Nicol, Mary; O'Brian, Michael; Page, Christopher; Pallant, Roy J.V.; Palmer, Debbie; Peake, Frank A.; Pearson, Leslie Trayer Holt; Powers, Margaret Fishback; Powers, Paul Radha, Swami Sivananda; Read, Wendy; Roddan, Sam; Sale, Thomas; Sanguin, Bruce; Schneider, Birgit; Schofield, Emily M.; Schwartzentruber, Michael; Sheepshanks, John; Snowber, Celeste; Sovereign, A.H.; Stouck, Mary-Ann; Szydlowski, Pawel; Talbot, Cathie; Taylor, James; Townsend, Arthur H.; Tyson, Janet; Underhill, Stuart; Upton, Primrose; Vessey, Mark; Ward-Harris, E.D.; Wellcome, Henry; Wentworth, Elaine; Weyler, Rex; Whitehead, Margaret; Williams, Cyril.

D.M. FRASER

Alongside Malcolm Lowry, singing in the highest choirs in B.C.'s literary heaven, resides a sensitive, alcoholic genius named D.M. Fraser. Hardly anyone knows he's up there.

Born in New Glasgow, Nova Scotia, in 1946, the only son of a Presbyterian minister and a high school teacher, Donald Murray Fraser grew up in coal-mining towns, particularly Glace Bay, and came west in 1967 to escape his background and to attend UBC. Instead he developed his astonishingly original prose style and published his first book of short stories, *Class Warfare* (1974), with Pulp Press, a loose, literary, left-leaning and self-mythologizing collective for which he served as an editor. Gentle and soft-spoken (his speech could be inaudible or slurred), Fraser was renowned as an habitué of east-side Vancouver bars. For many years he lived above a junk store at 28th and Main. In the wee hours he transcribed his estrangement into writing binges that culminated in a second brilliant collection, *The Voice of Emma Sachs* (1983). At the invitation of editor Bob Mercer, he wrote the short-lived column "Manners" in the *Georgia Straight*, and he also published infrequently in other small magazines. He succumbed to a lung infection at age 39 in 1985, unable to complete his novel called *Ignorant Armies*. It was later edited by Bryan Carson and released in 1990. Also released posthumously was *D.M. Fraser: The Collected Works, Volume One—Prelude* (1987).

Publisher of *Geist* magazine, Stephen Osborne, Fraser's closest literary acquaintance, once described Fraser as "a writer admired for the beauty of his prose and sought after for the pleasure of his conversation." Beneath Fraser's rumpled exterior was a sophisticated and highly sensitive self who often seemed like a refugee from an earlier age. He once said, "The society in which I grew up

The poignancy of D. M. Fraser was captured in this John Reeves photo from the 1970s.

was repressive psychologically. I was taught to keep my feelings to myself. To be reserved and reticent. Boy, that training took. There are periods when you can overcome it and there are periods when it closes in and you think, my god, I'm giving too much away here. But writing, that's what it's for. You have to give it away."

Fraser's stories resemble musical riffs more than conventional narratives, and several can be understood as fugues or variations on a repeating theme: in one story, written in 1973, a hair stylist inquires rhetorically: "Have you known the sweetness of life, do you remember it?" and goes on to ask, "Have you danced to the gentle strains of Pachelbel, in the stilly night? Have you loitered till dawn in waterfront bars, contemplating the mythic sailors who never appear? Have you ever wanted to be an antelope?"

Fraser's appearance in *The Essentials* is representative of literally dozens of accomplished fiction writers who could have been included in this book without much debate.

ROLF KNIGHT

Rolf Knight was a brave and little-heralded historian and a steadfast enemy of the notion that there exists such a phenomenon as the common man. Born in 1936, the son of an itinerant cook, Knight grew up in B.C. logging camps, gained his M.A. in anthropology at UBC in 1962, and a Ph.D. from Columbia University in 1968.

Knight's career path changed when he collaborated with his Berlin-born mother in *A Very Ordinary Life* (1974) to trace her difficult life from Germany to goldpanning in Lillooet and on to a succession of upcoast logging camps. After its release, Knight left his teaching job at SFU, disaffected by the narrowness of his fellow academics and the ignorance of his students. Knight drove a taxi in Vancouver, simultaneously producing a string of books that dignify, and show the complexity of, the so-called working class.

Knight's writing often bristles with impatience at shallow or conventional attitudes. "One of the great misconceptions of native Indian history in B.C.," he wrote in 1978, "is the vision of a golden past age. In this view, indigenous societies on the North Pacific coast existed in a veritable Garden of Eden where ready-smoked salmon flanks launched themselves, glittering, from the streams into trenches of salalberry and oolichan sauce, where a superabundance of foods was always and everywhere available with the merest of effort; a veritable land of Cockaigne. In such accounts, wars and raids were mainly rough games for prestige, slaves were not really slaves, chiefs were the servants of their people, all necessities were shared, and settlements were rife with co-operation and equity. Spiritualism and traditions reigned supreme and almost everyone was part of one big family. . . . Popular conceptions generally disregard or gloss over considerable evidence of suffering, hardships, and oppression between and within the indigenous Indian societies. While this is not a justification for the varied inequities which followed in the wake of European settlement, it should remind us that native Indian societies did not witness a fall from natural grace at the arrival of Europeans."

Rolf Knight also wrote or co-authored *Work Camps and Company Towns in Canada and the United States* (1975), *A Man of Our Times: A Life-History of a Japanese-Canadian Fisherman* (1976), *Stump Ranch Chronicles and Other Narratives* (1977), *Indians at Work: An Informal History of Native Indian Labour in British Columbia 1858–1930* (1978), *Along the No. 20 Line: Reminiscences of the Vancouver Waterfront* (1980), *Traces of Magma: An Annotated Bibliography of Left Literature* (1983), *Voyage Through the Mid-Century* (1988) and *Homer Stevens: A Life in Fishing* (1992).

For other authors writing about labour in British Columbia, see abcbookworld entries for Bains, Hardial S.; Baird, Irene; Belshaw, John Douglas; Bennett, William; Bergren, Myrtle; Bernard, Elaine; Braid, Kate; Brodie, Steve; Brooks, Carellin; Culhane, Claire; Diamond, Sara; Doherty, Bill; Dunaway, Jo; Edge, Marc; Griffin, Betty; Griffin, Harold; Hanebury, Derek; Hill, A.V.; Hinde, John R.; Hoar, Victor; Homer, Stevens; Howard, Irene; Howard, Victor; Latham, Barbara; Lazarus, Morden; Leier, Mark; Lembcke, Jerry; Liversedge, Ronald; Lowther, Bruce; MacKay, Charles Angus; Magee, Catherine J.; Mann, Geoff; Mayse, Susan; McEwan,

Tom; McMaster, Lindsey; Merkel, Robert; Munro, Jack; North, George; O'Hara, Jane; Palmer, Bryan D.; Parnaby, Andrew; Perry, Adele; Phillips, Paul; Robin, Martin; Schwantes, Carlos A.; Seager, Allen; Stanton, John; Stewart, Mary Lynn; Stonebanks, Roger; Swankey, Ben; Sykes, Ella; Tranfield, Pam; Tyler, Robert; Waiser, Bill; Warburton, Rennie; Wayman, Tom; Wejr, Patricia; White, Bill; White, Howard.

GEORGE MANUEL

The Fourth World: An Indian Reality (1974)
by George Manuel & Michael Posluns

According to historian Robin Fisher, at one time about one-third of the aboriginal population of Canada lived in what became British Columbia. The most well-known aboriginal from modern British Columbia is Chief Dan George, but possibly the most important aboriginal from B.C. is the political activist and organizer George Manuel, co-author of *The Fourth World: An Indian Reality* (1974).

Born in 1921 on Neskonlith Reserve within Secwepemc territory, George Manuel was raised by his grandparents and attended Kamloops Residential School until he contracted tuberculosis at age 12. He was confined to a sanatorium and never fully recovered from the experience. Mainly self-educated, he worked as a logger and boom boss in the forest industry.

With guidance from his mentor in politics, Andrew Paull, Manuel served for seven years as a Secwepemc chief and became president of the North American Indian Brotherhood in 1959. In an effort to speed up the process of reform and self-determination, Manuel took a position within the Department of Indian Affairs but became radicalized in opposition to the government when Prime Minister Pierre Trudeau issued the White Paper in 1969 that announced Canada's intention to promote "assimilation of Indian people into Canadian society."

To mobilize against the Trudeau plan, Manuel got himself elected as president of the National Indian Brotherhood. During this period of radicalization he was inspired and influenced by his personal audience with Julius Nyerere in Tanzania and a visit in 1971 to the Maori of New Zealand. "It was a Tanzanian [Nyerere] who said to me, 'When the Indian peoples come into their own, that will be the Fourth World,'" Manuel wrote. He also went to Washington, D.C., to contact his counterpart in the United States, Mel Tonasket, president of the National Congress of American Indians. This meeting led to an international agreement in 1973 to establish exchanges between the two aboriginal associations, thereby laying the groundwork for affiliations between indigenous peoples around the world.

To promote his message of unification for indigenous peoples of the world, Manuel travelled to aboriginal villages in northern Argentina, to Quechua villages in Peru, to Samiland in Sweden, to Indian reservations in the United States, to Yapti Tasbia in eastern Nicaragua, to Mapuche villages in Chile and to Mayan refugee camps on the border between Mexico and Guatemala. In the late 1970s, he made a speech to 15,000 indigenous Peruvians. "I told them that we have to have our own ideology," he said in 1983. "We don't fit into the Right and we don't fit into the Left. That's why we are fragmented completely; we are always on the losing end, the deprived end of the stick."

Manuel was instrumental in drafting the Universal Declaration on the Rights of Indigenous Peoples. He also developed the Union of British Columbia Indian Chiefs' Aboriginal Rights Position Paper and organized the Union's Indian Constitutional Express in 1980, sending a delegation of a thousand aboriginals to Ottawa by train in an attempt to delay patriation of Canada's constitution. He served as National Indian Brotherhood president from 1970 to 1976, as president of the Union of B.C. Indian Chiefs from 1979 to 1981, and as the first president of the World Council of Indigenous Peoples, from 1975 to 1981.

With Michael Posluns, Manuel co-authored *The Fourth World: An Indian Reality*, which promoted the rights of indigenous peoples. In the book, he writes, "At this point in our struggle for survival, the Indian peoples of North America are entitled to declare a victory. We have survived. If others have also prospered on our land, let it stand as a sign between us that the Mother Earth can be good to all her children without confusing one with another. It is a myth of European warfare that one's man victory requires another's defeat."

George Manuel died in Kamloops in 1989.

GERALD A. RUSHTON

Whistle Up the Inlet (1974) by Gerald A. Rushton

Gerald A. Rushton's classic history of the Union Steamship Company, *Whistle Up the Inlet* (1974), was followed by his illustrated history of "the lifeline of the coast," *Echoes of the Whistle*, in 1980. Founded in 1889, the Union Steamship Company developed a fleet of more than 40 vessels that stopped at almost every community and inhabited cove from Vancouver to Alaska, including the Queen Charlotte Islands, providing passenger and cargo services. The service began in response to the arrival of the Canadian Pacific Railway on the West Coast. The cross-Canada railway connection enabled the enclave of Gastown to be transformed into the port of Vancouver—and Vancouver began to rival Victoria as a transportation hub. Therefore, the Union Steamship Company of New Zealand decided to introduce a maritime transportation link between Vancouver and Australasia. With the support of the New Zealand–based company, the Burrard Inlet Towing Company was absorbed by the Union Steamship Company of B.C. Three freighters from Scotland were built in sections and reassembled in Vancouver. British shareholders also raised money for the passenger steamer, *Cutch*. The funnel colours and livery of the New Zealand firm were copied in Vancouver.

Union Steamships ceased operations on the West Coast on December 31, 1958. The remaining fleet was sold to the Northland Navigation Co. The gap in the transportation market for car ferries was partially filled by the Puget Sound–based Black Ball Ferries until the B.C. government in 1961 bought and renamed five Black Ball ships on behalf of the B.C. Toll Highway and Bridge Authority, for $6,690,000, giving rise to the "Dogwood fleet" of B.C. Ferries.

The main chronicler of the Union Steamship Company, Gerald Arnold Rushton, was born in Liverpool in 1898. After studying classics and fighting in France during WWI, he came to B.C. in 1920 and worked for Union Steamships as an office manager for 38 years. He died in Tsawwassen in 1993. Former Union Steamships purser Arthur Twigg published *Union Steamships Remembered, 1920–1958* (1997), a reference work devoted to ships and personnel. He had worked in the purser's office aboard every ship in the fleet that plied the coast between 1942 and 1950.

JACK HODGINS

Raised on a "stump ranch" at Merville, between Courtenay and Campbell River on Vancouver Island, Jack Hodgins has frequently recalled he felt "bush league" even in relation to people who lived in the nearby towns.

Encouraged by Earle Birney at UBC, Hodgins made a comet-like emergence with two audacious works of fiction, *Spit Delaney's Island* (1976), a light-hearted collection of stories that received the Eaton's Book Award, and *The Invention of the World* (1977), a magic realist novel that depicts the fictional Revelations Colony of Truth led by Donal Keneally, a religious leader inspired by the fraudulent occultist Edward Arthur Wilson, a.k.a. Brother XII.

"*The Invention of the World* ranks up there with *The Diviners* for me," says novelist Anne Cameron, who, along with Hodgins, was born in Nanaimo in 1938. "It made my personal reality visible and available to everyone. Somehow it no longer seemed quite the burden it had been to have been raised on this island, in Nanaimo, virtually cut off from the rest of the world."

Hodgins then gained broad recognition on the Canadian literary map when he won the Governor General's Award for Fiction for his light-hearted novel, *The Resurrection of Joseph Bourne* (1979), celebrating a potpourri of characters in the coastal town of Port Alice. He later received the Ethel Wilson Fiction Prize for *Broken Ground* (1998), a novelized tribute to the origins of Merville as a settlement for WWI soldiers and their families. Of his 14 books, his one non-fiction title is a *A Passion for Narrative* (1994).

Hodgins received the Canada-Australia Prize in 1986. In 2006, he was named the twelfth recipient of the George Woodcock Lifetime Achievement Award for an outstanding literary career in British Columbia. In that same year he received the Lieutenant Governor's Award for Literary Excellence. In 2009, he became a member of the Order of Canada.

KEN ADACHI

The Enemy that Never Was (1976) by Ken Adachi

The first authors to describe sympathetically the plight of Japanese Canadians interned in WWII, after their fishboats and belongings were confiscated, were Dorothy Livesay and Hubert Evans. His remarkable but little-known "No More Islands" was written and published in *Young People* while the forced relocation of Japanese Canadians was underway. The most important chronicler of the Redress Movement led by his brother, Art Miki, has been the award-winning poet Roy Miki. David Suzuki has written clearly and well about Japanese Canadians in his autobiography. And easily the best-known work about Japanese Canadians in B.C. is Joy Kogawa's novel *Obasan*.

But the flurry of books from *Obasan* onward was kick-started by *Toronto Star* books columnist Ken Adachi who wrote the fundamental history of Japanese Canadians from 1877 to 1975, *The Enemy that Never Was* (1976), commissioned by the National Association of Japanese Canadians. It took him ten years to complete. It was the first book on the subject that opened the way for the reparations movement.

Joy Kogawa wrote Obasan *(1981), the best-known book about Japanese Canadians.*

Barry Broadfoot published his laudable oral history *Years of Sorrow, Years of Shame* one year later.

Born in B.C. in 1928, Ken Adachi grew up in Vancouver, the youngest of five children, and was interned at age 13 with his family at Slocan in the interior of B.C. His mother died of a heart attack in what Adachi later described as a "jerry-built" hospital in Slocan in 1945. His father had operated a small hotel and confectionary store in Vancouver. Both were confiscated. His father never overcame the setback and was limited to menial jobs ever after.

"We were never to come together as a family unit," Adachi wrote, in a 1988 article.

Following WWII, at age 20, Adachi began to edit the *New Canadian*, a newspaper reflecting the concerns of Japanese Canadians. He became book pages editor at the *Toronto Star* in 1976. Five years later he became widely respected as the *Star*'s fair and intelligent literary columnist. Married to outgoing book editor Mary Adachi since 1962, Adachi was an esteemed presence in Canadian letters, winning a 1985 National Newspaper Award for critical writing. At age 60, Adachi committed suicide, following a second accusation of plagiarism. Adachi had inexplicably used three paragraphs from a *Time* magazine book review of 1982. Friends dismissed the notion that his suicide was somehow "Japanese." "If you want to know how Canadian Ken was," said theatre critic John Bemrose, "you should have seen him play hockey."

For other B.C.-related authors who have written about Japanese Canadians, see abcbookworld entries for Adachi, Pat; Awmack, Winifred J.; Ayukawa, Midge; Britton, Dorothy; Chu, Garrick; Enomoto, Randy; Fukawa, Masako; Fukawa, Stanley; Goto, Hiromi; Howes, John F.; Ito, Roy; Kitagawa, Muriel; Kobayashi, Cassandra; Kogawa, Joy; La Violette, F.E.; Lang, Catherine; Marlatt, Daphne; Matsura, Frank; Miki, Roy; Miyazaki, M.; Morita, A. Katsuyoshi; Moriyama, Raymond; Nakano, Takeo Ujo; Nakayama, Gordon; Oiwa, Keibo; Omatsu, Marka; Ozeki, Ruth; Patton, Janice; Roy, Patricia; Sando, Tom; Shibata, Yuko; Shimizu, Yon; Shiomi, Rick; Sugimoto, Howard Hiroshi; Sunahara, Ann; Suzuki, David; Takata, Toyo; Tanabe, Tak; Tanaka, Tosh; Taylor, Mary; Wakayama, Tamio; Watada, Terry; Webber, Bert; Yesaki, Mitsuo.

CHUCK DAVIS

The Vancouver Book (1976) by Chuck Davis

Once upon a time, there was a crusty, cranky, self-inflated, Welsh-born, New Zealand–raised amateur historian in Kitsilano named Major James Skitt Matthews who, having fought at Ypres in WWI, insisted he should be empowered to serve the City of Vancouver, both officially and unofficially, as its chief historian for almost 40 years. Matthews interviewed pioneers, including the namesake of his neighborhood, August Jack Khahtsahlano, and remained fiercely protective of his work until his retirement at age 91 in 1969. He died a year later.

In terms of omnivorous knowledge about Vancouver, trivia-buff and master gatherer Chuck Davis has been the obvious successor to Matthews ever since *Chuck Davis' Guide to Vancouver* (1973). Thereafter Davis, as a congenial radio host, quizmaster, newspaper columnist and author, has devoted his life to being *the* expert on the city's history and its environs. His landmark volume, *The Vancouver Book* (1976), for which he is listed as general editor, remains his foremost accomplishment, even though it was eclipsed in size by his 882-page omnibus, *The Greater Vancouver Book* (1997), co-produced with business partner John Cochlin. Self-published under his Linkman Press imprint, this enterprise proved disastrous on a financial level. "Memo to self," Davis wrote, "never publish, only write." An unstoppable public servant, and perhaps a glutton for self-punishment, Davis then proceeded to predict his next project, *The History of Metropolitan Vancouver*, will be "the Mother of all Histories of Greater Vancouver." It is, however, unlikely to match the cultural impact of his 1976 undertaking, a massive and astonishing accomplishment prior to the internet.

Born in Winnipeg in 1935, Chuck Davis was in broadcasting for many years, beginning with the Canadian Army radio station, before he came to B.C. His eagerness to spread lively information about Vancouver, while gaining precious little compensation for his indefatigable services, makes him worthy of a civic stipend. And he plays killer Scrabble.

THOMAS BERGER

The most influential B.C. author in Canadian history could be Thomas Berger who, as commissioner of the Mackenzie Valley Pipeline Inquiry, wrote an extensive report, *Northern Frontier, Northern Homeland* (1977), which has sold more copies than any other federal government publication. Berger's stalwart role in curbing development of the north for environmental and sociological reasons continues to have a profound impact on the people and ecology of Canada. In addition, Berger, as a lawyer, has fundamentally enhanced the concept and viability of self-government for aboriginal Canadians since the 1960s.

Thomas Berger's memoir *One Man's Justice: A Life in the Law* (2002) spans 40 years of precedent-making cases since 1957 and includes the landmark case of (Frank) *Calder v. British Columbia* in

Thomas Berger, one of B.C.'s most influential authors

1971, during which Berger asserted that aboriginal rights must have a distinct place in Canadian law. In 1973, the Supreme Court of Canada concurred. Berger's success in the Calder case laid the foundation upon which most modern treaty-making cases have been argued.

In his book *Fragile Freedoms: Human Rights and Dissent in Canada* (1981), Berger recounts his abiding concerns for civil rights, and in *A Long and Terrible Shadow* (1991) he surveys European and aboriginal relations in the Americas since 1492. In 1991, Berger was appointed Deputy Chairman of the first independent review commissioned by the World Bank to examine the implementation of resettlement and environmental measures in the Sardar Sarovar dam and irrigation projects in India. He co-authored a 360-page report critical of the World Bank's support for a project that would displace nearly 100,000 people. In 1997, he was part of an international human rights team that went to Chile to assess the social and environmental impact of a major dam project on the Biobio River.

Born in Victoria in 1933 of Swedish descent, Thomas R. Berger was called to the bar in 1957. He was later elected to serve the constituency of Vancouver-Burrard, both federally and provincially, and was narrowly defeated by Dave Barrett in his bid to become leader of the provincial New Democratic Party in the early 1970s.

Berger served as a B.C. Supreme Court judge from 1971 to 1983, during which time he conducted the aforementioned pipeline enquiry. Accorded more than a dozen honorary degrees, Berger has served as chair of SFU's J.S. Woodsworth campaign, which set out in 1984 to raise one million dollars for the J.S. Woodsworth Endowment Fund in the Humanities.

Berger received the Order of Canada in 1990 and the Freedom of the City of Vancouver in 1992.

After twelve years as a judge in the Supreme Court of British Columbia, Berger returned to the practice of law and represented the province in a lawsuit against tobacco companies. Berger is the subject of a biography by Carolyn Swayze called *Hard Choices: A Life of Tom Berger* (1987), and he remains active in the B.C. Civil Liberties Association. Other Berger titles are *Village Journey* (1985) and *Northern Frontier, Northern Homeland* (1988, rev. ed.). Other authors who have worked extensively in northern B.C. include linguist Sharon Hargus and anthropologists Diamond Jenness, Robin Ridington and Hugh Brody.

DOUGLAS COLE

The name Douglas Cole rings very few bells beyond academic circles, but his writing career was nothing short of exemplary. Cole was born in Mason City, west of Spokane, in 1938. As one of the foremost authorities on relations between First Nations and non-aboriginal cultures, Cole produced two essential volumes, *Captured Heritage: The Scramble for Northwest Coast Artifacts* (1985) and *An Iron Hand upon the People: The Law Against the Potlatch on the Northwest Coast* (1990), with Ira Chaikin. *Captured Heritage* has been hugely influential in the social movement to regain artifacts that were taken from B.C. As Joan Givner noted in a review of Cole's work, "It is said that by 1930 there were more Kwakwaka'wakw artifacts in Milwaukee than in Mamalillikulla, more Salish artifacts in Cambridge than in Comox."

With Bradley Lockner, Cole co-edited *The Journals of George M. Dawson 1875–1878* (1989) which shed new light on the explorer. These journals chronicled the survey process and exploration of the Interior of B.C., the Fraser River and the Queen Charlotte Islands. A second set of journals, dated 1879 to 1900, was in the process of being edited and prepared for publication when Cole died in 1997 of a heart attack.

Posthumously, Cole was credited as co-editor of *At Home with the Bella Coola Indians: T.F. McIlwraith's Field Letters, 1922–4* (2003), with John Barker, and, more significantly, *Franz Boas: The Early Years, 1858–1906* (1999). "Cole's account of Boas' early scientific work is important for anthropologists and the references to Boas' field work are of special interest to B.C. readers," wrote Joan Givner. "But this biography also paints a vivid picture of life in the Jewish communities of German provincial towns, it describes Boas' education at leading German universities and it recounts how and why Boas settled in New York as part of the German expatriate society there. Like all magisterial biographies, *Franz Boas: The Early Years* successfully depicts one man's life against the backdrop of his historical period."

As well, the third Eaton's B.C. Book Award went to Douglas Cole and Maria Tippett for their critical study of B.C. art, *From Desolation to Splendour* (1977), a study of changing European attitudes to West Coast landscapes. Prior to the creation of the B.C. Book Prizes in 1985, the Eaton's Book Award was widely considered to be the province's top literary prize. Its perennial judges Margaret Prang (UBC), Walter D. Young (UVic) and Gordon Elliott (SFU) maintained unusually high standards. For a complete list of Eaton's Book Award recipients from 1975 to 1983, search for "Eaton's" at www.abcbookworld.com.

Douglas Cole, a founding professor at SFU, died at age 58.

W. P. KINSELLA

Dance Me Outside (1977) by W.P. Kinsella

Baseball fan W.P. Kinsella is in a league of his own. Of his twelve books related to baseball, including a Japanese-only non-fiction study, *Ichiro Dreams: Ichiro Suzuki and the Seattle Mariners* (2002), the most famous is *Shoeless Joe* (1982), a novel that served as the basis for *Field of Dreams* (1989) starring Kevin Costner.

Shoeless Joe was written after a young editor in Boston named Larry Kessenich saw a brief synopsis of W.P. Kinsella's short story called "Shoeless Joe Jackson Comes to Iowa" in *Publisher's Weekly* and asked him to expand the storyline. It's the story of an Iowa farmer named Ray Kinsella who erects a baseball field in his cornfield to attract bygone baseball stars from the 1919 Chicago White Sox. Audaciously, the central character kidnaps J.D. Salinger as part of the plot. For the film rights, Kinsella only received $250,000, but he approves of the adaptation.

Before that Hollywood movie spread the phrase "built it and they will come" around the planet, Kinsella's career took off with the release of a brilliant collection of stories, *Dance Me Outside* (1977). This was the first of seven popular books of "Indian stories" mostly set on the Hobbema reserve of Alberta, near where Kinsella was raised as an only child. They feature Cree narrator Silas Ermineskin as a would-be writer and his outrageous entrepreneurial sidekick Frank Fencepost, as they invariably outwit white authorities. Kinsella flatly rejects criticism that he has demeaned aboriginals by resorting to stereotypes. His stories are about the comic foibles of human nature.

Born in Edmonton, in 1935, William Patrick Kinsella lives in Yale, B.C. He no longer writes books.

W.P. Kinsella, 1997

BARRIE SANFORD

McCulloch's Wonder: The Story of the Kettle Valley Railway (1977)
by Barrie Sanford

Completing the Kettle Valley Railway (KVR) easily ranks in the "top ten" of B.C. engineering feats. It took three decades to construct a rail line through five mountain passes, including the Coquihalla Pass and Myra Canyon. Hence the most difficult railway in Canada to operate, the KVR was often referred to as McCulloch's Wonder, citing the achievements of the turn-of-the-century engineer Andrew McCulloch.

Railway buff Barrie Sanford spent ten years researching the building of the KVR line for *McCulloch's Wonder: The Story of the Kettle Valley Railway* (1977) which has gone through numerous printings. Sales were boosted in 2003 by the forest fires south of Kelowna that destroyed some of the KVR's bridgework, bringing cross-Canada attention to the rail line that was once considered the lifeline of southern B.C. The KVR is also the subject of Sanford's pictorial history, *Steel Rails and Iron Men* (1990).

The best-known transportation author of B.C. is Robert Turner. For others, see abcbookworld

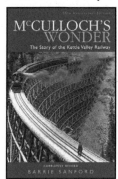

entries for Affleck, Edward L.; Anderson, J.F.; Armstrong, Cliff; Baird, Ian MacLeod; Bannerman, Gary; Barnard, John; Barr, James; Beaudoin, Ted; Bennett, Norma V.; Berton, Pierre; Booth, Jan; Bradley, Ken; Brown, Jim; Burrows, Roger; Clapp, Frank; Coates, Ken; Cockfield, Ian; Condit, John; Corley-Smith, Peter; Cotsworth, M.B.; Cox, Doug; Craig, Andy; de Goutiere, Justin; Doeksen, Gerry Corwin; Downs, Art; Duffy, Dennis J.; Ewert, Henry; Fleming, Sandford; Garden, John; Garner, Lloyd; Green, Mervyn; Grescoe, Paul; Gresko, Jacqueline; Griffiths, Garth; Hammer, Heinz; Harris, Lorraine; Harvey, R.G.; Hayman, Bob; Hearn, George; Henry, Tom; Hope, James; Horton, Timothy; Hungry Wolf, Adolf; Huntley, Edward (Ted); Kelly, Brian;

Kennedy, W.G.; Lamb, W.K.; Lanz, Walter; Leonard, Frank; Lewis, Donald C.; MacKay, Donald; Maiden, Cecil; Martin, J. Edward; Matheson, George; May, David; McAllister, Bruce; McKee, Bill; Moir, George Thompson; Muralt, Darryl; O'Neill, Wiggs; Ommundsen, Peter D.; Oum, Tae; Parker, Douglas; Patterson, Edward; Pendakur, Setty; Pole, Graeme; Preston, Dave; Rees-Thomas, David; Robb, Judy; Schofield, Jack; Secretan, J.H.; Skene, Wayne; Smith, Blake; Smuin, Joe; Spilsbury, Jim; Steed, Roger G.; Taylor, G.W.; Terpening, Rex; Twigg, Arthur M.; Volovsek, Walter O.; Wells, Martin; Whetham, Bob; White, Elwood; Whitesitt, Larry; Wilby, Thomas W.; Williams, Maurice; Wilson, Ralph.

CRAWFORD KILIAN

Go Do Some Great Thing (1978) by Crawford Kilian

The first non-fiction book about B.C.'s black pioneers, Crawford Kilian's *Go Do Some Great Thing* (1978), concentrates on the 19th-century migration of blacks from California, as encouraged by Governor James Douglas, and particularly the leadership of Mifflin Gibbs who was once told by an associate of Frederick Douglass to "go do some great thing."

Victoria city councillor Mifflin Wistar Gibbs was the first civic leader of black people in B.C. and the first widely-read black writer. He arrived in 1858, shortly after black pioneers arrived on the *Commodore* from California. Gibbs wrote many articles and speeches during his ten years in Canada. Had he remained on Vancouver Island and promises made to black pioneers been kept, Kilian has speculated, "Mifflin Gibbs might have become premier of British Columbia, or a businessman on the scale of a Dunsmuir."

Kilian's *Go Do Some Great Thing* inspired the likes of black film-maker Anthony Brown to make a documentary, *Go Do Some Great Thing*, and historian and poet Wayde Compton to generate his landmark anthology, *Bluesprint: Black British Columbian Literature & Orature* (2002). Compton also spearheaded Commodore Books, an imprint for black authors of B.C. that was named after the aforementioned ship.

Wayde Compton

Born in New York in 1941 and raised in Los Angeles and Mexico, Crawford Kilian, a white historian, worked at the Lawrence Radiation Laboratory in Berkeley prior to immigrating to Vancouver in 1967. He has taught English at Capilano College and written 19 other books, mostly speculative fiction novels.

Kilian has cited his debt to an unpublished UBC MA thesis by James W. Pilton, "Negro Settlement in B.C., 1858–1871," that was prepared in 1951. Commodore Books released a revised version of Kilian's history in 2008, 30 years after it first appeared, at which time he received an award of appreciation from Vancouver's black community.

For African Canadian authors, see abcbookworld entries for André, F.B.; Booker, Fred; Demming, Keita; Edugyan, Esi; Gale, Lorena; Garraway, Garbette; Gibbs, Mifflin; Green, Truman; Griggs, William E.; Odhiambo, David; Sarsfield, Mairuth Hodge; Sumter-Freitag, Addena; White, Evelyn C.

TERRY REKSTEN

Rattenbury (1978) by Terry Reksten

The great murder story of B.C. is Terry Reksten's non-fictional account of the life and death of Francis Mawson Rattenbury, the architect who designed the Empress Hotel, the Legislative Buildings and the Vancouver Courthouse (later transformed into the Vancouver Art Gallery). Reksten's involvement with successful efforts to preserve Crystal Gardens, a Victoria landmark designed by Rattenbury, led to her biography, simply entitled *Rattenbury* (1978), which received the fifth annual Eaton's Book Award.

Rattenbury immigrated to Vancouver in 1892, then relocated to Victoria where he enjoyed a distinguished career for three decades until he was embroiled in a land development scandal.

Equally problematic, he had divorced his first wife to marry Alma Clarke Pakenham, a lyricist for popular songs, who was 30 years younger.

The couple left B.C. in 1929 and settled in Bournemouth where the somewhat reclusive architect, nicknamed "Ratz," was murdered six years later at age 67 by his 38-year-old wife's 18-year-old chauffeur, handyman and lover, George Percy Stoner, on March 28, 1935. Allegedly high on cocaine-laced sandwiches, Stoner repeatedly bashed Rattenbury on the head with a carpenter's mallet, giving rise to a famous murder trial at the Old Bailey in May and June of 1935.

Investigations for the so-called Mallet Murder revealed that Stoner and Mrs. Rattenbury repeatedly slept together in her bedroom, with her six-year-old son in the room. In the witness box Mrs. Rattenbury described how she accidentally trod on her husband's false teeth when she discovered the body, then tried to insert the false teeth into his mouth to help him speak, if he was alive. The sordid affair generated headlines around the world.

The chauffeur was found guilty, but he was glad Alma was acquitted. "Deceitful bloody cow that she is," he exclaims in Terence Rattigan's play about the affair, "she's the only woman I ever had, ever loved."

Unable to endure the loss of her young lover, Alma went down to a river near her home and stabbed herself to death. Stoner's sentence was reduced to life imprisonment. Eventually he was released, although in the 1980s he was arrested on a morals charge.

Rattigan's play became the basis for a TV movie *Cause Célèbre*, starring Helen Mirren as Alma. It aired on PBS Mystery in 1987.

Terry Reksten wrote six other books, including two about the Vancouver Island–based coal mining dynasty of the Dunsmuir family, and *The Illustrated History of British Columbia* (2001), a useful, fair-minded work that does not attempt any overriding views or organizing principles. Born in England in 1942, she died in 2001.

HUGH JOHNSTON

The Voyage of the Komagata Maru: The Sikh Challenge to Canada's Colour Bar (1979) by Hugh Johnston

In 1914, some 376 British subjects, including 340 Sikhs, were stranded offshore for two months in the ship *Komagata Maru*, as they unsuccessfully challenged B.C. immigration policies in Burrard Inlet. The ship had been chartered for $66,000 by Gurdit Singh Sarhali, a Sikh entrepreneur, as a direct challenge to a restrictive policy that required all would-be immigrants from India to take direct passage to Canada—when no such direct passage from India existed. During the impasse, food and water aboard ship diminished and social unrest among the South Asian community of B.C. increased. An attempt to board the ship by 150 armed men, in support of a Canadian immigration official, was rebuffed. It took the arrival of the federal navy vessel H.M.C.S. *Rainbow* on July 23, 1914, to force the *Komagata Maru* to leave the city and return to Calcutta.

The stand-off has been documented and examined by Hugh Johnston in *The Voyage of the Komagata Maru: The Sikh Challenge to Canada's Colour Bar* (1979). Passing through Vancouver in 1914, Sir Arthur Conan Doyle remarked, "The whole incident seemed to me to be so grotesque—for why should sun-loving Hindoos force themselves upon Canada?"

Alan Dutton, Robert Jarvis, Sohan Sarinder Singh Sangha, Ajmer Rode and Kesar Singh have also written books on the *Komagata Maru* incident after Sharon Pollock led the way in 1976 with a play about the racist stand-off. In 1990, the Progressive Indo-Canadian Community Services Society also published the proceedings of a Vancouver conference, *Beyond the Komagata Maru: Race Rela-*

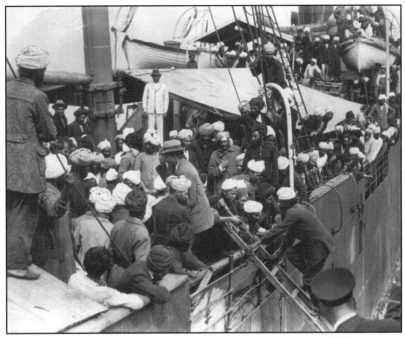
Negotiators board the Komagata Maru *in Vancouver harbour, 1914.*

tions Today, edited by Alan Dutton. With Tara Singh Bains, Johnston has also published *The Four Quarters of the Night: The Life-Journey of an Emigrant Sikh* (1995).

British Columbia has been steeped in racism. A chapter of the Ku Klux Klan opened in Vancouver in 1925 and attracted 500 people to a meeting in 1927. It argued for a ban on Oriental immigration and the confiscation of property owned by Asians— laying the groundwork for the government's expropriation of land and possessions from Japanese-Canadians during WWII.

A classic racist tract is Hilda Glynn-Ward's fear-mongering novel *The Writing on the Wall* (1921), published by the Sun Publishing Company. It concludes with Vancouver's white population dying from typhoid fever contracted from Chinese-grown vegetables and sugar to which local Chinese merchants had purposely added ty-phoid germs. In this story the Chinese and Japanese remain healthy because they have been "inured to it by countless generations of living without sanitation."

Patricia Roy has become the leading academic authority on anti-Asian policies in B.C. with books such as *A White Man's Province: British Columbia Politicians and Chinese and Japanese Immigrants, 1858–1914* (1989) and *The Oriental Question: Consolidating a White Man's Province, 1914–41* (2003). For a few of the many books about racism in B.C., see abcbookworld entries for Ito, Roy; Kitagawa, Muriel; Laut, Agnes; Lee, Jo-Anne; McAlpine, John D.; Miki, Roy; O'Keefe, Betty; Robin, Martin; Ward, W. Peter.

L.D. LOVICK

Tommy Douglas Speaks: Till Power is Brought to Pooling (1979)
edited by L.D. Lovick

It was never a bestseller. But if Tommy Douglas really is *the* greatest Canadian, as determined by a national 2004 CBC poll, surely *Tommy Douglas Speaks: Till Power is Brought to Pooling* (1979), edited by L.D. (Dale) Lovick, qualifies as a literary benchmark in the realm of B.C. books by politicians. It contains full texts or excerpts from 35 speeches spanning Douglas' 42-year political career.

Lovick was a professor of English and Canadian Studies at Malaspina College when he edited this B.C.-published collection of speeches. He cites Douglas' valiant denunciations of the War Measures Act ("his finest hour"), the sell-off of Canada's oil and gas, and the Columbia River Treaty.

Lovick describes Douglas as a classic liberal because "he believes that human beings are created good and are corrupted by the society and environment they inhabit." Some of the quotations from Douglas reveal his sparkling wit. "When a Yankee trader tells you that you are a tough negotiator," he said, "you know you have been taken to the cleaners."

For books by politicians, see abcbookworld entries for Bains, Hardial S.; Barrett, Dave; Brown, Rosemary; Campbell, Kim; Campbell, Larry; Carney, Pat; Edwards, Anne; Gibson, Gordon; Harcourt, Mike; Hardwick, Walter G.; Holt, Simma; Humphreys, Derrick; Jewett, Pauline; McGeer, Patrick; McWhinney, Edward (Ted); Mitchell, Margaret; Oberle, Frank; Petter, Andrew; Shelford, Cyril; Tyabji, Judi; Vander Zalm, Bill; Wilson, Gordon.

STAN PERSKY

Son of Socred (1979) by Stan Persky

Books about B.C. politics and politicians have become a weak spot in B.C. publishing. The more publishers must worry about getting their books into Chapters and retaining precarious funding, the less we see critical works about our society and its managers. A flood has turned into a trickle.

When Stan Persky was full of vigour, he led the way with a populist critique of the Social Credit government of Premier Bill Bennett, *Son of Socred* (1979). In this first volume in a series of lively paperbacks about B.C. politics, sold in supermarkets, Persky suggested that academics should "spend more of their time and skills addressing the general public rather than just talking to each other." A long-time sociology professor at Capilano College/University, Perksy co-founded the *Georgia Straight Writing Supplement* in the late 1960s, which led to the formation of New Star Books by Lanny Beckman. Politically and philosophically, Persky was influenced by Bob Rowan, one of the founders of the B.C. Civil Liberties Association and the Arts One curriculum at UBC. His literary mentor was his lover Robin Blaser. Since the release of *Buddy's: Meditations on Desire* (1989), Persky has leaned more towards self-referential writing and personal essays.

For other political books by non-politicians, see abcbookworld entries for Adam, Heribet; Antliff, Allan; Avakumovic, Ivan; Baldrey, Keith; Birney, Earle; Blake, Donald E.; Block, Walter; Boyle, Patrick T.; Brière, Elaine; Brunet-Jailly, Emmanuel; Bryden, P.E.; Byers, Michael; Cairns, Alan; Cameron, Stevie; Carr, Paul; Carty, Kenneth; Clearwater, John; Clements, Alan; Coats,

R.H.; Cohen, Lenard; Conway, Robert; Covell, Caroline; Cross, William; Day, J.C.; Ditmars, Hadani; Dobbin, Murray; Doyle, Charles; Eisenberg, Avigail; Engler, Allan; Engler, Yves; Enomoto, Randy; Evans, Elwood; Fenton, Anthony; Finlay, K.A.; Foster, Leslie; Friedrichs, Christopher; Garr, Allen; Gawthrop, Daniel; Gerolymatos, André; Godfrey, Sima; Grey, Deborah; Harding, Jim; Haskett, Michael J.; Head, Ivan; Herath, R.B.; Howlett, Michael; Jefferess, David; Johnson, Genevieve Fuji; Julian, Terry; Kavic, Lorne J.; Kay, William; Keene, R.; Knox, Paul; Leslie, Graham; Lewis, S.P.; Lund, Darren; MacMinn, George; MacPherson, Donald; Magnusson, Warren; Marchak, Patricia; Mathews, Robin; Mauzy, Diane K.; McClung, Nellie Letitia; Mgbeoji, Ikechi; Millard, Gregory; Moens, Alexander; Morley, Terry; Morton, James; Mugridge, Ian; Munro, John; Murray, Peter; Nadir, Leilah; Nixon, Bob; Onstad, Gary; Ore, Kenneth; Palmer, Bryan D.; Parker, Gilbert; Plant, Geoff; Plecas, Bob; Prentice, Roger; Prince, Michael J.; Resnick, Philip; Robin, Martin; Rodney, William; Rose, William; Rothenburger, Mel; Sajoo, Amyn B.; Sakolsky, Ron; Scott, Jack; Sharifad, Yadi; Shelton, George W.; Sherman, Paddy; Spector, Norman; Stankiewicz, W.J.; Steeves, Dorothy; Stephen, A.M.; Stevenson, Michael; Swankey, Ben; Townsend-Gault, Ian; Twigg, Alan; Varzeliotis, Tom; Walker, Len; Walker, Michael; Walker, Russell Robert; Webster, Daisy; Wharf, Brian; Wild, Roland; Williams, David Ricardo; Wilson, Donna; Woodsworth, Glenn; Ykelchyk, Serhy; Young, Lisa; Young, Walter D.

PHILIP J. THOMAS

Songs of the Pacific Northwest (1979) by Philip J. Thomas

The most essential book on music in British Columbia is *Songs of the Pacific Northwest* (1979) by Phil Thomas, the Pete Seeger of B.C. "A common theme is accepting one's destiny as a miner, fisherman or whatever," said Thomas. "Minor hardships are often made a grim joke in songs of places: the winters of the East Kootenays, the rains of Ocean Falls or Holberg. The bitter struggle of miners fighting for the right to have their own unions produced several B.C. songs, one of which was recorded 50 years after the events that sparked its creation."

Born in 1921, Thomas was a WWII veteran forced to take a teaching job in Pender Harbour in 1949 when he was suspected of being a communist by the Delta School Board. He taught grades six to ten in a small school where his students were mostly the children of fishermen and loggers. His neighbour was the author and fisherman Bertrand Sinclair who inspired Thomas to collect distinctly British Columbian songs. In the early 1950s, Thomas first adapted and augmented Sinclair's lyrics for a song, "The Bank Trollers," about commercial fishing (as distinguished from gillnetting and seining). His song collecting and field recording of original B.C. material soon became a lifelong passion, much influenced by the song-collecting of Edith Fowke in Ontario. Thomas contributed songs to some of her books and to a 16-part CBC radio series entitled *The Songs and Stories of Canada.*

Thomas' best-known song, "Where the Fraser River Flows," was written by Joe Hill and first sung in 1912. *Where the Fraser River Flows* was also the title of a CD made by Thomas. A CD entitled *Phil Thomas and Friends: Live at Folklife Expo 86* includes the song "Bank Trollers" which was first published in Thomas' *Twenty-Five Songs for Vancouver 1886–1986* (1986).

Thomas' *Songs of the Pacific Northwest* was revised and expanded in 2006. It included a dual-CD compilation from Cariboo Road Music, *Songs of the Pacific Northwest: A Tribute,* drawn primarily from songs Thomas had gathered through his field recordings and research. The audio collection features Thomas' final public performance as well as 40 other Northwest musicians singing 37 songs, 28 of which are in the book. In 2003, Jon Bartlett and Rika Ruebesaat released a CD drawn from Thomas' collecting work from the early 1950s to the late 1970s, *The Young Man from Canada: BC Songs from the PJ Thomas Collection.*

The approximately 500 songs in the P.J. Thomas Collection in the Sound and Moving Image Division of the Royal B.C. Museum mainly showcase indigenous songs of fishing, mining, logging and homesteading. Most were donated in 1975. Rare Books and Special Collections at UBC has 7,240 items in its Philip J. Thomas Popular Song Collection. Until he died at age 85 in 2007, Thomas remained active as a banjo player, singer and composer in the Alma Y Folk Circle, an organization that he and his wife Hilda Thomas co-founded with others in 1959. It later became the Vancouver Folk Song Society.

Dale McIntosh of the University of Victoria published *History of Music in British Columbia* (1989), a reference guide to B.C.'s musical ensembles and major musical personalities from 1850 to 1950. With ethnomusicologist Wendy Bross Stuart, John Enrico published a 519-page study, *Northern Haida Songs* (1996), which situates Haida music in the context of the Northwest Coast and presents a collection of 128 songs, fully transcribed and analyzed, representing some 20 types of songs. For other B.C. authors who have written about music—from Mart Kenney and Dal Richards to Will Millar and Joey Shithead—see abcbookworld entries for Adams, Bryan; Adaskin, Harry; Anstey, Robert; Armstrong, John; Bachman, Randy; Baldry, Long John; Bates, Morris; Becker, John; Bradshaw, M. Doris; Brown, Heide; Bruneau, William; Campbell, Amy; Case, George; Cavoukian, Raffi; Chesher, Deborah; Chesterman, Robert; Childerhose, Buffy; Chong, Kevin; Clyne, Dorothy; Crich, Tim; Cunningham, Rosemary; Densmore, Frances; Duke, David Gordon; Forbes-Roberts, Ron; Gati, Laszlo; Giese, Rachel; Gothe, Jurgen; Gray, Martin; Gregory, Hugh; hagarty, britt; Halpern, Ida; Headrick, Paul; Hendrix, James Al; Hicks, George; Hryniuk, Angela; Hughes, Mary E.; Jackson, Lorna; Keithley, Joe; Kendy, Emily; Kenney, Mart; Kivi, K. Linda; Konieczny, Vladimir; Le Bel, Pauline Eulalie; Lee, David; McGuire, Ra; McLaren, Jean; Millar, Will; Mitchell, Joni; O'Connell, Sheldon; Pearce, Christian; Potter, Greg; Reid, Jamie; Richards, Dal; Robinson, Red; Saidman, Sorelle; Salloum, Trevor; Schafer, R. Murray; Schwartz, Ellen; Setterfield, Gwenlyn; Slim, H. Colin; Slyne, Dorothy; Smith, Bill; Soret, Mike; Stevenson, Richard; Swanton, John; Tenzer, Michael; Thomson, Robert S.; Thrasher, Alan; Tidler, Charles; Truax, Barry; Tyson, Ian; Varty, Alex; Walker, Carl Ian; Walter, Chris; Wooton, Carol.

MARGARET TRUDEAU

Beyond Reason (1979) by Margaret Trudeau

M argaret Trudeau? An important author? Her memoir *Beyond Reason* (1979) will be read in the next century because she was one-half of the most famous couple in Canadian history. Born as Margaret Joan Sinclair in 1948, the so-called "flower child" was the daughter of West Vancouver's leading federal Liberal Party official, James Sinclair, a former federal Fisheries Minister. In 1971, she wed 51-year-old Prime Minister Pierre Trudeau in a private ceremony in Vancouver.

At age 18, she had first met Trudeau, then Minister of Justice, while vacationing in Tahiti, but this encounter was not particularly memorable for her. He nonetheless began to pursue her.

Prior to their separation in 1977, she gave birth to three sons, Justin, Sacha and Michel. She resented her husband's prolonged absences and was often criticized for her free-spirited behaviour at formal government events. "Tenderly, without realizing he was doing it, Trudeau set her inside a bell jar and cut her off from life," wrote Richard Gwyn in his Trudeau biography, *The Northern Magus*. It didn't help that she was rumoured to have had a romantic interlude with U.S. Senator Ted Kennedy or that she wore a see-through T-shirt while visiting Cuba, where the Trudeaus met Fidel Castro.

Intolerant of weakness, Pierre Trudeau was nonetheless compassionate about Margaret's bouts of depression. She spent her sixth anniversary with the Rolling Stones, having flown to Toronto and taken photos of them during their performance at the El Mocambo club. She was seen in Mick Jagger's limousine afterwards. It turned out she had a tryst with Rolling Stone guitarist Ronnie Wood. The *Daily Mirror* in London proclaimed "Premier's Wife in Stones Scandal." After the pub-

lic collapse of their marriage, she was the victim of sensational headlines linking her to drugs and actors Jack Nicholson and Ryan O'Neal.

Margaret Trudeau tried to rebound with two volumes of memoirs, *Beyond Reason* (1979), mainly about her life as Mrs. Trudeau, and *Consequences* (1982), about her "afterlife" outside of politics. "Fairy tales don't happen," she wrote. "Real life happens." Pierre Trudeau was re-elected to power in 1980, at which time both parents agreed to share custody of their children. The Trudeaus were

Margaret Trudeau with Prime Minister Pierre Trudeau and son at Vancouver's airport

divorced in 1984 but they increasingly set aside acrimony in order to work together constructively as parents. Margaret Trudeau had a brief career as a television host prior to marrying Ottawa real estate developer Fred Kemper, with whom she has two children.

Margaret Kemper's links to B.C. were tragically renewed in 1998 when her son Michel Trudeau died in an avalanche at Kokanee Lake, near Rossland. Margaret Kemper and Pierre Trudeau were seen hand-in-hand at Outremont's St. Viateur Church for Michel's funeral, reunited by grief. Margaret Kemper separated from her second husband Fred Kemper six months later, and rekindled her friendship with the ailing ex-Prime Minister. She was at Trudeau's bedside when he died in 2000.

Margaret Kemper became Honorary President of WaterCan, an Ottawa-based organization dedicated to helping the poorest communities in developing countries build sustainable water supply and sanitation services. She later became a board member of the Institute of Mental Health at UBC.

VII
1980s

ANNE CAMERON

Daughters of Copper Woman (1981) by Anne Cameron

If there's one work of identifiably British Columbian fiction that will outlast all others for a century, it could well be Anne Cameron's audacious *Daughters of Copper Woman* (1981), reprinted thirteen times. It has long been the bestselling work of fiction to be written and published in B.C. In recent decades, most fiction from B.C. writers is published in the Prairie provinces or Ontario.

Born in Nanaimo in 1938, and raised halfway between Chinatown and the Indian reserve, Anne Cameron says that the only place where she found order was in books, or her imagination. Married at a young age, she raised a family and divorced, and eventually gained her grade twelve education ("except in Math, and in that I have grade ten"). After she began writing theatre scripts and screenplays under the name Cam Hubert, her stage adaptation of a documentary poem developed into a play about racism, *Windigo*, which in 1974 was the first presentation of Tillicum Theatre, the first aboriginal-based theatre group in Canada.

In 1979, her film *Dreamspeaker*, directed by Claude Jutra, won seven Canadian Film Awards, including best script. It is the story of an emotionally disturbed boy who runs away from hospital and finds refuge with a First Nations elder, portrayed by George Clutesi, and his mute companion. Published as a novel that same year, *Dreamspeaker* won the Gibson Award for Literature.

Cameron's other credits as a screenwriter include *Ticket to Heaven*, *The Tin Flute* and *Drying up the Streets*, but she remains most widely known for the first of her two feminist renderings of Coast Salish and Nuu-chah-nulth legends, *Daughters of Copper Woman*. More than 20 books have followed, mainly novels about so-called working-

Reprinted thirteen times, Anne Cameron's *Daughters of Copper Woman* is one of the bestselling books of fiction published from and about British Columbia.

WINNER

ANNE CAMERON

Since 1995, *BC BookWorld* and the Vancouver Public Library have proudly sponsored the Woodcock Award and the Writers Walk at 350 West Georgia Street in Vancouver.

16TH ANNUAL
GEORGE WOODCOCK
LIFETIME ACHIEVEMENT AWARD

FOR AN OUTSTANDING LITERARY CAREER IN BRITISH COLUMBIA

ANNE CAMERON BIBLIOGRAPHY:
Novels & Short Stories: Dahlia Cassidy (2004) • Family Resemblances (2003) • Hardscratch Row (2002)
• Sarah's Children (2001) • Those Lancasters (2000) • Aftermath (1999) • Selkie (1996) • The Whole Dam Family (1995)
• Deeyay and Betty (1994) • Wedding Cakes, Rats and Rodeo Queens (1994) • A Whole Brass Band (1992) • Kick the Can (1991)
• Escape to Beulah (1990) • Bright's Crossing (1990) • South of an Unnamed Creek (1989) • Women, Kids & Huckleberry Wine (1989)
• Tales of the Cairds (1989) • Stubby Amberchuk & The Holy Grail (1987) • Child of Her People (1987) • Dzelarhons: Mythology of the Northwest
Coast (1986) • The Journey (1982) • Daughters of Copper Woman (1981) • Dreamspeaker (1979). **Poetry:** The Annie Poems (1987)
• Earth Witch (1983) **Children's Books:** T'aal: The One Who Takes Bad Children (1998) • The Gumboot Geese (1992)
• Raven Goes Berrypicking (1991) • Raven & Snipe (1991) • Spider Woman (1988) • Lazy Boy (1988) • Orca's Song (1987)
• Raven Returns the Water (1987) • How the Loon Lost her Voice (1985) • How Raven Freed the Moon (1985)

Vancouver Public Library reading Thursday, July 29th. Call 604-736-4011 for info.

FOR MORE INFO SEE WWW.ABCBOOKWORLD.COM

Anne Cameron won the George Woodcock Lifetime Achievement Award in 2010.

class life in coastal communities such as Powell River or Nanaimo. Most of her stories involve transformation and healing.

Cameron has been primarily concerned with the lives of women who keep the world turning, or dare to assert their independence with non-conformist behaviour. Long before the movie *Thelma and Louise*, Cameron wrote her cowgirl buddy western *The Journey* in which 14-year-old Anne, abused by her uncle, sets off on her own and teams up with Sarah, a prostitute who has been tarred and feathered by a vigilante killer and his supporters. The pair ride off into the sunset in the late nineteeth century, defending themselves as necessary.

For many years Anne Cameron and her partner lived near Powell River on a 30-acre farm. An exceedingly funny social critic, she now lives alone in Tahsis, minding her grandchildren, estranged from, and overlooked by, literary tastemakers. One suspects there lingers a mystified prejudice against any woman who swears openly. Her readership is international, her work remains uncompromising.

In 2010, Cameron received the George Woodcock Lifetime Achievement Award for B.C. literature.

HUGH BRODY

Maps and Dreams: Indians and the British Columbia Frontier (1981)
by Hugh Brody

Following his groundbreaking study *Indians on Skid Row* (1971), Hugh Brody spent 18 months with Beaver Indians in northeastern B.C. in response to proposals for an Alaska Highway natural gas pipeline. Fluent in French, German and Hebrew, Brody learned two Inuktitut dialects and concluded language is the key to understanding cultures. Collecting anecdotes, maps and research data, he wrote his best-known work, *Maps and Dreams: Indians and the British Columbia Frontier* (1981). He later wrote a clear explanation of what four million square miles of Canadian Arctic means to the Inuit, Déné, Cree, Naskapi, Innu and Métis in *Living Arctic: Hunters of the Canadian North* (1987), in conjunction with the British Museum and Indigenous Survival International.

Brody's work as a social scientist contradicts the stereotypes which imply that aboriginals never had, or sadly have lost, a sustainable economic life. "The W.A.C. Bennett Hydroelectric Dam," he writes, "illustrates the kind of disregard for the Indian interest that has accompanied northern development. The Bennett Dam created Williston Lake, the largest body of fresh water in British Columbia, over 250 miles in length, covering a total of 640 square miles. The flooded valleys were the principal hunting, trapping and fishing territories of several Sekani Indian bands. Their reserves were destroyed; they were dispossessed of the entire area of their traditional homeland, expected to move along, make do, or somehow disappear. And silently they did, withdrawing to higher ground, where they have lived ever since at the edge of other bands, in dire poverty and some social distress."

LYNNE BOWEN

Boss Whistle: The Coal Miners of Vancouver Island Remember (1982),
edited by Lynne Bowen

Harsh conditions encountered by miners in the Dunsmuir family mines on Vancouver Island gave rise to B.C.'s sometimes formidable labour movement, hence Lynne Bowen's *Boss Whistle* (1982) is a literary vein that leads to the heart of a province that has relied almost exclusively on resource-based industries such as mining.

Since 1849, when the Hudson's Bay Company sought coal on Vancouver Island, mining evolved into B.C.'s third-largest industry, in terms of dollar value, behind logging and tourism. But mining-related literature is miniscule compared to books on logging and fishing.

Culled from Myrtle Bergren's 130 hours of interviews, and sponsored by Nanaimo's Coal Tyee Society, *Boss Whistle: The Coal Miners of Vancouver Island Remember* (1982) is an indispensable oral

Irene Howard

history of Vancouver Island colliers and their families. After it received the Eaton's B.C. Book Award, Bowen dug deeper and provided a sequel, *Three Dollar Dreams* (1987), to outline the frequently violent labour history of coal mining on southern Vancouver Island from 1848 to 1900. This led to her study of coal baron, Robert Dunsmuir, also the subject of two plays by Rod Langley.

A mainland counterpart to *Boss Whistle* is Irene Howard's heart-wrenching tribute to her parents, *Gold Dust on His Shirt: The True Story of an Immigrant Mining Family* (2008). Doubling as a social history, *Gold Dust* is easily one of the most impressive family memoirs ever written about a B.C. working class family as it recounts the heroism of pioneer labour, generating profit for others.

If Woody Guthrie had visited B.C. mining camps, he might have written a song about Alfred and Ingeborg Nelson, Irene Howard's parents.

For other authors pertaining to mining, see abcbookworld entries for Aho, Aaro E.; Audain, James; Bain, David; Barlee, N.L.; Barr, David A.; Blake, Don; Brown, James N.J.; Brown, Murray; Caldwell, Francis E.; Cole, Sidney K.; Cox, Doug; Draper, Penny; Frolick, Vernon; Green, Lewis; Guppy, Walter; Hawkins, Elizabeth; Hedley, M.S.; Helm, Charles; Hemmingsen, John; Hines, Ben; Hudson, Rick; Hutchings, Ozzie; Jacobsen, Larry; Johnstone, Bill; Lammers, John; Laskowski, Janusz S.; May, David; Miller, Charles; Mouat, Jeremy; Newsome, Eric; Petersen, Eugene; Picard, Ed; Ramsey, Bruce; Rickard, T.A.; Roberts, W.R. (Bill); Robertson, Leslie A.; Taylor, G.W.; Trimble, William J.; Trueman, Allan Stanley; Warden, Geoff; Wilson, John; Zinovich, Jordan.

H. "DUDE" LAVINGTON

The Nine Lives of a Cowboy (1982) by H. "Dude" Lavington

Born in Content, Alberta (near Red Deer), Harold "Dude" Lavington grew up breaking horses and breaking bones, riding a bronco named Calamity. He arrived in the Chilcotin area, near Nasko, B.C., in 1931. Working with his brother Art, he mainly ranched in Baker Creek Valley, three hours from Quesnel. "A cowboy must be blessed (or cursed) with nine lives like the proverbial cat," Lavington wrote. "[Or else] he would never make it to the allotted three score and ten—or even to maturity."

Lavington provided a classic example of pioneering cowboy literature in his autobiography *The Nine Lives of a Cowboy* (1982), followed by a collection of mostly true ranching tales, *Born to be Hung* (1983), which went through nine printings.

Like a cowboy keeping track of heifers, Lavington, in February of 1991, could report precise sales for *The Nine Lives* (11,857) and *Born to be Hung* (8,198).

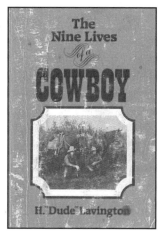

After his first wife, Ruth, a former schoolteacher, had died giving birth to his only child, a daughter, Lavington remarried in 1953 to Margaret Paul of Vancouver, who answered his newspaper personal ad for a wife.

H. "Dude" Lavington died in Salmon Arm in 1993 at age 85. Five years later he was inducted into the B.C. Cowboy Hall of Fame in Williams Lake in its inaugural year.

The battered front cover of
The Nine Lives of a Cowboy

DAVID RICARDO WILLIAMS

Trapline Outlaw: Simon Peter Gunanoot (1982)
by David Ricardo Williams

Robertson Davies said the fundamental difference between the U.S. and Canada is that the United States broke away from Britain, whereas Canada was the dutiful daughter. Consequently, Canadians are law-abiding, more orderly. The Mounties always get their man. This paradigm explains why Americans tend to revere their outlaws and gangsters, whereas Canadians, in general, do not.

In a province that reveres the so-called hanging judge, Judge Matthew Begbie, the classic B.C. outlaw book is David Ricardo Williams' *Trapline Outlaw: Simon Peter Gunanoot* (1982), an investigation of the capture of the fair-dealing and respected Gitksan outlaw who was accused of two separate murders, near Hazelton in 1906, after he was reputedly offended by one man's disparaging remark in reference to his wife and/or the morality of Gitksan women in general.

Rather than face a trial by a white jury, Gunanoot and his brother-in-law fled into the bush, where they eluded capture for thirteen years. Eventually, through an intermediary named George Beirnes, Gunanoot surrendered to the authorities, having acquired the services of a Vancouver lawyer named Stuart Henderson. Williams describes Henderson as "perhaps the most effective criminal lawyer British Columbia has known." After Gunanoot was acquitted in 1920, his brother-in-law Peter Hi-madan surrendered and was also acquitted. The missionary Thomas P. Kelley wrote a book about Gunanoot, *Run Indian Run*, which built up Gunanoot's folk hero status. Then along came Williams, an experienced biographer and lawyer, who debunked Gunanoot's Robin Hood–like reputation.

Williams' sobering indictment of Gunanoot (alternately spelled Gun-a-noot) was based on his interviews with Gunanoot's children and information not raised at the botched Vancouver trial during which the prosecution failed to provide evidence or witnesses. According to Williams' investigation, Gunanoot privately confessed to killing both Alec McIntosh and Max LeClair to his wife, to his father and to another man named Tom Lula. Gunanoot's co-defendant Peter Hi-madan implicated him and Gunanoot also told two of his sons he had committed the murders.

If labour activist Ginger Goodwin of Cumberland can be classified an outlaw, Susan Mayse's biography *Ginger: The Life and Death of Albert Goodwin* (1990) can be considered as a classic alongside *Trapline Outlaw*. Arriving on Vancouver Island in 1910, the socialist Albert "Ginger" Goodwin was a slight, red-haired man who was forced to take refuge in the wilderness around Comox Lake as a

Simon Peter Gunanoot

subversive. He had run unsuccessfully for parliament in 1916 and demanded an eight-hour day for miners in Trail. In 1917, he brought 1600 Consolidated miners to strike action, upsetting Canadian arms manufacturing. The shooting of the coal miner unionist in 1918 by Pinkerton constable Dan Campbell, at the behest of Canada's Dominion Police, sparked a 24-hour protest strike and labour unrest across Canada. Goodwin was a tubercular coal miner whose only crime was a belief in democracy.

Two other important books about B.C. outlaws are Peter Grauer's *Interred with Their Bones: Bill Miner in Canada, 1903–1907* (2006), a 600-pager that exhaustively recalls the four years spent in British Columbia by the chronically inept "gentleman bandit" Bill Miner, and George Bowering's novel *Shoot!* (1994), about the McLean gang from the Okanagan.

JEANNETTE ARMSTRONG

The most integral, contemporary figure in the growing constellation of aboriginal authors of British Columbia is Jeannette Armstrong. She grew up hearing stories about her mother's great aunt, the novelist Mourning Dove, who lived briefly in Oliver, B.C., and who also taught Armstrong's mother in school. Mourning Dove, who died in 1936, twelve years before Armstrong was born on the Penticton Indian Reservation in 1948, wrote *Cogewea, the Half-Blood* (1927), possibly the first novel to be written by an American aboriginal woman.

Armstrong was also influenced by the cadence of Pauline Johnson's poetry, the mentoring of Okanagan storyteller Harry Robinson and the proximity of Summerland-based playwright and novelist George Ryga who provided an introduction to Armstrong's first novel *Slash* (1985).

Reprinted more than ten times and adopted for use in schools, *Slash* recalls First Nations alienation and militancy during the period from 1960 to 1983. Despite ridicule from some friends, the protagonist Thomas Kelasket, nicknamed Slash due to a criminal incident, enjoys speaking the Okanagan language and attending powwows. Eventually he is forced to confront racism in a white-operated school. Sometimes angry and confused, he travels widely in North America to come to terms with himself and the world.

Slash was promoted in the Theytus Books catalogue as the first adult novel by a Canadian aboriginal woman. Lee Maracle's earlier *Bobbi Lee, Indian Rebel* (1975), as a synthesis of autobiography and fiction, gives some grounds for disputing that claim.

In 1989, in conjunction with Theytus Books and the En'owkin Centre in Penticton, Armstrong oversaw the creation of the En'owkin International School of Writing for Native Students in

Jeannette Armstrong (above) is related to the aboriginal novelist Mourning Dove.

conjunction with the University of Victoria's Bachelor of Fine Arts program and Okanagan College. It is now a focal point for aboriginal writing throughout North America. Started by Randy Fred in Nanaimo, Theytus Books is a publishing company named from a Salish word meaning "preserving for the sake of handing down." After Theytus Books became one of the first two aboriginal-owned publishing houses in Canada in 1980, it moved its headquarters to Penticton in the mid-1980s. Pemmican Books in Winnipeg was also started, by the Manitoba Métis Federation, in 1980.

Armstrong's best-known non-fiction book is *Native Creative Process* (1991), in collaboration with aboriginal architect Douglas Cardinal. She has edited, contributed to, and written numerous other works, including poetry.

Fluent in the Okanagan language, Armstrong has participated in international conferences around the world, received the Mungo Martin Memorial Award in 1974, the Helen Pitt Award in 1978, an Honorary Doctorate of Letters from St. Thomas University in New

Brunswick in 2000 and the 2003 EcoTrust Buffet Award for Indigenous Leadership. She was appointed one of seven Indigenous judges to the First Nations Court of Justice called by the Chiefs of Ontario. She received an Honorary Doctorate of Laws from UBC Okanagan in 2006.

For other First Nations authors of British Columbia, see abcbookworld entries for Adams, Howard; Alfred, Agnes; Alfred, Gerald Taiaiake; Antoine, Irene; Archibald, Jo-Ann; Arima, Joshua; Arnott, Joanne; Assu, Frank; Assu, Harry; Atleo, E. Richard; Augaitis, Daina; Baker, Marie Annharte; Baker, Simon; Barbetti, Louise; Bates, Morris; Batiste, Francis; Battiste, Marie; Beynon, William; Bird, Catherine; Blackstock, Michael (Ama Goodim Gyet); Borrows, John; Bose, Chris; Boyd, Laura Marie; Brooks, Cheryl; Brown, J.N.J.; Bruce, Skyros; Caffey, John; Calihoo, Robert; Capilano, Chief Joe; Charleyboy, Orrey; Charlie, Domanic; Chelsea, Phyllis; Chrisjohn, Roland; Clamhouse, Louis; Clements, Marie; Clutesi, George; Cohen, Bill; Collins, Theo; Collison, Nika; Cook, Margaret; Courtoreille, Fred; Craigan, Charlie; Cranmer, Agnes; Crey, Ernie; Cuthand, Beth; Davidson, Florence; Davidson, Robert; Dixon, Stan; Dove, Mourning; Dumont, Marilyn; Einarson, Earl; Eustache, Harold; Felix, Dolly; Fife, Connie; Framst, Louise Susy; Gawa, Edith; George, Charlie; George, Chief Dan; George, Leonard; Ghandl, (Walter McGregor); Gottfriedson, Garry; Guerin, Arnold; Hager, Barbara; Hale, Janet Campbell; Hall, Lizette; Hamilton, Ron; Hanna, Darwin; Harris, Heather; Harris, Kenneth B. (Hagbegwatku); Harris, Martha Douglas; Harry, Celina; Hart, Jim; Henry, Mamie; Highway, Tomson; Hill, Gord; Hungry Wolf, Beverly; Hunt, George; Ignace, Ron; Ironstand, Raphael; Jack, Agnes; Jacobson, Diane; Jensen, Doreen; John, Gracie; John, Mary; John, Peter (Adahdah); Johnson, Emily Pauline; Johnson, Mary; Jones, Charles; Joseph, Gene; Jungen, Brian; Jules, C.T. Manny; Kew, Della; Khahtsahlano, August Jack; Kirkness, Verna; Koon, Danny; LaRue, Frank; Lawrence, Mary; Lecoy, Denise; Longman, Mary; Loring, Kevin; Louis, Shirley; Loyie, Larry; Mack, Charlie; Mack, Clayton; MacLeod, Heather Simeney; Malloway, Richard; Manuel, George; Manuel, Vera; Maquinna George, Earl; Maracle, Lee; Marchand, Len; Marsden, Solomon; McIvor, Dorothy Matheson; Michell, Teresa; Morin, Peter; Morisset, Jean; Mowatt, Ken; Nahanee, Gloria; Napoleon, Art; Neel, David; Nowell, Charles James; O'Connor, Joseph; Odjig, Daphne; Patrick, Betty; Patrick, Dorothy; Paul, Frances Lackey; Paul, Philip Kevin; Pennier, Henry; Pielle, Sue; Pierce, William H.; Prince, Louis-Billy; Reid, Bill; Reid-Stevens, Amanda; Robertson, Gordon; Robinson, Eden; Robinson, Gordon; Robinson, Harry; Rogers, Janet; Rosetti, Bernadette; Sam, Lillian; Sam Sr., Stanley; Scofield, Gregory; Scow, Alfred; Seaweed, Willie; Seletze, D. Johnnie; Sepass, Chief William (K'HHalserten); Sewid, James (Poogleedee); Sewid-Smith, Daisy (My-yah-nelth); Silvey, Diane; SKAAY, (a.k.a. John Sky); Smith, Howard; Smith, M. Jane; Speck, Chief Henry (Ozistalis); Stanley, Robert E.; Sterling, Shirley; Stevens, Russell; Stump, Sarain; Stump, Violet; Swan, Luke Francis; Tappage, Mary Augusta; Tate, Henry; Taylor, Drew Hayden; Tetso, John; Van Camp, Richard; Vickers, Roy Henry; Wagamese, Richard; Walkem, Ardith; Walkus Sr., Simon; Wallas, James; Watts, Annie; Webster, Gloria Cranmer; Webster, Peter; Wheeler, Jordan; William, Gerry; Williams, Lorna; Wilson, Ardythe (Skanu'u); Wilson, Beatrice; Wilson, Solomon; Windsor, Evelyn Walkus; Wolf, Annabel Cropped Eared; Wolters, Brent Leonard; Wright, Marion; Wright, Walter; Yahgulanaas, Michael Nicoll; Yellowhorn, Eldon; York, Annie; Young-Ing, Greg.

DAVID MITCHELL

W.A.C. Bennett and the Rise of British Columbia (1983)
by David Mitchell

O nce featured on the cover of *Time* magazine, W.A.C. "Wacky" Bennett cast an overbearing shadow on British Columbia for 20 years during an era of robust expansion. Like his notorious Highways Minister Phil Gaglardi, who famously remarked that "pollution is the smell of money," Bennett was a talker, not a literary man—although the Simon Fraser University Library bears Bennett's name. His only credited publication was *A Personal Report from the Premier: 20 Years of Achievement—and Now, the Kelowna Charter* (1972). Regardless of whether New Brunswick–born Bennett is venerated or despised, his stature as the province's most influential politician will likely never be erased.

W.A.C. Bennett

The most useful synopsis of the life and times of the province's longest-in-power premier is David Mitchell's *W.A.C. Bennett and the Rise of British Columbia* (1983). It arose from 30 hours of interviews with Bennett, as well as many hours spent interviewing members of the Bennett family. "The distance between biographer and subject is exceedingly small," wrote John English in *BC Studies*, "and the tone is excessively chatty and sententious. By the end of the book, the reader knows that the subject has captured the biographer, and the mediation which the skilled biographer offers both to subject and reader thoroughly breaks down." But the Mitchell biography remains the best reference volume available on its subject.

Two sycophantic books on Bennett are Paddy Sherman's *Bennett* (1966) and Ronald Worley's *The Wonderful World of W.A.C. Bennett* (1971). In contrast, Martin Robin's *Pillars of Profit: The Company Province 1934–1972* (1973) describes early Socreds under Bennett as a "drab collection of monetary fetishists, British Israelites, naturopaths, chiropractors, preachers, pleaders and anti-semites."

WILLIAM GIBSON

Neuromancer (1984) by William Gibson

With the publication of his first novel *Neuromancer* (1984), William Gibson achieved unprecedented success by winning the Hugo and Nebula Awards for best science fiction and fantasy novel, plus the Philip K. Dick Award for best original science fiction paperback. Two years after the movie *Blade Runner* (1982), the emergence of Gibson's realm of "cyberspace" coincided with the cultural deluge of the internet. Computer geeks and hackers could be heroes, or at least dramatic characters. Gibson became the newly crowned godfather of cyberpunk, a movement that has given rise to a spate of futuristic films, some cheesy, some brilliant. Gibson's world-ranging fiction is an interplay between dread and ecstasy, with riffs about technology as if it is a new drug.

William Ford Gibson, the "King of Dystopia," was born in Conway, South Carolina, in 1948. His father, who worked on the Manhattan Project in Oak Ridge, Tennessee, where the first atomic bombs were made, died accidentally on a business trip. After that, he grew up in the small mountain town of Wytheville in southwest Virginia, which he disliked, until he was 15. When the family TV set finally was able to receive programs, he became greatly enamoured of a show called *Tom Corbett, Space Cadet*, and sent away to receive a ray gun and space helmet. At age 13, he decided he should become a science fiction writer. He attended boarding school in Arizona and developed an interest in the science fiction of Ray Bradbury. Gibson's other early literary influences included Bruce Springsteen, William Burroughs and Thomas Pynchon. He once told *Rolling Stone* magazine, "I want to eroticize computers the way Bruce Springsteen eroticized cars."

William Gibson

At age 18, in response to what he calls the "Kafka-esque" possibility of being drafted, he came to live in Toronto's Yorkville district where he met Deborah Thompson. They travelled in Europe, married, and came to Vancouver in 1972 to be near her parents. Gibson's first published story, "Fragments of a Hologram Rose," appeared in Boston's *UnEarth* magazine in 1977. It was written as a course assignment at UBC, and he earned $23 for it.

He graduated from UBC and began writing science fiction in 1980. In 1981, *Omni* magazine bought the first story he sent them, "Johnny Mnemonic," for $2,000, and asked for another, whereupon Gibson was encouraged to complete a novel. In 1986, Gibson sold the screen rights for *Neuromancer* and published his second novel in his Sprawl trilogy, *Count Zero* (1986), containing some of *Neuromancer*'s characters. Mona Lisa Overdrive (1988) completed the trilogy. Gibson has been hired to write screenplays, including a draft for *Aliens 3*. One of his short stories became the basis for the 1995 movie *Johnny Mnemonic* starring Keanu Reeves; another was the basis for the 1999 movie *New Rose Hotel* starring Christopher Walken, Willem Dafoe and Asia Argento. The stork-like, bespectacled Gibson made a cameo appearance in the mini-series *Wild Palms* and was interviewed by *Playboy*. His writing reportedly inspired U2's song "Zooropa," and the rock band's Zoo TV tour.

THOM HENLEY

*Islands at the Edge: Preserving the Queen Charlotte
Islands Wilderness* (1984) edited by Thom Henley

The first European who wrote about the southern Queen Charlotte Islands and their people in detail was James Colnett in the late 1700s. The American lawyer Newton Chittenden was the first white man to explore the interior of those islands, as described in *Settlers, Prospectors and Tourists Guide or Travels Through British Columbia* (1882). Irish-born William Henry Collison was reputedly the first missionary to preach to the Haida, Nisga'a and Tsimshian in their own languages, as described in his often condescending memoir *In the Wake of the War Canoe* (1915). Kathleen Dalzell self-published *The Queen Charlotte Islands, Volume 1: 1774–1966* (1968) and *The Queen Charlotte Islands, Volume 2* (1973), both popular for decades. After an article in the *New Yorker*, John Vaillant skillfully wove together Haida Gwaii–related material for a prize-winning bestseller, *The Golden Spruce* (2005).

The turning point for recognition of Haida Gwaii as a separate culture—the book that, more than any other, made it acceptable and even preferable to refer to the place as Haida Gwaii—was *Islands at the Edge: Preserving the Queen Charlotte Islands Wilderness* (1984), a co-operative project largely engineered and written by Thom Henley. Later renamed *Islands at the Edge: Preserving the Queen Charlotte Archipelago*, this political milestone was accorded the first Bill Duthie Booksellers' Choice Award in 1985. At the gala event on Granville Island, Henley asked artist Bill Reid to give an acceptance speech. Reid's riveting denunciation of modern B.C. society was not only the highlight of an evening that marked the coming-of-age of B.C. writing and publishing with the creation of

Bill Reid calling white civilization "the worst plague of locusts" in 1985

the B.C. Book Prizes, it signalled to the mainland that Haida culture would henceforth aggressively seek self-definition. Quivering with Parkinson's disease, Reid reminded the audience of the ravages of white civilization, calling it "the worst plague of locusts." *Islands at the Edge* was a powerful ambassadorial force in the successful preservation of South Moresby Island as a park. Its success begat a string of well-researched coffee table books to protect the environment, notably *Stein: The Way of the River* (1988) by Michael M'Gonigle and Wendy Wickwire, and *Carmanah: Artistic Visions of an Ancient Rainforest* (1989), spearheaded by Paul George, who had produced a similar book about Meares Island in 1985.

For other authors pertaining to Haida Gwaii / Queen Charlotte Islands, see abcbookworld entries for Adams, Dawn; Bancroft, J. Austen; Barbeau, Marius; Blackman, Margaret; Bodega y Quadra, Juan Francisco; Boelscher, Marianne; Bolton, Herbert E.; Bowditch, Dan; Burling, Samuel; Caamaño, Jacinto; Calder, J.A.; Cameron, June; Carey, Neil; Carter, Anthony; Crespi, Juan; Curtis, Edward S.; Davidson, Robert; Dawson, George M.; Deans, James; Dixon, George; Douglas, Sheila; Drew, Leslie; Duff, Wilson; Dunn, John; Ellis, David W.; Enrico, John; Ernst, Maria; Fedje, Daryl; Fischer, George; Fleurieu, Charles; Foster, J.B.; Garner, Joe; Gazetas, Mary; Gessler, Trisha; Gill, Ian; Gray, Robert; Hale, Amanda; Harrison, Charles; Hart, Jim; Haswell, Robert; Hatt, D.E.; Hearne, Margo; Henderson, Fern; Henderson, R.W.; Hoover, Allan; Horwood, Dennis; Houston, James; Ingraham, Joseph; Johnson, Ebenezer; Karstad, Aleta; Lasser, Peggy; Lillard, Charles; Long, Bob; MacDonald, George F.; MacDonald, Joanne;

Macnair, Peter; Marchand, Etienne; Mayol, Lurline Bowles; Musgrave, Susan; Newton, Norman; Oliviero, Jamie; Osgood, Wilfred; Patterson, Samuel; Pena, Tomas de la; Peron, Francois; Perouse, Jean-Francois de la; Poole, Francis; Razzell, Mary; Reid, Martine; Reynolds, Stephen; Ricketts, Ed; Ross, Michael Lee; Scudder, G.G.E.; Sheehan, Carol; Simpson, S.L.; Siska, Heather; Smith, Robin Percival; Smyly, John; Spilsbury, Jim; Steltzer, Ulli; Stuart, Wendy Bross; Swan, James G.; Swanton, John; Taylor, Andrew Bracey; Taylor, Roy; Turner, Nancy; Turner, William O.; Van den Brink, J.H.; Ward, David; Westergaard, Ross; White, April; Wright, Robin K.; Wyatt, Victoria; Yates, J. Michael.

ALFRED G. DAVY

The Gilly: A Flyfisher's Guide to British Columbia (1985)
edited by Alfred G. Davy

Gilly is a term to describe a guide who accompanies and helps an angler to fish. As a high school teacher in Kelowna, Alf Davy edited and co-authored *The Gilly: A Flyfisher's Guide to British Columbia* (1985) to describe advanced techniques for fly tying, rod building and fly casting. With line drawings by Steve Carter and more than 75 colour photos of B.C. flies by Jim Crawford, *The Gilly*, with twelve contributors, became one of the bestselling fishing books from B.C., selling more than 50,000 copies before it went out-of-print in 2006. The popularity of *The Gilly* enabled Sandhill Book Marketing, the province's main outlet for marketing independent titles, to gain access to sales in Smithbooks across the country. Proceeds were allocated to the B.C. Federation of Flyfishers, generating more than $150,000 of accumulated interest for conservation projects. With its eleven printings, *The Gilly* is an example of why every great book need not be in a league with Alice Munro's short stories. There is a lifetime of learning and sophistication packed into *The Gilly*, but it will never be cited as a great book unless you love to fish.

There is no shortage of B.C. books on fishing, only a shortage of fish. Experts in print have included Gordon Davies, Robert H.

Jones, Art Lingren, Jack Shaw, *Province* outdoors editor Mike Cramond, entrepreneur Charlie White, conservationist Roderick Haig-Brown, Tyee Club historian Van Gorman Egan, union leader Homer Stevens, *New Yorker* contributor Edith Iglauer, League of Canadian Poets president D.C. Reid and academic analyst Diane Newell.

For other authors pertaining to fishing in British Columbia, see abcbookworld entries for Alexander, George J.; Arnold, David F.; Bell-Irving, Rob; Bennett, Marilyn; Blyth, Gladys Young; Bowling, Tim; Boyanowsky, Ehor; Brandt, Charles A.E.; Brown, Dennis; Bruhn, Karl; Burrows, Bruce; Campbell, K. Mack; Carrothers, W.A.; Childerhose, R.J.; Cohen, Fay C.; Coward, Harold; Denham, Joe; Drake, Allene; Downs, Art; Farson, Negley; Fennelly, John F.; Foerster, R.E.; Forester, Anne D.; Forester, Joseph E.; Gauvin, Brian; Glennie, Rory E.; Grain, John; Grundle, Jack; Gudgeon, Chris; Hagelund, William A.; Haig-Brown, Alan; Haig-Brown, Roderick; Harris, Douglas C.; Heighton, Hugh; Hill, A.V.; Hohizaki, Bill; Hume, Mark; Jennings, Neil L.; Jensen, Vickie; Keller, Betty; Kilburn, Jim; Knight, Rolf; Landale, Zoe; Langer, Otto; Legault, Stephen; Lewis, Adam; Lichatowich, Jim; Long, Bob; Lorenz, Claudia; Lyon, Robert; Lyons, Cicely; Macdonald, W.A.; Mair, Rafe; Marchak, Patricia; Maximchuk, Yvonne Caroline; Maxwell, Michael; McDaniel, Neil; McKay, Will; McKervill, Hugh; McPhail, J.D.; Meggs, Geoff; Merriman, Alec; Muszynski, Alicja; Norris, Pat Wastell; North, George; Nuttall, David; Ommer, Rosemary E.; Passek, Rick; Pearse, Peter; Peppar, Albert H.; Pierce, William H.; Pitcher, Tony; Pollard, Doug; Read, Stanley E.; Robson, Peter; Roche, Judith; Roos, John F.; Rose, Alex; Sharcott, Margaret; Shaw, Ralph; Shibata, Yuko; Skogan, Joan; Smith, Brian; Stacey, Duncan; Stefanyk, Larry E.; Stewart, Dave; Sullivan, Heidi H.; Thornton, Barry M.; Upton, Joe; Wickham, Eric; Will, George Stuart; Wooding, Frederick.

For many readers in B.C., Alfred G. Davy is a more important author than Alice Munro.

PETER MURRAY

The Devil and Mr. Duncan: A History of the Two Metlakatlas (1985)
by Peter Murray

The most extraordinary and controversial missionary of British Columbia—and that's saying a lot—was William Duncan, whose story is told in Peter Murray's *The Devil and Mr. Duncan: A History of the Two Metlakatlas* (1985). A bastard son who escaped poverty by becoming a travelling leather salesman, Duncan was born in Yorkshire in 1832 and apprenticed with the Church Missionary Society in London. Having gained schoolmaster training from 1854 to 1856, Duncan was chosen by the Missionary Society to work among the Tsimshian on the northern B.C. coast to learn their language and hear their "heathen cry." Duncan never sought to be ordained; he would later refuse ordination repeatedly to maintain his independence.

Duncan quickly learned enough Tsimshian at Fort Simpson to teach the singing of hymns and "God Save the Queen." All nine Tsimshian tribes had converged around the Hudson's Bay Company fort, making them convenient targets for the American liquor traders. Liquor purchases were often financed by prostitution. After four years, knowing the fort environment was detrimental to his converts, Duncan was intrigued to learn some of his followers wished to return to their former village of Metlakatla (also spelled Metlakahtla and meaning "water passage") 25 kilometres down the coast. Moses-like, Duncan led 60 followers in 1862 to the site where ten Tsimshian were still living. With authoritarian diligence, he founded a strict Christian village called Metlakatla where Victorian values were rigidly superimposed. Within a year, the population rose to nearly a thousand. Whereas some five hundred small-

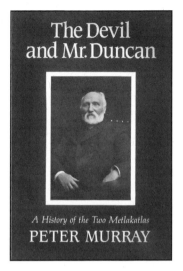

The Devil and Mr. Duncan

A History of the Two Metlakatlas

PETER MURRAY

pox deaths were reported at Fort Simpson, only five smallpox deaths were reported at Metlakatla where Duncan had quickly vaccinated his followers. Forsaking face-painting and the potlatch, Duncan's followers built houses, observed the Sabbath, paid taxes, established a sawmill, a newspaper and a salmon cannery. There was a uniformed Tsimshian police force, a brass band and a church choir. No other white man was allowed to camp within four miles of the town. Punishments were meted out by Duncan. His word was law. In 1867, Duncan hired architect Edward Mallandaine, Sr. to draw plans for a church, but he returned the drawings and refused to pay him. A year later, William Duncan presided over an 800-seat Gothic cathedral, the largest church north of San Francisco and west of Chicago.

Duncan made trips back to England to learn various trades and to publicize his increasingly famous mission: Africa had David Livingston; the wilds of British Columbia had William Duncan. But problems with Victoria and schisms with church authorities arose as a result of his dictatorial approach. Duncan maintained that his Metlakatlans ought to be able to live outside the Indian Act and that he should control property ownership. In 1887, the mercurial Duncan took 823 members of his flock northward to establish New Metlakatla on a site provided by the United States government on Annette Island in Alaska. Increasingly intransigent, Duncan encountered more problems with American authorities. He limited education to age 14, and there were allegations of financial mismanagement and sexual misconduct. The United States government seized the New Metlakatla property in 1915. Duncan remained there until he died three years later with almost $300,000 to his name, about half of which was in a Seattle bank account.

RICK HANSEN

Rick Hansen: Man in Motion (1987)
by Rick Hansen with Jim Taylor

Touted as the largest first printing for any B.C. book, Rick Hansen's *Man in Motion* (1987), co-written with sportswriter Jim Taylor, reportedly had an initial print run of 65,000 copies. It was featured on the cover of the inaugural issue of *B.C. BookWorld* in 1987.

Born in Port Alberni in 1957, Rick Hansen lost the use of both his legs in a Williams Lake traffic accident when he was 15 and was paralyzed thereafter due to spinal cord injuries. He became a wheelchair athlete, winning 19 marathons, three world championships as well as competing in an exhibition event at the 1984 Olympics. Having commenced his Man in Motion World Tour in 1985, pushing his wheelchair more than 40,000 kilometres through 34 countries to raise $26 million for spinal cord research, rehabilitation and sport, Hansen rolled back into Vancouver as B.C.'s most popular citizen on May 22, 1987, buoyed by a theme song provided by Victoria composer and arranger David Foster. The story behind the story of the book was that Jim Taylor's daughter Teresa had become a quadriplegic in 1976 at age 14, as the result of a skiing accident. Hansen and Taylor verbally agreed to do the book together on the night before Hansen's world tour began.

Prior to re-entering Canada, after his tour of 33 countries, Hansen had raised only $174,000. Newfoundlanders made the difference, having missed out on the cross-country fundraising marathons of Terry Fox and Steve Fonyo. The enthusiasm for Hansen in Newfoundland kindled a "St. Elmo's fire" of appreciation that swept across Canada in 1987. *Rick Hansen: Man in Motion* became one of the most successful sports titles ever published in B.C. Hansen soon married his physiotherapist Amanda Reid, daughter of Expo '86 organizer Patrick Reid. The marriage did not go the distance but Hansen's self-promotional zeal was unabated. He co-authored a motivational book with psychologist Joan Laub.

For other B.C. books pertaining to sports, see abcbookworld entries for Ackles, Bob; Adachi, Pat; Anstey, Robert; Arnason, Kathleen; Banks, Kerry; Bascomb, Neal; Beardsley, Doug; Bjarnason, Paul; Bowering, George; Bowlsby, Craig; Brill, Debbie; Brodsgaard, Shel; Caron, Marnie; Carroll, M.R.; Carver, John Arthur; Childerhose, R.J.; Clerk, Blair M.; Cowley, Glen; Cruise, David; Dawe, Alan; Diersch, Sandra; Edge, Marc; Farris, Jason; Fox, Terry; Fraser, Fil; Galloway, Steven; Gaston, Bill; Getty, Ian; Gregson, Ian; Greig, Murray; Harrison, Pat; Harrison, Patricia; Johnston, Mike; Johnston, Tom; Kew, Trevor; Khan, Karim; Laumann, Silken; Mackin, Bob; McCredie, Andrew; McKinley, Michael; Meraw, Ann Mundigel; Miller, Saul; Mooney, Maggie; Morrison, Janet Love; Nash, Steve; Nicol, Eric; Norton, Wayne; Petersen, Carl W.; Reid, D.C.; Ross, Jesse; Ross, Julian; Rossiter, Sean; Sauerwein, Stan; Savelieff, David S.; Scott, Chic; Shaw, Chris A.; Sheepshanks, John; Smith, Pat; Square, David; Stewart, Barbara; Stott, Jon; Sturrock, Doug; Triano, Jay; Twigg, Alan; Urefe, Frank A.; Waiters, Tony; Walter, Ryan; White, Silas; Whitfield, Simon; Wilberg, Karl; Williams, Tiger; Yzerman, Steve.

JIM SPILSBURY & HOWARD WHITE

Spilsbury's Coast: Pioneer Years in the Wet West (1987)
by Jim Spilsbury & Howard White

Raised in a tent, the Savary Island–based renaissance man, inventor, entrepreneur and quintessential West Coaster Jim Spilsbury co-wrote one of the classics of B.C. literature, *Spilsbury's Coast: Pioneer Years in the Wet West* (1987) with Howard White, cementing his reputation as perhaps the most ingenious character in coastal history. He excelled in communications, transportation and art.

Jim Spilsbury was born in Derbyshire, England, in 1905, and was brought to the B.C. coast in his infancy. His mother was a trouser-wearing suffragette and his father was Cambridge-educated.

Fascinated by the wireless as a boy, Spilsbury invented radio gear out of mail-order catalogue items that he received on Savary Island, a summer haven for well-to-do families from Vancouver. As a poor, year-round resident, Spilsbury fell in love with a rich girl and vowed to make himself worthy by earning his own fortune. He never got the girl, but he got rich.

Starting as a salesman for his own radios in coastal logging camps, Spilsbury became Canada's largest exporter of radio-telephone equipment, first manufacturing small radios in the 1920s. In 1941,

Howard White

he founded Spilsbury and Hepburn Ltd., which was later renamed Spilsbury and Tindall Ltd., and his products were used worldwide. One of his radio-telephones accompanied a Japanese climber who made a solo ascent of Mt. Everest.

One successful business wasn't enough. Realizing that he could better serve his customers with a seaplane, Spilsbury co-founded Queen Charlotte Airlines (QCA) in the 1940s, and it became a lifeline for the "loggers, fishermen, stump ranchers, hermits, remittance men, Greek scholars, ex-prostitutes and outright lunatics" who had bought his radios. Spilsbury's planes were known as "whistling shithouses" at the outset, because of their extremely rudimentary toilet facilities, but by the time QCA merged with Pacific Western Airlines in 1955, Spilsbury had become co-owner of Canada's third largest airline. Ironically, as outlined in Spilsbury's second co-authored bestseller, *The Accidental Airline* (1988), a fatal air crash early in the history of QCA actually helped the fledgling outfit by providing much-needed national publicity. Many years later, when he became the subject of a documentary film screened nationally on CBC as *Spilsbury's Coast*, the feisty octogenarian was not averse to chuckling about this fact.

Upon retirement from business, Spilsbury developed his third vocation as a raconteur and painter of coastal scenes. At 81, he had his first art exhibit. He also published a collection of his coastal photographs called *Spilsbury's Album* (1990). His enormous archive of self-developed, meticulously catalogued black-and-white photographs is housed at UBC Special Collections. Jim Spilsbury died in 2003. The Canadian Museum of Civilization in Gatineau later erected an exhibit with a Spilsbury radio telephone to represent West Coast culture.

The first two coastal history books about the life and times of Jim Spilsbury were co-authored by his publisher, Howard White, winner of the Leacock Medal for Humour for his non-fiction collection *Writing in the Rain* (1990). For more information on B.C. publishers as authors, and B.C. publishing, see abcbookworld entries for Aligizakis, Manolis; Anastasiou, Kip; Anstey, Robert; Antonson, Rick; Barlee, N.L.; Basque, Garnet; Bendall, Raymond; bissett, bill; Brett, Brian; Bringhurst, Robert; Brown, Earl; Brown, Jim; Budd, Ken; Campbell, Betty; Campbell, Gray; Castle, Stephanie; Chaplin, Robert M.; Coney, Michael Greatrex; Douglas, Diana; Downs, Art; Elsted, Crispin; Fred, Randy; Fredeman, Jane; Garden, John; George, Paul; Goldsmith, Penny; Grundle, Jack; Gursche, Siegfried; Hancock, David; Hanebury, Derek; Hatch, Ronald; Heal, S.C.; Hoffer, William; James, Jack; Katz, Michael; Kaufman, Brian; Kirk, H.; Lester, David; Lorimer, Rowland; Lugrin, Nora de Bertrand; Mallandaine, Edward; Marks, Vic; Matheson, George; Mayne, Seymour; McConnell, William; McDonald, Herbert; Milton, Ralph; Mitchell, Howard; Olafson, Richard; Opre, Kal; Osborne, Stephen; Pass, John; Persky, Stan; Plant, Judith; Reid, Robert; Rimmer, Jim; Ross, Julian; Safarik, Allan; Schwartzentruber, Michael; Siegler, Karl; Smith, Cherie; Smith, Ron; Soules, Gordon; Sturmanis, Dona; Such, Peter; Taylor, Andrea; Thomson, Robert S.; Touchie, Rodger (and Pat); Tyrrell, Bob; Varney, Edwin; Wakan, Naomi; Walker, Michael; Werschler, Terri; West, Ann; White, Silas; Wilmott, Norah Mannion; Wilson, Cynthia; Windsor, John; Yandle, Anne; Yates, J. Michael; Zebroff, Kareen; Zonailo, Carolyn.

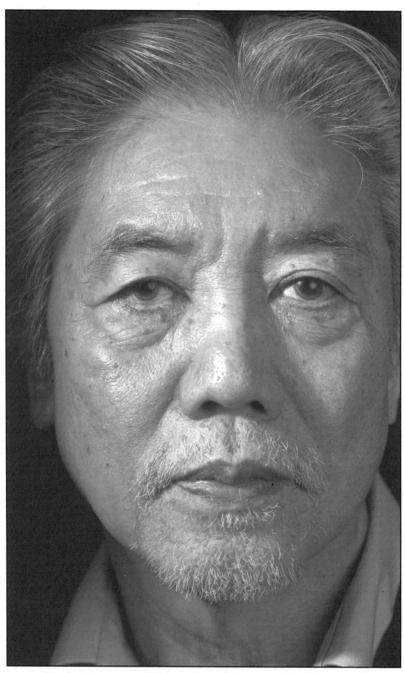

John Beebe's portrait of Wayson Choy, author of The Jade Peony *(1995)*

VIII
1990s

R. WAYNE CAMPBELL

The Birds of British Columbia (1990–2001)
by R. Wayne Campbell et al

Since the arrival of botanists José Mariano Moziño and Archibald Menzies, and the ground-breaking treks of naturalist David Douglas, there have been hundreds of "outdoors" titles from and about B.C. but few qualify as classic works of natural history. Of these, the co-authored, four-volume compilation known as *The Birds of British Columbia* is perhaps the most impressive, but one could also cite recent titles by the Cannings twins, Richard and Robert, as well as Andy Lamb and Phil Edgell's *Coastal Fishes of the Pacific Northwest* (1986), and Andy Lamb and Bernard Hanby's *Marine Life of the Pacific Northwest: A Photographic Encyclopedia of Invertebrates, Seaweeds and Selected Fishes* (2005).

The Birds of British Columbia is a 25-year project (with publications ranging from 1990 to 2001) led by R. Wayne Campbell, one of its seven co-authors. The others are Neil K. Dawe, Ian McTaggart-Cowan, John M. Cooper, Gary W. Kaiser, Andrew C. Stewart and  Michael C.E. McNall. The four volumes in *The Birds of British Columbia* provide a wealth of information on the "ornithological history, environments, habitat, breeding habits, migratory movements, seasonality and distribution patterns" of 472 species of birds. A longtime curator of ornithology at the Royal B.C. Museum, Campbell also co-wrote *The Reptiles of British Columbia* (1984), a series of bird books for Lone Pine Publishing and co-compiled *A Bibliography of British Columbia Ornithology, Vol-*

R. Wayne Campbell

ume 1 (1979). Campbell's scientific forefather was the eminent UBC zoologist Ian McTaggart-Cowan who taught from 1945 to 1975, serving as head of the zoology faculty from 1953 to 1964, and who served as a model for David Suzuki, hosting two widely seen programs on national television in the 1960s, *The Living Sea* and *The Web of Life.* McTaggart-Cowan died in 2010 at age 99.

For other authors pertaining to natural history in British Columbia, see abcbookworld entries for Bandoni, R.J.; Blood, Donald A.; Bodsworth, Fred; Brayshaw, T. Christopher; Brown, Robert; Burbridge, Joan; Busch, Robert H.; Campbell, Susan; Carefoot, Thomas; Carrick, Doug; Corkran, Charlott; Croft, Philip; Davidson, John; De Maddalena, Alessandro; Delehanty Pearkes, Eileen; Douglas, George; Forsythe, Robert; Green, David M.; Greenfield, Tony; Gregory, Patrick T.; Guiguet, C.J.; Harcombe, Andrew; Hardy, G.A.; Hearne, Margo; Hitchcock, C. Leo; Horwood, Dennis; Hoyt, Erich; Hume, Mark; Hunter, Tom; Hutchings, Kevin; Jones, David; Kaiser, Peter; Klinka, A.; Kosloff, Eugene N.; Kozloff, Eugene; Lambert, Philip; Lansdowne, Fenwick; Lord, John Keast Ludvigsen, Rolf; Martin, Carol; Matsuda, Brent; McTaggart-Cowan, Ian; Merilees, Bill; Mudd-Ruth, Maria; Munro, J.; Nagorsen, David; Osgood, Wilfred; Owen, Audrey; Parham, H.J.; Parsons, Harry; Pasco, Juanita; Pearse, Theed; Penn, Briony; Pojar, Rosamund; Power, Margaret; Ricketts, Ed; Scagell, Robert; Seavy, Mary Lynn; Shackleton, David M.; Sheldon, Ian; Taylor, Keith; Taylor, T.M.C.; Waaland, Robert; Weston, J.; Whittington, Bruce; Yip, Mike.

LEONARD FRANK

An Enterprising Life: Leonard Frank Photographs 1895–1944 (1990)
edited by Cyril Leonoff

Leonard Frank, B.C.'s pre-eminent commercial photographer for the first half of the century, documented the rise of British Columbia, as showcased in Cyril Leonoff's *An Enterprising Life: Leonard Frank Photographs 1895–1944* (1990).

Born in Germany in 1870 as the son of a photographer, Leonard Frank went to the California gold fields at age 22 and gravitated north to Port Alberni, B.C., where he managed a general store. Following his move to Vancouver in 1917, he became the most successful photographer in the city, documenting the growth of vibrant industries. From 1920 until his death in 1944, Frank was the official Dominion of Canada photographer on the West Coast. He also documented the internment of Japanese-Canadians during WWII for the B.C. Security Commission, generating the impression that the confiscation of property and the evacuation and forced incarceration of thousands was orderly and humane. Photographer Otta Landauer purchased and continued Frank's business after his death in Vancouver in 1944.

Including a biography of Frank, Cyril Leonoff's coffee table book, *An Enterprising Life*, won numerous awards including the City of Vancouver Heritage Award and a B.C. Historical Association Award. Leonoff also published *Leonard Frank, Bridges of Light: Otto Landauer of Leonard Frank Photos 1945–1980* (1997) and an important pictorial history of Jews in B.C. and the Yukon.

NICK BANTOCK

Griffin & Sabine (1991) by Nick Bantock

Nick Bantock's first unconventional art-novel *Griffin & Sabine: An Extraordinary Correspondence* (1991) provides letters and postcards between lovers separated by continents. Griffin Moss is a lonely artist in London who receives mail from a mysterious woman named Sabine Strohem, living on an island in the South Pacific. Each page of the book contains a postcard or a letter, including an envelope. The reader removes each different message. Some are handwritten and some are typed, complete with spelling mistakes.

Initiated by San Francisco's Chronicle Books, *Griffin & Sabine* was followed by *Sabine's Notebook*, which received the Bill Duthie Booksellers' Choice Award in 1993. Subsequent titles in a similar vein have included *The Golden Mean: In Which the Extraordinary*

Correspondence of Griffin & Sabine Concludes, The Gryphon (which introduces the reader to a new couple) and *Alexandria*. Bantock completed his labyrinthine series of "visual literature" with the final volume of his second trilogy, *The Morning Star*, in 2003. After a combined run of more than a hundred weeks on the *New York Times* bestseller lists, the Griffin & Sabine series was revived by Bantock for a romantic drama at the Arts Club Theatre in 2006.

The phenomenal success of British-trained designer Bantock's series of "pop-up books for adults" began quite by accident. According to Bantock, the rough manuscript for his *Griffin & Sabine* was discovered only after an American editor happened to notice some of Bantock's personal doodlings. Bantock had gone to California to pitch conventional projects. "It was at the bottom of my clothes bag," he says. "I was only taking it along to show to a friend. As I threw the other dummies back on top, my red socks parted to reveal the dummy of *Griffin & Sabine*. The editor reached over and said, 'What's that?'" The curious American editor, Victoria Rock, took it to her senior editor at Chroni-

Nick Bantock

cle Books. It was published in Canada by Raincoast Books, who would hit the jackpot a second time by serving as the Canadian publisher for the *Harry Potter* series.

In much the same way that sampling in the music industry has become legitimate for recording artists, or poets publish "found poems," technology has enabled the easy "borrowing" of imagery for rejuvenated art by graphic designers. In the wake of his commercial success with the *Griffin & Sabine* books, original in both shape and design, Nick Bantock has been a pioneer in this emerging field of found art within books, along with Vancouver designer and author Barbara Hodgson, who co-founded Byzantium Books with Bantock.

DOUGLAS COUPLAND

Generation X: Tales for an Accelerated Culture (1991)
by Douglas Coupland

Douglas Coupland has proven himself—with 21 books in 19 years—to be unfailingly original, tirelessly inquisitive and an artist unafraid to take risks. It's a slam dunk to include Coupland's famous "magazine-style" first novel *Generation X* (1991) when citing the foremost titles by B.C. authors, so much so that one can easily overlook its important subtitle. Just as George Orwell's *Animal Farm* was first released as *Animal Farm: A Fairy Story*, Coupland's round-the-world-in-multiple-translations debut has a seldom-mentioned subtitle, *Tales for an Accelerated Culture*, which indicates Coupland operates as a social commentator as much as a novelist. His increasingly poignant, barometer-like readings of popular culture bristle with a reluctant wit.

Born in 1961 on a Canadian Armed Forces Base for NATO in Germany, Coupland attended Sentinel High School in West Vancouver where he had a non-religious upbringing. His adjunct career as a sculptor led him to attend the Emily Carr College of Art and Design in Vancouver, the Hokkaido College of Art and Design in Sapporo and the Istituto Europeo di Design in Milan. In 1987, he began describing his own "twentysomething" generation for *Vancouver* magazine, edited by Malcolm Parry. During a stint with *Vista* magazine, he revised his *Vancouver* article on Gen-X as a comic strip. He was subsequently contracted to write a non-fiction handbook on Generation X. Coupland went to Palm Springs and completed his "edgy, funny and hip" story of three young refugees from the world of yuppie wannabe-ism who are under-employed, over-educated and intensely private. The manuscript was rejected by 15 Canadian publishers and 14 American publishers before it appeared in 1991.

Since then Coupland has been increasingly concerned with characterization in his novels, while also working as a designer and visual artist. Recent novels have dealt with faith, or acknowledgement of God, or lack thereof, amid the diversions of a consumer culture and technology. *Hey Nostradamus!* (2003) explores the aftermath of a fictional shooting spree in North Vancouver's Delbrook High School cafeteria. *Microserfs* (1995) used the corporate backdrop of Microsoft headquarters in Seattle to depict the high-tech and somewhat geeky lives of employees "who realize they don't have lives." Some plots can be far-fetched. In *Girlfriend in a Coma* (1998), a high school senior named Karen Ann McNeil descends into a coma after a skiing accident—and gives birth to a child nine months later. She remains comatose for 18 years. Set in the near future when honeybees are almost extinct, *Generation A* (2009) starts when five people around the world are stung simultaneously. Coupland has produced eight non-fiction titles, including appreciations of Terry Fox, the city of Vancouver and Marshall McLuhan. In 2010, he began his own clothing label with Roots.

RON LIGHTBURN & SHERYL MCFARLANE

Waiting for the Whales (1991)
by Sheryl McFarlane, illustrated by Ron Lightburn

Founded by Bob Tyrrell and now co-owned by Andrew Wooldridge, Orca Books evolved from its initial regional focus to become one of Canada's most successful imprints for children's and young adult literature. As much as any other title, it was *Waiting for the Whales* (1991), illustrated by Ron Lightburn, that turned the tide. It received the Governor General's Award for

Illustration by Ron Lightburn from Waiting for the Whales

Children's Illustration. The story by Sheryl McFarlane concerns a grandfather who conveys to his granddaughter his deep pleasure in the seasonal cycles of nature. After his death, the child gains comfort from the seasonal return of the orcas.

For his coloured pencil illustrations in *Waiting for the Whales*, Ron Lightburn used friends and family members to pose for the major characters and proceeded to photograph them. "You're the cinematographer and the producer," he said. "I explained the story very carefully to them, then gave directions on how and where to look. This is a classic tradition in illustration, as old as photography." Once the editor approved his colour roughs, he projected them onto larger pieces of paper. Lightburn has compared "the transition between spreads in a picture book to the editing cuts in a film." Born in Cobourg, Ontario, and raised in West Vancouver, Ron Lightburn settled in Victoria in 1975, then relocated with his wife and co-author, Sandra Lightburn, to Nova Scotia in 1997.

Lightburn has won numerous other awards, but his Governor General's Award remains particularly significant because it drew national attention to the children's list of Orca Books in Victoria. "That's how you get good manuscripts," Orca founder Bob Tyrrell has commented, "by winning awards."

B.C.'s maven of children's literature, Judith Saltman, points to Ann Blades' self-illustrated *Mary of Mile 18* (1971) as her choice for a breakthrough illustrated title by a B.C. writer. The published-from-Ontario story is based on Blades' experiences as a teacher at Mile 18, a village on the Alaska Highway. The Vancouver Art Gallery exhibited paintings for the book and the Canadian Association of Children's Librarians chose it as Book of the Year in 1972. Among Blades' more than twenty titles, her enduring and charming picture book, *A Salmon for Simon* (1978), with text by Betty Waterton, was the first published-in-B.C. children's book to win a Governor General's Children's Literature Award and the Amelia Frances Howard-Gibbon Illustrator's Award.

For other B.C. book illustrators, see abcbookworld entries for Banks, Robert; Bateman, Robert; Berman, Rachel; Bevis, Vivian; Bonder, Dianna; Bridgeman, Kristi; Calvert, Lissa; Campbell, Laila; Campbell, Ruth; Clover, Gordon; Cohen, Bill; Coleman, Sue; Corbel, Eve; Coulson, Evi; Courbault, Martine; Cowles, Rose; Craigan, Charlie; Czernecki, Stefan; Daniel, C. Stuart; Deas, Mike; Eidlitz, Barbara; Einarson, Earl; Elsner, Gretchen; Ferguson-Dumais, Maggie; Filbrandt, Rod; Flett, Julie; Fodi, Lee Edward; Forsyth, Bonita; Gait, Darlene; George, Jr., Leonard; Godin, Tom; Gordon-Findlay, Lynn; Gourbault, Martine; Griffiths, Dean; Guzek, Greta; Hamelin, Marie-Micheline; Harrington, Jennifer; Harrison, Ted; Hill, Stephanie; Hobson, Megan; Houston, Deryk; Huber, June; Hunter, Helen Downing; Juhasz, George; Kazenbroot, Nelly; Kimber, Murray; Kyle, Margaret; La Fave, Kim; Larson, Joan; Leger, Michael; Leist, Christina; Littlechild, George; Longman, Mary; Lott, Sheena; Lovett, Glen; Maté, Rae; Mayne, Elizabeth; McAusland, William; McCallum, Stephen; McPhail, David; Morstad, Julie; Mowatt, Ken; Norris, Len; Nugent, Cynthia; Osborne, Tom; Penn, Briony; Phillips, W.S.; Randall, Wally; Ritchie, Scot; van Sandwyk, Charles; Shefrin, Sima Elizabeth; Shoemaker, Kathryn; Sinclair, Jeff; Swannell, Anne; Syme, Marion; T'Kenye, Caddie; Valerio, Geraldo; Visser, Tineke; Wakelin, Kirsti Anne; Wang, Jacqueline; Wapp, Josh; Wilson, Janet; Wolsak, Jane; Wolsak, Wendy; Woods, Emily H.

ALEXANDRA MORTON

Siwiti: A Whale's Story (1991) by Alexandra Morton

Alexandra Morton is the province's leading critic of fish farms. She first rose to prominence as the author of *Siwiti: A Whale's Story* (1991), winner of the Sheila A. Egoff Prize for Children's Literature.

Brought up in Connecticut, Morton moved to California in 1976 in order to research marine mammals. "When I was 18," she recalls, "I naively thought that if I looked hard enough, I could understand the communication between two whales in a tank in Los Angeles. I was wrong." She arrived to study orcas in B.C. in 1979. Six years after her marriage to filmmaker and photographer Robin Morton in 1980, her husband died while filming whales, one day before *National Geographic* was scheduled to record the couple's work. Morton remained at Echo Bay and took a job as a seasick, green-horn deckhand on Billy Proctor's fishboat, while raising her son and daughter on a boathouse at Echo Bay in Simoom Sound.

Siwiti is her charming personal account of one year in the life of a young whale. It was also a launching pad for Morton's two decades of public advocacy work for the protection of the Broughton Archipelago and for the elimination of fish farms. She now collects research to prove the biological threat of industrial net-pen feedlots that are accorded use of the oceans. Morton maintains, "The science is clear these operations risk wild fish populations by intensifying disease, they deplete world fishery resources to make the feed. They privatize ocean spaces and threaten our sovereign rights to food security."

She is a co-author of the anti–fish farming compendium, *A Stain Upon the Sea* (2004), winner of a Roderick Haig-Brown Regional

Prize, followed by *Beyond the Whales: The Photographs and Passions of Alexandra Morton* (2004) in which she writes, "Some time ago I was given the opportunity to meet Jane Goodall. I was spellbound by my childhood idol. She radiated grace, and the wisdom of the Earth. When a lull in the conversation opened, I stepped forward and asked, 'Jane, do you think there is hope?' Her answer came back crystal clear, 'Yes.'"

In 2010, Morton organized the Get Out Migration protest walk through Vancouver Island communities, as a call to action to make the provincial government aware that wild salmon should be given a higher priority than farm salmon. With Billy Proctor, a lifelong resident of the Broughton Archipelago, Morton also co-wrote *Heart of the Raincoast: A Life Story* (1999), followed by her autobiography, *Listening to Whales: What the Orcas Have Taught Us* (2002). Morton's life and work are the subject of a documentary film, *Alexandra's Echo*, released in 2003.

For books pertaining to other female activists, see abcbookworld entries for Baxter, Sheila; Culhane, Clare; Day, Shelagh; Edwards, Anne; Finlay, K.A.; Guiled, Brenda; Holt, Simma; Howard, Irene; Jewett, Pauline; Kivi, K. Linda; Krawczyk, Betty; Lewis, S.P.; McAllister, Karen; McClung, Nellie Letitia; Mitchell, Margaret; Nickerson, Betty; Rempel, Sharon; Thobani, Sunera; Zimmerman, Lillian.

JOHN OLIPHANT

Brother Twelve: The Incredible Story of Canada's False Prophet (1991)
by John Oliphant

There was never a more outrageous charlatan in B.C. history than Edward Arthur Wilson, the English sea captain and occultist who became The Brother XII (a.k.a. "Brother Twelve"). In 1927, he formed the Aquarian Foundation on Vancouver Island at Cedar-by-the-Sea, south of Nanaimo, with adjunct settlements on De Courcy and Valdes islands. The financial and sexual scandals that arose have led to comparisons with Rasputin, scientologist L. Ron Hubbard and Jamestown fanatic Jim Jones.

The Brother XII succeeded in bilking his followers of a fortune before he fled court challenges and possible jail terms in the early 1930s, accompanied by his dictatorial and fraudulent paramour, Madame Zee, who intimidated colony members with her riding crop. There are numerous books about The Brother XII. Easily the most in-depth study is John Oliphant's ten-years-in-the-making biography, *Brother Twelve: The Incredible Story of Canada's False Prophet* (1991), republished in an expanded edition by Oliphant in 2006. Pearl Luke has written a fictionalized portrait of Wilson's mistress, *Madame Zee* (2006).

Wilson first came to Victoria, B.C., around 1910, working as the driver of a delivery wagon. In his book *Foundations, Letters and Teachings* (1927) he claims to have undergone a mystical Ceremony of Dedication in 1912 that appointed him as a seeker and bringer of truth. He was a member of the Theosophical Society from 1913 to 1918. In Victoria, Wilson also worked as a clerk in the Dominion Express office, handling the Wells Fargo account, until he requested an exorbitant pay increase to match the salary of the president of the Canadian Pacific Railway. He left Victoria in 1914. Wilson supposedly apprenticed with the Royal Navy and earned his living as a merchant mariner until the 1920s. Abandoning his wife and children, he claimed to have heard the voice of an Egyptian deity while he was destitute in southern France. In Genoa, Italy, by the process of automatic writing, he received the text for his book *The Three Truths* from a mystical master he called the Twelfth Brother of the Great White Lodge. His Master instructed him to adopt the moniker The Brother XII. The Great White Lodge consisted of twelve groups around the globe who represented the twelve astrological houses.

Wilson gained followers in England in 1926 with his series of articles in *The Occult Review* in which he foretold Armageddon. Heeding The Brother XII's prophecies, a contingent of about twelve mostly wealthy and well-educated followers arrived on Vancouver Island with Wilson, via Southampton, in the spring of 1927.

They were encouraged to surrender all their earthly possessions to him. One of the first dwellings built at Cedar-by-the-Sea, according to journalist B.A. McKelvie, who visited in 1928, was the House of Mystery into which only The Brother XII was allowed to enter. By establishing his Aquarian Foundation, Wilson believed he was carrying forward the work of Madame H.P. Blavatsky, a founder of the Theosophical Society, and welcoming the new age of Aquarius. Approximately two thousand well-to-do and prominent American, British and Canadian seekers of truth enrolled in the movement for the privilege of sitting beneath the Tree of Wisdom, a moss-draped maple tree, where The Brother XII held court.

JAMIE CASSELS

The Uncertain Promise of Law: Lessons from Bhopal (1993)
by Jamie Cassels

Academics in B.C. have contributed greatly to society. To alert British Columbians to an under-publicized issue, John Calvert protested the privatization of B.C.'s rivers for power supply purposes in *Liquid Gold: Energy Privatization in British Columbia* (2008); Paul Tennant received the Roderick Haig-Brown Regional Prize for *Aboriginal Peoples and Politics: The Indian Land Question in British Columbia, 1849–1989* (1990), the first comprehensive treatment of aboriginal land claims in B.C; sociologist Becki L. Ross shed light on an unexamined subject with *Burlesque West: Showgirls, Sex, and Sin in Postwar Vancouver* (2009).

To pick one worthwhile academic title to represent many, it is hard to overlook Jamie Cassels' *The Uncertain Promise of Law: Lessons from Bhopal* (1993), a thorough investigation of the world's worst industrial accident (with the possible exception of the Chernobyl nuclear explosion, for which the long-term effects are still unknown). On December 2, 1984, a massive explosion and discharge of lethal gas from the Union Carbide factory in Bhopal, India, killed thousands of people in their sleep, blanketing the city for miles. The Bhopal plant manufactured pesticides and insecticides, including Sevin. The gas leak lasted for two hours, injuring people up to eight kilometres downwind. As a University of Victoria professor of law, Cassels examined the tragic accident and its complex aftermath. By 1992, the death toll around Bhopal was officially estimated at more than four thousand though victims' organizations placed that figure higher. Approximately thirty to forty thousand people were maimed or injured. Total claims for damages amounted to approximately 80 times the available funds, and the disaster gave rise to the world's largest lawsuit. Seven years later, the Government of India and Union Carbide were satisfied; the victims were not. "The only tests that ultimately matter are whether safety has been improved, and whether the innocent victims of industry are treated justly," Cassels concluded. "On both counts, the story of Bhopal cannot yet be viewed with any satisfaction. Too little has been delivered so far to restore our faith in the uncertain promise of law."

ROBERT HARE

Without Conscience: The Disturbing World of Psychopaths Among Us
(1993) by Robert Hare

When O.J. Simpson was rolling down the freeway in his white Bronco, *Larry King Live* phoned Robert Hare at his home but the UBC psychology professor would not agree to be part of a media circus. Always worried that his expertise will be misinterpreted or sensationalized, Hare has twice turned down appearances on the *Oprah Winfrey Show*. He did, however, agree to help actress Nicole Kidman prepare for her role as a psychopath in the movie *Malice*.

It is not easy to be one of the world's foremost experts on psychopaths—and still be taken seriously. Ever since UBC psychology professor Hare developed his Psychopathy Checklist—adopted worldwide as a standard measure for use by researchers—he has been a widely travelled public lecturer keen on ensuring his work is not simplified or misused.

Robert Hare's bestseller *Without Conscience: The Disturbing World of Psychopaths Among Us* (1993) evolved from his doctoral thesis on punishment, based on research undertaken at the federal penitentiary in New Westminster. After conducting experiments, Hare outlined the origins and nature of psychopathic behaviour.

Written for the lay reader, *Without Conscience* defines psychopaths, explains where their disorders come from, and alerts readers to the telling signs. His research determined that psychopaths are inordinately unconcerned with fear and punishment. He or she may masquerade as a friendly banker, loving spouse, a soothing doctor or an empathetic counsellor, but in the end the "average" psychopath will violently take what he or she wants, with no concern for morals or consequences. Robert Hare claims there are 300,000 psychopaths in Canada, but only a tiny fraction of that one percent of the Canadian population are violent offenders like Paul Bernardo and Clifford Olson. Most are "sub-clinical" psychopaths who operate as charming predators and superb liars. They love chaos and hate rules.

There are several hundred B.C. authors who have written books concerned with health; far too many to list.

Notably, physician Gabor Maté has risen to literary prominence with a series of psychotherapy titles. As a founding father of the alternative health movement, Dr. Abram Hoffer, the Victoria-based medical doctor and father of bookseller William Hoffer, influenced the work of Linus Pauling and Ewan Cameron with vitamin C. The son of novelist Kurt Vonnegut, Jr., Mark Vonnegut, briefly worked at Duthie Books before he lived on a hippie commune and wrote *The Eden Express: A Memoir of Insanity* (1975).

RONALD B. HATCH

Clayoquot & Dissent (1994) edited by Ronald B. Hatch

In 1993, in response to a B.C. government decision to allow logging in two-thirds of the old growth forest in Clayoqout Sound, more than 12,000 people attended blockades on Vancouver Island, resulting in more than 850 arrests. It was the largest collective act of peaceful civil disobedience in Canadian history.

That summer of protest and its legal aftermath are the subjects for *Clayoquot & Dissent* (1994), edited by Ron Hatch, with essays by Tzeporah Berman, Maurice Gibbons, Gordon Brent Ingram, Christopher Hatch and Loÿs Maingon. These essayists reveal the lack of a scientific basis for forestry decisions, explain why Canada's forests continue to be destroyed, and propose alternatives for conservation. The first logging blockades in Canada had occurred in the same region, on Meares Island, in 1984.

Clayoquot blockades received world attention when the Australian rock group Midnight Oil gave a concert in the protestors' "peace camp." But the logging company, Macmillan Bloedel (MB) in the short term, won the fight, with the support of the courts.

"The whole experience has deepened the sense of what we have to fight against," said Ron Hatch, a UBC professor. "We discovered during the trials that the RCMP had been giving information to Macmillan Bloedel on a daily basis. The police, wittingly or unwittingly, were aligning themselves with MB. At the same time, you begin to realize how much the court system is slanted towards the logging companies. We soon found ourselves fighting the courts instead of fighting MB. The courts took the heat off Macmillan Bloedel and the province paid for the process. By the time the sentencing was over, the process didn't satisfy anybody except

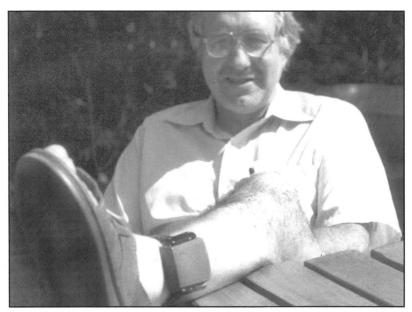

As one of hundreds arrested for protesting logging in Clayoqout Sound, editor Ronald B. Hatch displays the electronic monitoring device he was forced to wear around his ankle.

Macmillan Bloedel. The judges were unhappy, the protestors were unhappy, and the general public was unhappy. The courts failed to understand that civil disobedience could be done, as Martin Luther King said, 'lovingly,' with respect for the law one is breaking."

Hatch pleaded not guilty to criminal contempt and was sentenced to 20 days under electronic surveillance, 25 community hours and probation for the rest of the year. "On the day of my sentencing, I tried to be calm and logical. But I was really angry. We were never allowed to justify our actions. Given the sort of charge it is, the judges believe it's possible to infer your motives. At the time of our trial in Victoria, we flew over environmental planner Brent Ingram from UBC to speak about old growth forests. He's an internationally recognized expert but the judge decided he couldn't offer evidence. The only time we were allowed to say anything of substance was at our sentencing."

UNESCO made Clayoquot Sound into a World Biosphere Reserve in 2000. First Nations timber companies now control licences for 90,000 hectares of its forest, including old-growth valleys.

SAGE BIRCHWATER

Chiwid (1995) by Sage Birchwater

There are several superb books about aboriginal women. *The Days of Augusta* (1973) came first, a tribute to the hard life of Mary Augusta Tappage, born at Soda Creek in 1888, followed by *During My Time: Florence Edenshaw Davidson, A Haida Woman* (1982). Carrier woman Mary John's memoir, *Stoney Creek Woman* (1989), co-written with Prince George social worker Bridget Moran, was for many years the bestselling title from Arsenal Pulp Press. Published more than 50 years after her death, *Mourning Dove: A Salishan Autobiography* (1990), recalls the ground-breaking literary achievements of American-born Okanagan writer Mourning Dove. Shirley Sterling retold her experiences in the Kamloops Residential School for a children's book, *My Name is Seepeetza* (1992). The first autobiographical portrayal of a Kwakwa̱ka̱'wakw matriarch, *Paddling to Where I Stand* (2004), recalls the life and times of storyteller Agnes Alfred.

But the most memorable portrait is the shortest, *Chiwid* (1995), by Cariboo journalist Sage Birchwater, in which he profiles the Tsilhqot'in woman who lived outdoors for most of her adult life.

Chiwid (also Chee-Wit, or "Chickadee") was widely known as a crack shot who moved her solitary campsite according to the seasons, protected only by a tarp. Rumoured to have spiritual powers, she was born as Lily Skinner, daughter of deaf and mute Luzep, a Tsilhqot'in from Redstone, and Charley Skinner, a white settler in the Tatlayoko–Eagle Lake area.

Chiwid married Alex Jack and they had two daughters, but her life changed irrevocably when her husband beat her mercilessly with a heavy chain. Remorseful, Chiwid's husband drove several

Chiwid, a crack shot, moved her solitary camp according to the seasons.
This photo was taken by Veera Bonner of Big Creek, one of the Witte sisters.

head of cattle to Chezacut and sold them to Charlie Mulvahill to raise money to send his beautiful wife to Vancouver for treatment, but thereafter Chiwid left her husband in order to roam the Chilcotin, from Anahim Lake to Riske Creek, sometimes with an old horse and a dog. Many people tried to assist her, offering firewood, food or clothes, which she gratefully accepted, but Chiwid maintained her independence, fearing she would become sick if she remained too long indoors. Ill, aged and going blind, Chiwid eventually consented to spend her final years in the Stoney Creek Reserve home of Katie Quilt, where she died in 1986.

WAYSON CHOY

The Jade Peony (1995) by Wayson Choy

Wayson Choy has emerged foremost among Chinese Canadian fiction writers for his novel *The Jade Peony* (1995), an inter-generational saga about an immigrant family, the Chens, during the Depression.

Born in Vancouver in 1939, Wayson Choy was the only son of two working parents. He was cared for in a variety of Chinese Canadian households in the Strathcona neighbourhood, dreaming of becoming a cowboy. He grew up being told his absent father was a cook on a Canadian Pacific ship.

Choy often attended Chinese opera with his mother and became the first Chinese Canadian to enroll in a creative writing course (taught by Earle Birney) at UBC. There he began writing a short story that turned into his best-known novel, *The Jade Peony*, some 30 years later.

The Jade Peony won both the City of Vancouver Book Award and the Trillium Award in Ontario. It has been anthologized more than 25 times. While on a publicity tour for the novel, Choy received an unexpected phone call from a woman who had been his babysitter, during which, at age 56, he learned he had been adopted. This led him to write *Paper Shadows* (1999), a memoir of the 1940s.

Choy returned to the Chen family for *All That Matters* (2004), a prequel told through the eyes of eldest son Kiam-Kim, who arrives by ship with his father and grandmother Poh-Poh, in 1926. For his writing, Choy has said it has been essential to trust the point of view of others. "My character, Kiam-Kim, is heterosexual which I am not. You have to risk everything to make a breakthrough. Be on the side of the monster. Until we can make someone understand that any of us could have been the guard at a Nazi concentration camp or the uncle that abused his niece or the soldiers that napalmed Vietnam, until we can make others see that, it is not literature. A writer has to reverse things to get at what they know."

The flourishing of Chinese Canadian literature was kick-started by UVic historian David Chuenyan Lai and Vancouver cultural activist Jim Wong-Chu who co-edited a breakthrough anthology, *Many-Mouthed Birds* (1991), with Bennett Lee. Since then Paul Yee has gained considerable success as a children's book author and Denise Chong has earned widespread notice for her non-fiction family stories. For seven years, Louis Luping Han helped his mother, Dr. Li Qunying—a medical doctor who had worked in China through WWII, the Chinese Civil war, and the Korean War—to write her riveting memoir of her experiences under repressive communism, *The Doctor Who Was Followed by Ghosts* (2007).

For other books written by or about Chinese Canadians, see abcbookworld entries for Chan, Anthony Bernard; Chan, Gillian; Chang, Ginger; Chen, Ying; Cheng, Tien-fang; Chow, Lily; Chu, Garrick; Chung, Tsai Chih; Con, Harry; Hong, W.M.; Jew, Anne; Kwa, Lydia; Lai, Larissa; Lam, Fiona; Lau, Evelyn; Lee, Jen Sookfong; Lee, SKY; Li, Donghai; Li, Huai-Min; Li, Julia; Lim, Sing; Lu, Henry; Ma, Ching; Moosang, Faith; Ng, Wing Chung; Price, Lily Hoy; Quan, Andy; Quan, Betty; Tan, Jin-Yan; Wong, Kileasa; Wong, Marjorie; Wong, Rita; Woon, Yuen-Fong; Zhao, Yuezhi. For other authors who have also written about China or Chinese Canadians, see abcbookworld entries for Anderson, Kay; Dionne, JoAnn; Hayter-Menzies, Grant; Hemmingsen, John; Johnson, Graham; Maartman, Ben; Morton, James; Overmyer, Daniel L.; Owen, Patricia; Phillips, Molly; Roth, Terrence; Roy, Patricia; Stursberg, Richard; Ward, N. Lascelles; Wickberg, Edgar; Worrall, Brandy Lien; Wright, Richard.

JOHN ENRICO

The translator seldom gets the glory. Until her death in 2007, the English language translator of Heinrich Böll, Leila Vennewitz, lived quietly and largely unnoticed near Lost Lagoon in Vancouver for more than 50 years. Similarly, prior to Robert Bringhurst's reworkings of Haida storytellers, as transcribed by anthropologist John Swanton, John Enrico had translated and edited Swanton's original 1905 transcriptions as *Skidegate Haida Myths and Histories* (1995) with minimal notice. It has been suggested by Enrico that Bringhurst's higher-profile revival of the "classic" Haida storytellers in three hardcover editions provides a less than sufficient ackowledgement of Enrico's spadework.

John Enrico began his studies of Haida music in 1975. Arguably, Enrico has done more than any other scholar to make the Haida language accessible as one of the best documented indigenous languages of North America.

In his two-volume, 1387-page *Haida Syntax* (2003), Enrico provides a comprehensive description of the syntax of two Haida dialects, partially based on the materials that were collected by Swanton in the early 20th century, enhanced by his 25 years of fieldwork in the Haida community. With ethnomusicologist Wendy Bross Stuart, Enrico also published a 519-page study, *Northern Haida Songs* (1996), which situates Haida music in the context of the Northwest Coast and presents a collection of 128 songs, fully transcribed and analyzed, representing some 20 types of songs. Enrico's other published works include *The Lexical Phonology of Masset Haida* (1991) and a Haida reader for juveniles.

Other authors of First Nations language resources include Wayne Suttles and Jay Powell. Suttles published *Musqueam Reference Grammar* (2004). In 1968, as a graduate student in anthropology, Powell first visited La Push on the Olympic Peninsula where Fred "Woody" Woodruff, one of the last remaining Quileute speakers, had the patience to teach his language to Powell. Photographer Vicki Jensen joined him there in 1972. Since then Jensen has shot more than 50,000 photographs and Powell has become the most essential linguist on the West Coast. For over 40 years, the couple has helped produce more than 40 language and culture books for the Quileutes, the Kwakwaka'wakw, the Halkomelem, the Eastern and Western Gitksan, the Shuswap and the Nuu-chah-nulth. "A language is like a species of bird," Powell has said, "that has evolved across thousands of generations. How hard would we work to save such a bird from becoming extinct?"

Translation of First Nations materials is a growing field, whereas relatively few literary works in other languages are translated for publication in B.C. See abcbookworld entries for Aligizkis, Manolis; Binning, Sadhu; Boyce, Pleuke; Bullock, Michael; Downes, Gwladys; Good, Graham; Hatch, Ronald; McWhirter, George; Rhenisch, Harold; Siegler, Karl.

BIRUTÉ GALDIKAS

B iruté Mary Galdikas is the foremost protector of orangutans on the planet. Also known as Biruté Marija Filomena Galdikas, she is frequently described as the third woman sent by paleontologist Dr. Louis B. Leakey to study primates in their natural habitat, after Dian Fossey and Jane Goodall, and is therefore known as one of Leakey's Angels. Although she was dubbed "Queen of the Orangutans" in Italy and profiled by the *New York Times* and *Time*, she has not been one to play to the media. She is the only foreign-born person to win the Hero of the Earth Award (Kalpataru), from the Indonesian government. She has studied and protected orangutans in Tanjung Puting National Park, Indonesia, since 1971, and she has also long been associated with the Department of Archaeology at Simon Fraser University.

Galdikas' parents met in a refugee camp after fleeing Lithuania

Biruté Galdikas of SFU has studied and protected orangutans in Indonesia since 1971.

at the end of WWII. She was born in West Germany in 1946 but came to Canada at age two, settling in Toronto, then moving to Vancouver in 1962. She married Rod Brindamour while attending the University of California. After attending a Leakey lecture in Los Angeles, she asked Leakey for his help in order to study orangutans. "Are you willing to have your appendix removed?" Leakey asked. It was a test. Galdikas offered to have her tonsils taken out, too. Leakey suggested Brindamour accompany her to Borneo to photograph orangutans. Three years later, in 1971, the young couple left for Borneo, stopping at *National Geographic* headquarters in Washington, D.C., for training and equipment. They flew to Kenya to visit Leakey, briefly acquired some field training from Goodall in Tanzania, stopped in Pakistan, India and Nepal, and then arrived in Jakarta. "At first I thought we would be just holding down the fort until reinforcements came," she recalls. "I never envisioned that we were the cavalry."

Gradually they accumulated sightings, allocating names according to Jane Goodall's method: related apes were always given names beginning with the same letter of the alphabet. "What started out as an academic study," she says, "quickly evolved into a passion." Dr. Leakey died of a heart attack in 1972 but Goodall encouraged Galdikas and Brindamour to persist. *National Geographic* arrived with a camera crew in 1975. Binti Paul Galdikas Brindamour was born in 1976 and grew up with orangutans as playmates, imitating orangutans as his siblings. The marriage buckled but Galdikas didn't. Rod Brindamour left for Canada to pursue a career in computer science. In 1981, Galdikas married her co-worker Pak Bohap and they have several children. Galdikas' *Reflections of Eden: My Years with the Orangutans of Borneo* (1995) was followed by *Orangutan Odyssey* (1999) and *Great Ape Odyssey* (2005).

Galdikas has proven that orangutans have the longest birth intervals of any mammal: a wild adult female has young once every eight years. Orangutan females give birth alone. Mothers will carry their young for four years; some are not weaned until six or seven years. Male-to-male competition for females is fierce. Forced copulation exists. Orangutans share 97% of human DNA, making them the third-closest relations to humans after chimpanzees and gorillas.

JOHN VANDERPANT

Underlying Vibrations: The Photography and Life of John Vanderpant (1995) edited by Sheryl Salloum

In terms of productivity, Leonard Frank was the pervasively dominant photographer during the first half of the 20th century, but arguably the most sophisticated photographic artist during roughly the same era was John Vanderpant, ably represented by Sheryl Salloum's coffee table collection, *Underlying Vibrations: The Photography and Life of John Vanderpant* (1995).

Born in the Netherlands in 1884, John Vanderpant was a photojournalist who immigrated to southern Alberta in 1911. In 1919, he opened a portrait studio in New Westminster, then moved to Vancouver. He was recognized in the 1920s and 1930s for his black-and-white bromide prints, his modernist views of surfaces, industrial views and his close-ups of vegetables. He also took some memorable portraits, including those of Bliss Carman, A.Y. Jackson, Jean Coulthard and Rabindranath Tagore.

While promoting and selling works by the Group of Seven, Vanderpant Galleries was a portrait studio that doubled as a mini-Mecca for avant-garde artists of Vancouver from 1926 until Vanderpant's death in 1939. His daughters operated his studio as a gallery in the 1940s. Thereafter the building served as the Cote d'Azur restaurant until its demolition. In 1976, the National Gallery of Canada issued a Vanderpant catalogue.

With 80,000 images of Vancouver taken during the second half of the 20th century, Fred Herzog is the city's premier street photographer, having focused on store fronts, cafés, barber shops, pedestrians, cars and signs since his emigration from Germany in 1952. "It was my goal from the start to show city vitality," he said. His mostly colour images suggest Vancouver was more vibrant and unselfconscious in the fifties and sixties when it was a bustling city in which the working class could still afford to live. Herzog began to sell his work only in 1970. His book, accompanying a retrospective at the Vancouver Art Gallery, is *Fred Herzog: Vancouver Photographs* (2007), with textual contributions from Grant Arnold and Michael Turner.

Vancouver's Jeff Wall has been British Columbia's most successful photographer internationally.

For other authors pertaining to photography, see abcbookworld entries for Adams, Bryan; Adney, Tappan; Allen, Richard Edward; Andrews, Ralph; Baker, Carol; Ballantyne, Bob; Ballard, Jill; Barnholden, Michael; Bartosik, John; Birrell, Andrew J.; Blevins, David; Blohm, Hans; Bourdon, Donald; Breen, David; Brière, Elaine; Butler, A.P.; Campbell, Betty; Campion, David; Carey, Wendy; Carter, Anthony; Cheadle, Chris; Chesher, Deborah; Clarkes, Lincoln; Congdon-Martin, Douglas; Cox, H.G.; Curran, Douglas; Currie, Rod; Curtis, Edward S.; Cyr, Helene; Czolowski, Ted; De Volpi, Charles P.; Dekur, William; Denton, Don; Douglas, Stan; Dowden, Graham; Emmons, George Thornton; Ernst, Trent; Fiegehen, Gary; Fischer, George;

Fitzharris, Tim; Francis, Daniel; Galloway, C.F.J.; Garnier, Karie; Garrett-Petts, W.F.; Gauvin, Brian; Gilbert, Paul; Goering, Dag; Grant, Peter; Gregory, Doane; Griggs, William E.; Haegert, Dorothy; Hainsworth, Gavin; Hanby, Bernard; Harmon, Byron; Harris, Brian; Harris, Chris; Harvey, Al; Harvey, Gail; Hayward, Alex Waterhouse; Heinl, Russ; Herger, Bob; Herrmann, Karl; Hobbs, Jared; Howell, Brian; Hunter, Kendall; Jeffries, Bill; Jennings, Neil L.; Jerome, Gillian; Jerritt, Boomer; Jones, David; Jurome, William Bradley; Kraulis, J.A.; Lee, Evan; Lloyd, Tanya; Lyon, Jim; Madsen, Ken; Marshall, Denis; Matsen, Bradford; Matsura, Frank; Mattison, David; McKeever, Harry P.; McLaren, Keith; McQuarrie, John; Mearns, Lindsay; Milne, Courtney; Minden, Robert; Moe, Karen; Mooney, Shirley; Moosang, Faith; Morgan, Rowland; Morgan, Sher; Morrow, Patrick; Nazemi, Akbar; Neel, David; Nelson, Colleen; Newman, Nancy; Norbury, Rosamond; Nunuk, David; Oke, Kevin; Onley, Yukiko; Orton, Michael; Osborne, Graham; Oulton, Dick; Owen, Tony; Parker, Terry; Parnell, Vene; Patterson, Helen; Patterson, Terry; Pedrick, Barbara; Pettit, Donald A.; Philipson, Claire Leila; Radul, Judy; Reksten, Terry; Reynolds, Reg; Riley, Linda; Robideau, Henri; Ryan, Jim; Ryan, Liz Mitten; Savard, Dan; Sherwood, Jay; Shymanksi, Wendy; Silversides, Brock V.; Sommer, Robin; Sparks, Jean; Speitz, Karl; Spilsbury, Jim; Steltzer, Ulli; Stewart, Susan; Sutherland, Tom; Tepper, Leslie; Tewinkel, Wim; Thirkell, Fred; Timms, Philip; Touchie, Rodger; Vogel, Aynsley; Waite, Donald Ender; Ward, Robin; Warick, Bob; Watts, Ron; Weiser, Judy; Whetham, Bob; White, Cliff; White, Peter; Wigle, Michael; Wilks, Claire Weissman; Williams, Carol; Windh, Jacqueline; Wolf, Jim; Woodcock, Ingeborg; Woodley, Barbara; Woodward, Meredith Bain; Woodward, Ron; Wyatt, Victoria; Yip, Mike; Young, Cameron.

THE WITTE SISTERS

Chilcotin: Preserving Pioneer Memories (1995) by the Witte Sisters

Never mind Arthur Erickson's SFU campus, the Marine Building or the BowMac sign. The top engineering feat of B.C. is either Mungo Martin's 39-metre totem in Beacon Hill Park or Rudy Johnson's bridge that was erected without government support in 1968. With typical Cariboo-Chilcotin grit and ingenuity, Rudy Johnson purchased a 200-ton, 300-foot long steel bridge in Alaska and reassembled it across the Fraser River, with the help of engineer Howard Elder, in six months for only $200,000. It allowed him to cut 30 miles off his trips between his Buckskin Ranch and Williams Lake.

Rudy Johnson is just one of the countless hardy souls featured in *Chilcotin: Preserving Pioneer Memories* (1995), a 432-page who-was-who assembled, as much as written, by the three Chilcotin-born Witte sisters—Irene, Veera and Hazel—all raised at Big Creek. As the granddaughters of pioneers Tom Hance and Nellie Verdier Hance—reputedly the Chilcotin's first white female resident, who rode side-saddle for 400 miles to get there in 1887—Irene E. Bliss, Veera Bonner and Hazel Henry Litterick were raised by their mother Hattie Witte, who drove a six-horse freight wagon through Bull Canyon in the 1920s. The three sisters continued to live in the Cariboo-Chilcotin and co-wrote their book under the name of the Witte Sisters. It arose from an out-of-print 1958 Centennial project published as *History and Legends of the Chilcotin*. Veera Bonner did most of the actual writing for their jointly authored book but she credits her sisters as instrumental in gathering the stories.

In 1941, Veera Witte married John Bonner, and they had two children. When the marriage ended, she took her children to live on Fletcher Lake near Big Creek where she started a resort business called Bin-Goh-Sha, renting log cabins, boats and camping facilities. There she became the "rural correspondent" for the *Williams Lake Tribune* at the behest of its publisher Clive Stangoe. Veera Bonner's text is communal, charming and often fascinating—and captures the spirit of the Cariboo-Chilcotin with unpretentious pride. The story of Veera's birth, one month premature, on August 25, 1918, has been recorded by Linda-Lou Howarth in an equally remarkable collection *Gumption & Grit: Women of the Cariboo Chilcotin* (2009).

There have been countless books from and about the Cariboo-Chilcotin since Margaret McNaughton published *Overland to Cariboo* (1896). For other Cariboo-Chilcotin non-fiction authors, see abcbookworld entries for Baity, Earl S.; Barlee, N.L.; Beeson, Edith; Brown, Darlene; Brown, James N.J.; Champness, W.; Cochran, Lutie Ulrich; Cridland, June L.; Currie, Vera Baker; Decker, Karla; Downie, William; Elliott, Gordon; Elliott, Marie Anne; Futcher, Winnifred; Galloway, C.F.J.; Harris, Lorraine; Holley, D.A.; Hong, W.M.; Innes, Roy; Jenkins, Chuck; Kind, Chris; Klan, Yvonne; Laut, Agnes; Lee, Eldon; Lee, Norman; Lee, Todd; Leiren-Young, Mark; Lindsay, Frederick William; Logan, Don; Loggins, Olive Spencer; Ludditt, Fred; Patenaude, Branwen; Place, Marian T.; Price, Lily Hoy; Ramsey, Bruce; Rhenisch, Harold; Riley, Bill; Roberts, J.A.; Schreiber, John; Skelton, Robin; Speare, Jean; Stangoe, Irene; Sullivan, Alan; Townsend, Arthur H.; Turkel, William J.; Wade, Mark Sweeten; Waite, Donald Ender; Williams, David Ricardo; Wilson, Diana; Wood, June; Wright, Richard.

GEORGE BOWERING

George Bowering's *Bowering's B.C.: A Swashbuckling History* (1996) proves he knows British Columbia as much and as well as anyone. Even if Bowering is addicted to his own cleverness, this is one of the best books ever written about his home province—the sort of history book they wouldn't allow in schools because it says too much.

". . . people in B.C. have to be taught to be Canadians," he writes. "This is done by the Canadian Broadcasting Corporation and the *Globe and Mail.* But most British Columbians don't listen to the CBC or read the *G&M.*"

More conventional histories by Jean Barman, Terry Reksten, George Woodcock and Geoffrey Molyneux have tended to overshadow *Bowering's B.C.* And his title didn't help either. But Bowering's shrewd, sometimes cynical take on human nature and politics is unfailingly provocative as an educational force.

Bowering's B.C. harkens back to Hubert Howe Bancroft. Bowering is fascinated by, and dedicated to, uncovering and discussing what might be *original* about British Columbia. There are precious few writers in Bowering's league when it comes to a comprehensive understanding of the maverick characters and odd stories that are unique to B.C. Howard White of Harbour Publishing might be his only peer in this regard.

Born in Penticton in 1935 and raised in nearby Oliver as the son of a high school chemistry teacher, Bowering was a Royal Canadian Air Force photographer (1954–1957) who subsequently attended Victoria College and UBC in the early 1960s. He taught at SFU for 29 years (1972–2001). The most opinionated and outspoken writer to emerge from the UBC-based TISH collective, Bowering has received Governor General's Awards for fiction and poetry, a rare feat. In some respects the writing game is competitive and Bowering has been a hard-working and bright force. He has published more than 60 books in various genres and was selected to serve as the country's first Parliamentary Poet Laureate (2002–2004). His approach to making books is invariably experimental.

For other authors pertaining to the TISH movement, see abcbookworld entries for Dawson, David; Davey, Frank; Hindmarch, Gladys; Kearns, Lionel; Marlatt, Daphne; McLeod, Dan; Reid, Jamie; Tallman, Warren; Wah, Fred. Outside, on the periphery of the TISH vortex, were Belford, Ken; bissett, bill; Brown, Jim; Copithorne, Judith; Coupey, Pierre; Gadd, Maxine; Gilbert, Gerry; Kiyooka, Roy; Lane, Pat; Lane, Red; Lawrence, Scott; McKinnon, Barry; Mayne, Seymour; Newlove, John; Persky, Stan; Robinson, Brad. The alleged American focus of TISH no longer generates debate. TISH graduates have become mainstream in universities.

MARIA COFFEY & DAG GOERING

Sailing Back in Time (1996) by Maria Coffey & Dag Goering

Using simple hand tools, Allen Farrell designed and built more than 40 boats on the coast, often out of driftwood, with the help of his wife Sharie, whom he met in Pender Harbour in 1945. The bohemian pair built their first sailboat, the 36-foot *Wind Song*, in 1949, and sailed to the South Pacific in the early 1950s. When they reached their eighties, they sold most of their possessions and flew to Mexico to live on the beach. She was the favourite subject for his many paintings until she died in 1996.

One year earlier, in 1995, in a refitted dory called *Luna Moth*, powered by sail and sculling oar, Maria Coffey and her photographer husband Dag Goering completed a three-month journey around Georgia Strait with the Farrells, tagging behind the couple's fourth hand-built cruising boat, the 42-foot *China Cloud*, designed to resemble a Chinese junk. To complement Goering's 65 photos, Coffey recorded the Farrells' memories and observations for *Sailing Back in Time: A Nostalgic Voyage on Canada's West Coast* (1996), a visually stunning tribute to two highly original and inspiring characters.

An affectionate biographical tribute by Dan Rubin, *Salt on the Wind* (1996), also traces the octogenarians' lives from Allen's birth in Vancouver in 1912, and Sharie's birth in Ontario in 1908, including some of the technical details for Farrell's ingenuity as a boat-builder. Sharie Farrell was introduced to the wayfaring life at sea in the 1930s and early 1940s by the German-born sailor and author George Dibbern, after he arrived in Vancouver aboard his sailboat *Te Rapunga*, disavowing citizenship to any country.

Allen Farrell's reputation as a craftsman, painter, scrounge artist, recycler and nomad has made him one of the coast's most famous characters, on a par with the inventor and entrepreneur Jim Spilsbury. "But it is the Farrells' humility and humanity that makes them such endearing characters," Alan Haig-Brown wrote. "After building a dream boat, the Farrells sail it to the South Pacific, grow homesick for the Pacific Coast and then either sell or sail the boat home. It they still have the boat when they return, they will sell it shortly after. With complete freedom from materialism, the boat is sold to the "right person" rather than the highest bidder. In between sailing trips, the Farrells lived on land, in houses they built themselves, occasionally squatting."

For other authors of maritime titles, see abcbookworld entries for Andersen, Doris; Anderson, Hugo; Anderson, Suzanne; Armitage, Doreen; Ashenfelter, Pete; Barnes, Gordon; Barr, James; Beavis, Lancelot; Belyk, Robert; Bendall, Pamela; Bown, Stephen R.; Brevig, Anne E.; Burrows, James; Burtinshaw, Julie; Calhoun, Bruce; Cameron, June; Campbell, John; Carey, Wendy; Chettleburgh, Peter; Converse, Cathy; Copeland, Andy; Cran, George A.; Cummings, Al; Dalton, Anthony; Davidson, George; Dawson, Will; Delgado, James; Dibbern, George; Dook, Catherine; Douglass, Don; Downie, William; Duggan, Barbara; Dyson, George; Eardley, Wilmot; Evans, Clayton; Favelle, Peter; Foster, John; Fukawa, Masako; Gibson, John Frederic; Gleeson, Paul; Goddard, Joan; Golby, Humphrey; Gough, Barry; Graham, Donald; Greene, Ruth; Grundle, Jack; Grundmann, Erika; Hacking, Norman; Hadley, Michael; Hagelund, William A.; Haigh, Val; Harbo, Rick M.; Harvey, Robert; Heal, S.C.; Hewett, Shirley; Hick, W.B.M.; Hill, Beth; Holloway, Godfrey; Howay, F.W.; Hulsizer, Elsie; Imray, James; Innes, Hammond; Irving, William; Jackman, S.W.; James, Rick; Jane, Cecil; Jensen, Vickie; Jupp, Ursula; Keating, Bern; Kelly, William; Koch, Tom; Lamb, W.K.; Lange, Owen; Lawrence, Iain; Leighton, Kenneth Macrae; Levy, Paul; Longstaff, F.V.; Lower, Arthur; Lundy, Derek; Luxton, Norman; MacCrostie, M. Watson; Manby, Thomas; Mansbridge, Francis; Marc, Jacques; Mayne,

Richard Charles; McCann, Leonard G.; McCulloch, Tom; McKee, William; McKinney, Sam; McLaren, Keith; Meares, John; Millar, Will; Mofras, Eugene Duflot (de); Morris, Robert; Morris, Wilfred H.; Murray, Peter; Nash, Ronald J.; Neitzel, Michael; Newell, Gordon; Newsome, Eric; Nicolls, Nan; Norris, Pat Wastell; Palmer, Ron; Paterson, T.W.; Portlock, Nathaniel; Proctor, Bill; Ricketts, Ed; Roberts, Harry; Roberts, John E. (Ted); Robson, Peter; Rogers, Fred; Rothery, Agnes; Sager, Eric W.; Sauer, Martin; Schade, Marv; Scott, Robert; Sharcott, Margaret; Skogan, Joan; Smeeton, Miles; Sparham, Adrian; Stone, David Leigh; Struthers, Andrew; Tamm, Eric Enno; Taylor, G.W.; Taylor, Jeanette; Teece, Philip; Theriault, Walter; Tovell, Freeman M.; Twigg, Arthur M.; Van der Ree, Freda; Vancouver, George; Varzeliotis, Tom; Vassilopoulos, Peter; Vipond, Anne; Voss, John; Wahl, Ryan; Wallace, Scott; Watmough, Don; Wells, Martin; Wells, R.E.; Westergaard, Ross; White, Bill; Wilson, James Ted; Winters, Barbara; Witt, Eugene; Wolferstan, Bill; Wright, E.W.; Yeadon-Jones, Anne.

———>◦◦◦◦⊂———

IAN MCALLISTER

The Great Bear Rainforest: Canada's Forgotten Coast (1997)
by Ian McAllister et al

One of the most influential Canadian books—ever—is *The Great Bear Rainforest: Canada's Forgotten Coast* (1997), co-authored by Ian McAllister, Karen McAllister and Cameron Young, with a foreword by Robert Kennedy, Jr. It successfully sparked awareness and engendered protective legislation to conserve the northern half of B.C.'s west coast, one of the northern hemisphere's richest unprotected wildlife habitats and home to Canada's largest grizzly bears.

From 1991 to 1996, the McAllisters charted an ecosystem which stretches from Knight Inlet to Alaska, taking thousands of photos, keeping journals, making seven pilgrimages in seven years, building their vision to protect a 2,000-kilometre strip of bear habitat. Like modern-day Darwins in a rain-soaked Galapagos, the McAllisters succeeded, in the spring of 1996, in reaching Smokehouse Creek off Smith Inlet, the last valley on their list. The couple often used a trimaran to explore an area where approximately two thousand grizzly bears reside, where "white spirit"

Environmentalists Karen and Ian McAllister

Kermode bears roam, where spring migration of eulachon can attract thousands of eagles, where pictographs abound and where an overzealous photographer can get bruised on the chin by a flying salmon—yes, it happened. All this was undertaken in order to present their anti-logging perspective on behalf of the Raincoast Conservation Society, an organization which they co-founded with Ian's father and some friends in 1990.

After the British Columbia government introduced measures to protect some of the Great Bear Rainforest in 2006, promising in February to allocate $30 million if the federal government matched that commitment, in February of 2007, the federal government pledged to spend $30 million to help preserve 1.2 million hectares of rainforest, the largest intact temperate rainforest left on earth. An additional $60 million was raised by private organizations and philanthropic groups. *Time* magazine heralded co-authors Ian and Karen McAllister as environmental leaders for the 21st century and credited their coffee table book as "the centrepiece for

Greenpeace International's North American forest campaign."

As a founding member of the Raincoast Conservation Society, Ian McAllister is not satisfied with the extent to which the Great Bear Rainforest has been protected and preserved. For his follow-up natural history title, *The Last Wild Wolves: Ghosts of the Great Bear Rainforest* (2007), he tracked, photographed and wrote about wolves over a five-year period during which he and his wife were living mainly in the outport of Shearwater on Denny Island.

DEREK HAYES

If geography were an Olympic event, they'd accuse Derek Hayes of being on steroids. During the first decade of the new millennium, Hayes compiled, designed and wrote ten atlases and illustrated histories, starting with his self-published *Historical Atlas of British Columbia and the Pacific Northwest* (1999), winner of the Bill Duthie Booksellers' Choice Award. Since that debut, Hayes has won many awards for tracing the exploration and settlement patterns of areas throughout Canada and the U.S.

The first Hayes atlas was followed by *Historical Atlas of the North Pacific Ocean* (2001) and *First Crossing: Alexander Mackenzie, His Expedition across North America, and the Opening of the Continent* (2001). With 370 maps charting the growth of Vancouver and its environs, Hayes' sixth large format atlas, and his eighth book, *Historical Atlas of Vancouver and the Lower Fraser Valley* (2005), traces the region's development from the days when the village of Granville, with 30 buildings, was divided into lots in 1882 for a city to be called Liverpool. Hayes received the Lieutenant Governor's Medal for best B.C. history book from the B.C. Historical Federation.

"I collected stamps as a child," Hayes explains, "and I wanted to know where they all came from, hence out came the atlas. Then I got into geography academically, then city planning. I like to think that if a picture is worth a thousand words, a map must be worth ten thousand. Having said that, I would emphasize I try to write history using maps as the primary illustration. This has a wider audience than if I only wrote books about maps."

Two other outstanding geography books are editor Albert L. Farley's revisions of a 1956 atlas for *Atlas of British Columbia: People, Environment and Resource Use* (1979), a key reference work with 115 maps for the general public and scholars; and Bruce Macdonald's innovative *Vancouver: A Visual History* (1992), a chronological atlas with a full-colour repeating grid format in which each ten-year period of the city is examined with the same criteria over a 140-year span.

Other geography authors of B.C. include Atkeson, Ray; Barnes, Trevor; Berelowitz, Lance; Blomley, Nick; Cameron, Laura Jean; Clapp, C.H.; Forward, Charles N.; Fraser, William Donald; Gregory, Derek; Gunn, Angus; Halseth, Greg; Hardwick, Walter G.; Harris, Cole; Holbrook, Stewart; Kistritz, Ron; Koroscil, Paul M.; Lai, David; Leigh, Roger; McGillivray, Brett; Minghi, Julian; O'Neill, Thomas; Penlington, Norman; Pierce, John; Robinson, J. Lewis; Sandwell, R.W.; Slaymaker, Olav; Townsend-Gault, Ian; Wilson, James W. (Jim); Wynn, Graeme; Yorath, Christopher John.

Laura Sawchuk's portrait of Ivan E. Coyote on the cover of B.C. BookWorld

NEW MILLENNIUM

DANIEL FRANCIS

The Encyclopedia of British Columbia (2000)
edited by Daniel Francis

If one were forced or instructed to select one book, above all others, that should be found in every B.C. household, one would have a hard time not selecting *The Encyclopedia of British Columbia* (2000). No other book has given British Columbians a better mirror in which to see themselves.

It is important for British Columbians to know about the world champion Trail Smoke Eaters or the explosion of Ripple Rock. Or how the Quaker lawyer Irving Stowe founded the Don't Make A Wave Committee, giving rise to Greenpeace. Or the Hope Slide. Or the soccer-playing Lenarduzzi brothers. That's why the *Encyclopedia* is the most essential book for and about B.C. It is both populist and smart. It efficiently reminds us of how and why we are unique, as a psychological and historical zone, west of the Rockies, where maverick sensibilities have thrived. It is remarkably comprehensive, lively and accurate.

Accepting the Roderick Haig-Brown Regional Prize for best book about B.C. in 2001, editor Daniel Francis said, "The whole project is based on a conversation Howie [White] and I had over a decade ago. I never had a contract with him; the project was not based on a business relationship, it was based on a friendship, one that miraculously survived some very tense moments. For most of the project Howie had no outside support. Much of the help was voluntary and it felt at times that we were flying by the seat of our pants. But we both knew that if we waited for the money and set up the committees and consulted all the experts and drew up a flow chart, we'd never get the damn thing done. So instead, we just went ahead and did it. I wouldn't recommend this as the best way, but it seems to me to be a typically B.C. way, and it worked."

Francis wrote approximately 80 per cent of the 4,000 entries, and Howard White, a long-time Pender Harbour resident, who also co-conceived the *Raincoast Chronicles* series with his wife Mary, was the driving force behind the project. He conceived it, took the financial risk, and *believed* it was both necessary and viable, even though Mel Hurtig's *The Canadian Encyclopedia* project had met with financial ruin.

The future of books is now uncertain. Small bookstores are closing; electronic media is increasingly prevalent. The proliferation of Chapters outlets across Canada has influenced the book trade enormously. Hence the successful release of the million-word, 824-page *Encyclopedia of British Columbia* in 2000 marked the pinnacle of a thirty-six year progression for a provincial industry that engendered the highest per capita book reading rate in Canada.

LINCOLN CLARKES

Heroines (2002) by Lincoln Clarkes

How should society recognize and remember its most dreadful events? *Province* reporter Salim Jiwa has written two books about the two Air India terrorist bombings in 1985, one of which ripped open a jumbo jet from Vancouver over the Irish Sea, murdering 329 people. Journalists Damian Inwood and Jon Ferry wrote *The Olson Murders* (1982) and Ian Mulgrew provided *Final Payoff: The True Price of Convicting Clifford Robert Olson* (1990).

For years, Vancouver Mayor Philip Owen and the police board failed to recognize that a serial killer could be responsible for the spate of missing women from Vancouver's Downtown Eastside. To ensure society didn't "invisibilize" such women again, Lincoln

A photo from Lincoln Clarkes' exhibition and book Heroines *(2002)*

Clarkes published photos of their peers. His controversial black-and-white album of marginalized women posing in Vancouver's Downtown Eastside, *Heroines* (2002), is arguably one of the most timely, necessary and respectful books ever published in B.C.

A resident of the Downtown Eastside, Clarkes is a professional photographer who began in 1996 to take photos of the women he met in his neighborhood, many of whom were prostitutes or drug addicts. By treating his subjects with the same respect he would accord Sharon Stone, one of his movie business clients, he assembled a photographic documentary that served as the basis for an award-winning documentary film with original poetry read by Susan Musgrave. *Heroines: A Photographic Obsession* opened the Leipzig Documentary Film Festival and has been shown nationally in Canada. The art exhibit and documentary film led to the publication of *Heroines*, the book, with commentaries from author Barbara Hodgson, social advocate Elaine Allan, 20th-century photo collector Patricia Canning and art curator Ken Dietrich-Campbell. In 2003, *Heroines* was named co-winner of the Vancouver Book Award for best book about the city.

The barbaric murders of women associated with the pig farm managed by Robert Picton and his brother have been documented by various journalists, and Maggie de Vries wrote *Missing Sarah* (2003) after Vancouver police gave her the news in 2002 that a sample of her younger sister Sarah's DNA (from a tooth) had been found on the Port Coquitlam property of Robert Pickton, the accused serial killer of Vancouver prostitutes. Maggie de Vries's 28-year-old sister had vanished from the corner of Princess and Hastings on April 14, 1998. Maggie de Vries' heart-rending memoir won both the first annual George Ryga Award for Social Awareness in B.C. Literature and the 13th annual VanCity Book Prize for women's issues.

TOM THURSTON

Strongman: The Doug Hepburn Story (2003) by Tom Thurston

Homegrown heroes such as swimmer Elaine Tanner, skater Karen Magnussen, sprinter Harry Jerome—the first Canadian to officially hold a world track record—and weightlifter Doug Hepburn all learned the hard way that society only loves a winner.

Harry Jerome's story is especially compelling because he overcame racial hurdles as the only black athlete in his North Vancouver high school. Doctors predicted Jerome would never walk again after he suffered a severe injury at the Perth Commonwealth Games in 1962 but he set seven world records, running the 100 metres in 10.2, 10.1 and 10.0 seconds successively. Fil Fraser's biography *Running Uphill: The Short, Fast Life of Canadian Champion Harry Jerome* (2006) merits consideration as an essential B.C. sports title.

Equally engaging, and better material for a movie, is *Strongman: The Doug Hepburn Story* (2003) by Tom Thurston. Born cross-eyed and with a club foot in Vancouver in 1927, the intensely shy and self-taught weightlifter Doug Hepburn miraculously became the world's strongest man and the West Coast's answer to eastern Canada's Louis Cyr.

Bullied at school, he also had to contend with an alcoholic father at home. Like Charles Atlas, he became obsessed with the compensatory activity of lifting weights. He dropped out of high school and developed his own training regimen and a 10,000 calorie-a-day menu. Hepburn broke all existing records in competitions in B.C.—only to have the Canadian Amateur Athletics Union (CAAU) continuously reject his results. After Hepburn won the U.S. weight lifting championship in Los Angeles in 1949, the CAAU governing body continued to resent Hepburn's independence. In February of 1950, he wrote a letter describing his plight to Charles A. Smith, a magazine editor, based in White Plains, New York, and a world authority on strength. After several months, a letter came that began Smith's mentoring relationship with Hepburn that endured until Smith's death in 1991.

Based in Montreal, the CAAU refused to allow Hepburn to represent Canada in the 1952 Olympic Games. Their rejection had emotional and economic repercussions. Everywhere that Hepburn went to compete, he had to raise his own funds for travel. Hepburn, on his own nickel, proceeded to win the 1953 World Weightlifting championship in Stockholm. He also won the gold medal in the 1954 British Empire and Commonwealth Games in Vancouver. For that latter competition, the mayor of Vancouver had hired him as a bodyguard so that he would have time to train. Hepburn refused to take any of the performance-enhancing drugs that were being used by his competitors. It was a source of pride to him that he was "clean." Later on, however, his inherited predilection for alcohol proved a major hurdle. He courageously overcame that obstacle, too, and became an advocate of vitamins, writing a book on the subject.

Hepburn was offered opportunities to make his living in commercial wrestling, but he disliked violence—and once claimed he was one of the first hippies. Hepburn tried his luck as a nightclub singer, with moderate success, and eventually he became an inventor of training devices, such as the Hepburn Exerciser, the Dynatron, and the Powermaster 3. Although Hepburn was granted a U.S. patent, his machines brought little financial reward. He was sometimes able to raise some money for himself by performing feats of strength in public, but he was happiest in the gym, advising others, mentoring young athletes, and training so that he continued to establish records for weightlifting in his own age group. If he could no longer lay claim to the title of strongest man in the world, he could at least boast he was the strongest 68-year-old man in the world.

In honour of the 50th anniversary of Doug Hepburn's Stockholm triumph, the 2003 World Weightlifting Championships were held in Vancouver, but Hepburn had died three years earlier, in 2000. He had spent his final years in obscurity. Like the troubled North Vancouver–raised sprinter Harry Jerome, who had won a bronze medal in the Olympics, Hepburn was a homegrown world-class athlete who couldn't, or wouldn't, fit into any media-friendly mould.

JOEL BAKAN

The Corporation: The Pathological Pursuit of Profit and Power (2004)
by Joel Bakan

No book by a British Columbian has stirred as much critical debate as Joel Bakan's *The Corporation: The Pathological Pursuit of Profit and Power* (2004), the print version of a feature film that won the top documentary award at Robert Redford's Sundance Film Festival.

Having co-developed the notion of a program that traces the origins and history of corporations with filmmaker Tom Shandel,

Joel Bakan and his creative partner Mark Achbar, one of the makers of *Manufacturing Consent: Noam Chomsky and the Media,* attended the Banff Television Festival in 1999, ostensibly as reporters for *B.C. BookWorld,* so they could pitch their project.

"Achbar and I brought a 25-page treatment document to Banff, a model of concision," Bakan recalls. "Few wanted to read it. 'Get it down to two pages,' was the straight-faced advice from one Canadian broadcaster heavy. That seemed generous compared to the high-brow BBC, which wanted only one page. Television people want to hear you, not read you." Miraculously, the film appeared in a timely fashion—boosted by a publishing contract with Penguin Books.

The Corporation was partially sparked by the anti-APEC protests at UBC in 1997, during which Bakan looked out his office window, grabbed his library card—to identify himself as a professor—and took his copy of the Constitution of Canada with him to monitor the Sgt. Pepper Spray demonstrations. It proved to be a memorable day. The mounting frustration of demonstrators as they tried to scale a fence made a strong impression on Bakan: Canadians who were protesting the presence of dictators in their own country were portrayed on the evening news as anti-social elements. Bakan and Mark Achbar roamed the UBC campus with Achbar shooting proceedings with his video camera. That day became a turning point in their efforts to make *The Corporation.*

"Most students in the mid-1990s were building investment portfolios, not social movements," writes Bakan in *The Corporation.* "Yet here they were, thousands of them, braving pepper spray and police batons to fight for ideals. Even more unusual, the students were protesting against corporations—against their destruction of the environment, exploitation of workers and abuses of human rights." Anti-globalization protests followed in Seattle, Prague and Geneva. Wall Street scandals—at Enron, WorldCom and Tyco—confirmed suspicions that large corporations were often corrupt and largely out of control. "There's a sense out there today that because corporations can be socially responsible," says Bakan, "they can regulate themselves, and we no longer need regulation from the government in the form of laws. There's a real pairing of deregulation on the one hand and the appearance of social responsibility on the other, and that's the point to which I object. It's fine if CEO guys and gals want to be decent, but corporate benevolence is not a replacement for legal standards that constrain what corporations can and should do." Or, as Noam Chomsky has pointed out, "it is better to ask why we have tyranny than whether it can be benevolent."

REX WEYLER

Greenpeace: How a Group of Ecologists, Journalists and Visionaries Changed the World (2004) by Rex Weyler

The creation of the world's leading organization for environmental activism is probably the greatest achievement of British Columbia as a distinct society, so if the *Encyclopedia of B.C.* ranks as the most important volume ever published in B.C., it's easy to argue that Rex Weyler's *Greenpeace: How a Group of Ecologists, Journalists and Visionaries Changed the World* (2004) must be considered as a close second.

Weyler's summary of Greenpeace Foundation activities between 1970 and 1979 was endorsed by Greenpeace pioneer Robert Hunter as "a masterpiece." It does a better job than Hunter's own personalized account to set the record straight, without undue boosterism, and clearly recalls how a Quaker lawyer named Irving Stowe and a bunch of so-called hippies rented the converted *Phyllis Cormack* to sail north on a Quixotic and dangerous mission to stop nuclear testing, greatly boosted by the public relations savvy of on-board journalist Ben Metcalfe, thereby igniting an explosion of ecological awareness around the world.

Yale-educated Stowe suffered from seasickness, so he stayed on

Rex Weyler (right) with Vancouver cameraman Ron Precious in the mid-Pacific, 1976

shore to coordinate political pressure, but it was his Don't Make A Wave Committee, the forerunner of Greenpeace, that organized the 1971 fundraising concert with Joni Mitchell, James Taylor and Phil Ochs, and chartered the boat to "bear witness" (a Quaker tradition of silent protest) after Committee member Marie Bohlen had suggested sending a vessel northward to serve as a floating picket line.

Rex Weyler was an apprentice engineer for Lockheed Aerospace, south of San Francisco, when he stumbled upon the Summer of Love in 1967. He marched with students of the Sorbonne during the Paris riots of 1968 and witnessed the demise of the Love Generation at the Rolling Stones concert at Altamont, California, in 1969. In 1972, he crossed the 49th parallel as one of the last of some 150,000 draft evaders to enter Canada, the largest single political exodus in U.S. history. In Vancouver he met *Phyllis Cormack* veterans Bob Keziere (photographer) and Bob Cummings (*Georgia Straight* correspondent) and learned about the Greenpeace initiative to halt French nuclear tests in the South Pacific at Moruroa. He became a director of the Greenpeace Foundation and its campaign photographer from 1974 to 1979, an editor and publisher of *Greenpeace Chronicles* magazine from 1975 to 1979, a co-founder of Greenpeace International, and a director of Greenpeace Canada until 1982.

In the 1990s, Rex Weyler helped draft legislation for B.C.'s new pulp mill effluent regulations, limiting dioxin releases into the Georgia Strait. A co-founder of the Hollyhock Educational Institute, he has contributed to publications that include the *New York Times, Smithsonian, Rolling Stone* and *National Geographic.* Weyler has also been publisher and editor of *Shared Vision* magazine. More recently he wrote *The Jesus Sayings: The Quest for His Authentic Message* (2008).

GARY GEDDES

Gary Geddes has been one of the most influential literary figures in B.C., having edited a widely used university text, *20th Century Poetry & Poetics* (1969) and one of the first modern anthologies of distinctly British Columbian literature, *Skookum Wawa* (1975), as well as *Vancouver: Soul of a City* (1986).

Born in Vancouver in 1940 and raised in the Commercial Drive area, Geddes was described as Canada's best political poet by George Woodcock.

Geddes founded two literary presses in Ontario, Quadrant Editions, in 1981, and Cormorant Books, in 1986. He then returned to British Columbia where he lives with novelist Ann Eriksson. With more than 35 titles and counting, Geddes lives by his wits, veering increasingly towards non-fiction.

An exemplary Geddes title is *Falsework* (2007), an historical memoir and long poem in many voices about the disastrous collapse of the Second Narrows Bridge, now called the Ironworkers Memorial Bridge, in North Vancouver, during its construction in

June of 1958. Eighteen workers were killed as well as a rescue diver. The tragedy occurred in the month that Geddes graduated from King Edward High School. "I was working at the time on the waterfront at BC Sugar Refinery," he recalls, "loading boxcars with 100-pound sacks of pure, white and deadly sugar, so the news did not take long to reach me. What I did not know at the time was that my father had been called out as a former navy diver to stand by in the search for bodies in the wreckage. I've carried for a long time the image of him dangling from his umbilical cord of oxygen in that cauldron of swirling water and twisted metal."

On the same subject, Eric Jamieson received the Lieutenant Governor's Medal for Historical Writing for his thorough non-fiction response to the event, *Tragedy at Second Narrows: The Story of the Ironworkers Memorial Bridge* (2008).

Other major disasters that occurred within B.C. have been identified by historian Derek Pethick as the Smallpox Epidemic (1862); the Bute Inlet Massacre (1864); the Barkerville Fire (1868); the Loss of the S.S. *Pacific* (1875); the Vancouver Fire (1886); the Nanaimo Coal Mine Disaster (1887); the Fraser Valley Flood (1894); the Point Ellice Bridge Disaster (1896); the New Westminster Fire (1898); the Victoria Fire (1910); the Hell's Gate Slides (1913, 1914); the Loss of the *Princess Sophia* (1918); the Influenza Epidemic (1918–1919); the Great Depression (1929-1939); and the Fraser River Flood (1948).

To Pethick's list should be added the Fernie Mine Explosion (1902); the Shipwreck of the *Valencia* (1906); the Rogers Pass Avalanche (1910); the Vancouver Waterfront Fire (1945); the Second Narrows Bridge Collapse (1958); the Port Alberni Tsunami (1964); the Hope Slide (1965); the B.C. Interior Firestorm (2003); and three airline crashes (1956, 1965, 1978) that killed 157 people in total.

For other authors associated with B.C. disasters, see abcbookworld entries for Abernethy, Don; Anderson, Charles; Anderson, Frank; Belyk, Robert; Draper, Penny; Freake, Ross; Hagelund, William A.; Hoolihan, Tony; Jiwa, Salim; Johnson, Peter; MacLeod, Joan; Marc, Jacques; Miller, Archie; Neitzel, Michael; Norton, Wayne; O'Keefe, Betty; Paterson, T.W.; Pethick, Derek; Rogers, Fred; Sanderson, Eric; Soames, Jorie; Turnbull, Elsie Grant; Watt, K. Jane; Wells, R.E.; Wilson, Diana.

FREEMAN M. TOVELL

At the Far Reaches of Empire: The Life of Juan Francisco de la Bodega y Quadra (2008) by Freeman M. Tovell

As the pre-eminent Spanish captain who explored the Pacific Northwest coast prior to 1800, Peruvian-born Juan Francisco de la Bodega y Quadra is the subject of Freeman M. Tovell's impressively sober, extensively researched, non-fanciful biography, *At the Far Reaches of Empire: The Life of Juan Francisco de la Bodega y Quadra* (2008), the first in-depth profile of Bodega y Quadra in English. It received the Keith Matthews Award from the Canadian Nautical Research Society for best book on a Canadian nautical subject.

Tovell, a former diplomat who served in Peru, points out that his subject is more commonly known as Bodega or else Bodega y Quadra in Spain, the United States, Mexico and Peru—rather than simply Quadra.

In terms of sophistication and accomplishments, Quadra's only rival during his era was the Italian-born Malaspina. Both were gentlemen who deserve greater recognition.

Bodega's reputation suffers because there is no genuine portrait of him, a fate that has also befallen the remarkable pathfinder David Thompson. "His enlightened policy toward the Nuuchah-nulth people and his close association with Chief Maquinna are a matter of record," writes Tovell, "and his cordial hospitality to all, including his British rival George Vancouver, has been universally admired.

"Such praise is deserved, but Bodega had his imperfections. He incurred enormous debts when his overreaching ambition to make a name for himself in his chosen career exceeded his financial circumstances. Serving on the outer edge of the empire, he lacked the support of an influential patron at the Spanish royal court. Furthermore, as a colonial-born subject from Peru, he was hampered by the governmental prejudice that hindered colonial subjects seeking high rank in the church and government. Despite his constant efforts to be promoted from four-ring captain to flag rank, he was never able to gain full recognition for his achievements from his naval superiors and political masters."

After Captains Bodega y Quadra and George Vancouver met at Nootka Sound in 1792, hosted by Maquinna, to dissolve simmering hostilities between Spain and England, maps soon thereafter ascribed the name "Vancouver and Quadra's Island" to what later became known as Vancouver Island. The Hudson's Bay Company expunged the Spaniard's name. The island opposite Campbell River, originally called Valdes Island, was renamed Quadra Island in 1903. The extent to which British Columbia could have been "Spanish Columbia" is not fully realized by most residents of B.C.

BUD OSBORN

B ud Osborn has been the unofficial archivist of Canada's poorest neighbourhood and its most eloquent and forceful author and spokesman, publishing six books since 1995. "We have become a community of prophets," writes the Downtown Eastside poet, "rebuking the system and speaking hope and possibility into situations of apparent impossibility." Along with City of Vancouver's Drug Policy Coordinator Donald MacPherson and UVic academic Susan Boyd—who lost her sister Diana to a drug overdose—Osborn has documented the social justice movement that culminated in the opening of North America's first supervised drug injection site in Vancouver's Downtown Eastside in the trio's impolitely-titled *Raise Shit! Social Action Saving Lives* (2009).

Bud Osborn (above) has portrayed the "scorned and scapegoated" of his Downtown Eastside neighbourhood as brave souls fighting for their dignity.

A former addict who was "seven years clean," Osborn became a board member of the Vancouver/Richmond Health Board, the Carnegie Centre Association Board and Vancouver Area Network of Drug Users (VANDU). In the process he began working closely with MP Libby Davies and advocating for the introduction of free injection sites. "I realize there are not many people who can advocate from the bottom, who have lived at the bottom," he says.

As a City Council candidate, Osborn became a fierce adversary of Mayor Philip Owen and met with federal Health Minister Allan Rock. Osborn did remarkably well at the polls for someone who might have been dismissed as a former alcoholic and drug addict. Mayor Owen eventually reversed his stance and accepted most of the policies that Osborn and Davies had been advocating.

Osborn's former life as a lost soul on the mean streets of Vancouver has been dramatized in an award-winning film called *Keys to Kingdoms,* made by Nathaniel Geary. Osborn's subsequent chapbook called *Keys to the Kingdom* received the City of Vancouver Book Award in 1999.

For other authors pertaining to the Downtown Eastside, see abcbookworld entries for Atkin, John; Ballantyne, Bob; Baxter, Sheila; Brodie, Steve; Cameron, Sandy; Cameron, Stevie; Campbell, Bart; Canning-Dew, Jo-Ann; Clarkes, Lincoln; Craig, Wallace Gilby; Cran, Brad; Daniel, Barb; Douglas, Stan; Fetherling, George; Gadd, Maxine; Gilbert, Lara; Greene, Trevor; Herron, Noel; Itter, Carole; Knight, Rolf; Lukyn, Justin; Mac, Carrie; Maté, Gabor; Murakami, Sachiko; Murphy, Lorraine; Reeve, Phyllis; Robertson, Leslie A.; Robinson, Eden; Roddan, Andrew; Swanson, Jean; Taylor, Paul; Tetrault, Richard; Vries, Maggie de; With, Cathleen.

JACK WHYTE

A dozen or so highly successful commercial novelists have arisen in B.C. during the past three decades. Of these, with the publication of *The Forest Laird: William Wallace* (2010), the first novel in his new trilogy about the Scottish Wars of Independence in the 14th-century, Jack Whyte stands a good chance of having the most enduring canon.

Jack Whyte's preceding two series of novels about King Arthur and the Knights Tempar have reputedly sold more than a million copies. Simply put, his novels are gripping, well-researched entertainment, often overlooked by overtly "literary" types because they are so popular. He doesn't win prizes, he wins readers.

At age 52, Scottish-born Whyte burst onto the writing stage with *The Skystone* (1992), the first of a projected quartet of Arthurian novels in a series called A Dream of Eagles (and called The Camolud Chronicles in the U.S.). Nine Arthurian titles later, in 2006, he launched a trilogy about the original nine Templar Knights, commencing with the madness and cruelty of the First Crusade in 1088.

A Bard for the Calgary Highlanders, a founder of both the Burns Club of Calgary and the Burns Club of Vancouver, and a former corporate communications consultant, Whyte is also an avid golfer and stage performer who sings in eight languages. His poetry-laden memoir *Jack Whyte: Forty Years in Canada* (2007) steers clear of intimate information.

Other unabashedly commercial novelists of B.C. who have gained far-flung readerships include Jo Beverley (romance), William Deverell (mystery), Vanessa Grant (romance), Kay Gregory (romance), Naomi Horton (romance), Daniel Kalla (medical thriller), Spider Robinson (sci-fi), Michael Slade (horror), Ian Slater (disaster) and Chevy Stevens (thriller).

At the opposite end of the scale, sophisticated do-it-yourselfer Ernest Hekkanen of Nelson, B.C., is a literary outsider by temperament and necessity, but probably not by choice. With more than 40 fiction titles, Hekkanen has done too much, too well, too fast, too independently, too far away from Ontario, to be fashionable.

The 880 pages and 73 stories of Volumes I and II of *The Collected Stories of Ernest Hekkanen: Naturalistic, Modern Gothic & Postmodern* (2010) represent an astonishing range and depth of over 40 years of highly original storytelling. His work has been seriously comic, absurdist, theatrical, iconoclastic, psychologically probing and shrewd. Along the way, the Seattle-born Hekkanen, of Finnish descent, has rivalled Adolf Hungry Wolf as B.C.'s most prolific and dedicated self-publisher.

MARK ZUEHLKE

Mark Zuehlke would agree with Leonardo da Vinci who said, "Work is the law." A Pierre Berton without the bow tie, Zuehlke has quickly become one of Canada's pre-eminent war historians with a spate of activity rivalled only by the pace of George Woodcock. In an age when creative non-fiction is chic, he does old-fashioned research.

To produce 23 titles in 18 years, Zuehlke has not busied himself with chapbooks, poetry titles or personal ramblings. He has somehow researched and written twelve thick military histories in only

14 years, simultaneously producing a trilogy of detective novels, plus eight other books since 1992, including the first and only book to examine the phenomenon of remittance men in B.C., *Scoundrels, Dreamers and Second Sons: British Remittance Men in the Canadian West* (1994).

In the eighth and final volume of his Canadian Battle Series, *On to Victory* (2010), Zuehlke recalls the fiercely fought and bittersweet liberation of Holland, incorporating the views and words of men on the ground. Never mind hockey—this was the greatest Canadian victory. It cost more than four billion dollars and the lives of 1,482 Canadians, as well as 6,298 casualties, but the Dutch remain grateful.

Born in Vernon in 1955, Mark Zuehlke has received the City of Victoria Butler Book Prize for *Holding Juno* (2005) and the Canadian Authors Association Lela Common Award for Canadian History for *For Honour's Sake: The War of 1812 and the Brokering of an Uneasy Peace* (2006). In his spare time he won the Arthur Ellis Best First Novel Award from the Crime Writers of Canada for *Hands Like Clouds* (2000).

For other authors who wrote about war, see abcbookworld entries for Adams, LaVerne; Allinson, Sidney; Allister, William; Alvarez, Manuel; Andrews, Allen; Barnholden, Michael; Bell, Gordon; Bjarnason, Bogi; Bourret, Annie; Bowman, Phylis; Briemberg, Mordecai; Broadfoot, Barry; Brodsky, G.W. Stephen; Brown, Atholl Sutherland; Browne, Donald Elgin; Cambon, Kenneth; Childerhose, R.J.; Clarke, Jay; Clavell, James; Cobley, Evelyn; Cohen, Stan; Cowling, Tony; Coyle, Brendan; Crawford, Scott; Crooks, Sylvia; Culhane, Claire; de Groot, Jan; Dixon, Jack; Drabek, Jan; Eagle, Raymond; Evans, Hubert; Fairclough, Gordon; Ferguson, Julie H.; Filter, Bo; Floris, Steve; Francis, Daniel; Galipeau, John; Garnett, Heidi; Gibson, John Frederic; Gleason, Mona; Godwin, George; Gough, Kathleen; Greenwood, Alexander; Greer, Rosamond; Gregory, Roxanne; Harker, Douglas Edward; Kahn, Leon; Keith, Agnes Newton; Leighton, Frank; Linn, Ruth; Lovatt, R.; Martin, Nikolaus Claude; McDowell, Jim; McInnes, Harvelyn Baird; McLeod, Gould L.; McMahon, John; McWilliams, James; Meade, Edward F.; Meyers, Edward; Mickleburgh, Rod; Mielnicki, Michel; Moszkiewiez, Helen; Mumford, Gordon; Murray, Keith; Napier, Roger; O'Kiely, Elizabeth; Oberle, Frank; Patterson, Kevin; Priebe, Eckehart; Propp, Dan; Purdy, Verity Sweeny; Ralph, Wayne; Rayment, Hugh; Reid, Charles; Rieger, Carla; Robertson, Alan; Rogow, Sally; Russell, Chester; Sager, Arthur; Sharifad, Yadi; Sheed, David J.; Sheffield, R. Scott; Slater, Ian; Smith, Blake; Spector, Norman; Steele, Samuel Benfield; Stofer, Ken; Stursberg, Peter; Sturze, Klaus G.M.; Taylor, Mary; Thomas, Elizabeth; Thorn, J.C.; Tobler, Douglas Hugen; van Oort, Boudewijn; Wade, Frank; Wagner, Gordon; Wilkes, Helen Waldstein; Williams, Jana; Wilson, John; Windsor, John; Wood, James A.; Young, Albert Charles.

DAVID SUZUKI

One of the few British Columbians who needs little or no introduction is the geneticist-turned-broadcaster-turned-environmentalist David Suzuki—author or co-author since 1988 of some 40 books in 22 years.

Born in Vancouver in 1936, David Takayoshi Suzuki was interned with his family in Slocan, B.C., during WWII. He grew up in southern Ontario. Like many Japanese Canadians who were interned and had some of their family holdings confiscated or sold, Suzuki was both embittered and emboldened—seemingly intent on proving his worth to society beyond any doubt. In 1963, he joined the UBC Zoology Department and won the award for outstanding Canadian research scientist under the age of 35 three years in a row.

He brought science to the masses via television, starting with *Suzuki on Science* in 1971, leading to his long association with *The Nature of Things* on CBC, from 1979. "When I began to work in television in 1962," he wrote, "I never dreamed that it would ultimately occupy most of my life and make me a celebrity in Canada." As well, Suzuki hosted *Science Magazine* on CBC TV and served as the first host of CBC Radio's *Quirks and Quarks* from 1975 to 1979.

David Suzuki titled his first autobiography *Metamorphosis: Stages in a Life* (1987) to echo his groundbreaking studies of mutations in fruit flies. It was expanded and reissued as *David Suzuki: The Autobiography* (2005), covering his accomplishments after age 50. In the second volume, Suzuki recalls how he proposed to his second wife, Tara Cullis, on Hollyburn Mountain in December of 1972. They have two daughters, Severn and Sarika. Suzuki also has three children, Tamiko, Troy and Laura, from a marriage that ended in 1964. "My children have been my pride and joy," he

Laura Sawchuk portrait of David Suzuki, dubbed "one of the planet's leading thinkers"

writes, "but getting Tara to marry me was the greatest achievement of my life." With Tara Cullis, he co-founded the David Suzuki Foundation and received countless honours including the Order of Canada in 1977 and the Order of B.C. in 1995.

With a foreword by Margaret Atwood, *The Legacy* (2010) is an expanded version of a lecture, released as a film, which offers "An Elder's Vision for Our Sustainable Future." David Suzuki argues that humans must join together as a species to respond to the problems we face, and accept that the laws of nature must take precedence over economics.

In terms of planetary influence, few B.C. authors can match or surpass David Suzuki. His politics are global and environmental— and he does things his own way. Still campaigning for change, he represents the best that British Columbia has to offer.

IVAN E. COYOTE

What is the future of B.C. writing? One answer is Ivan E. Coyote, as original and humorous as they come. As Coyote hones her talents as an onstage comedian and spoken word recording artist, she keeps producing subversively comic and poignant stories of consistently high quality, leading to her sixth book in ten years, *Missed Her* (2010), another collection of gender-bending memoirs.

Born and raised in Whitehorse, Yukon, Ivan E. Coyote is the daughter of a welder and a government worker. "Although technically I fall into the biologically female category," she writes in one of her stories entitled "If I Was a Girl," "I do lack most of the requirements for membership in the feminine realm." A founding member of Taste This, a Vancouver performing group, Coyote released three collections of autobiographical writing prior to *Missed Her*. The *Ottawa XPress* has observed, "Coyote is to CanLit what k.d. lang is to country music: a beautifully odd fixture."

"I had a sex change once," she wrote, "when I was six years old." That summer her mother bought her a bikini for a beginner's swimming class for ages five to seven. Trouble was, the top easily slid over her flat chest. "I was an accomplished tomboy by that time," she says, "so I was used to hating my clothes." Arriving at the pool, she didn't wear the top. When the swimming instructor, a human bellhorn, blew her silver whistle, aggressively dividing them into two camps along sexual lines, short-haired Ivan crossed over.

"It only got easier after that first day," she recalls in her story "No Bikini." "I wore my trunks under my pants and changed in the boys' room after that first day. The short form of the birth name my parents bestowed on me was androgynous enough to allow my charade to proceed through the entire six weeks of swimming lessons, six weeks of boyhood, six weeks of bliss." When her parents received a glowing report card from the swimming camp, citing their son's excellent performance—"He can tread water without a flotation device"—the ruse was discovered and her parents were upset. Since then Ivan has "crossed over" as an openly butch lesbian. She looks like a man and she writes like an angel.

Remarkably, Coyote has the manners and wit to be accepted by the mainstream, while retaining her integrity as an artist who can only survive on the fringe.

Her debut novel *Bow Grip* (2006) received the ReLit Award for best novel from an independent Canadian publishing house in 2007 and was shortlisted for the Lambda Literary Award, the Ferro-Grumley Award for LGBT Fiction and the Vancouver Public Library's "One Book, One Vancouver" competition.

"The question for Coyote's fans was whether she would have the staying power for a longer work," wrote reviewer Grant Shilling. "The answer is a definite yes. *Bow Grip* is a heartfelt, amusing page turner with characters recognizable from the working class walk of life. It's the story of a good-hearted, forty-something mechanic from Drumheller, Alberta, who was happily married to Alison. His buddy Mitch Sawyer runs an Esso station and his wife Kathleen is a quiet kindergarten teacher. Mitch and Joey played hockey together. Now they share some news; their wives have ran off with each other and—as is the case in a small town—everyone knows."

In 2009, Ivan E. (Elizabeth) Coyote was the writer-in-residence for the Vancouver Public Library. Even ten years earlier, that would have been unthinkable.

INDEX

Boldface numbers refer to photos

Volume 1

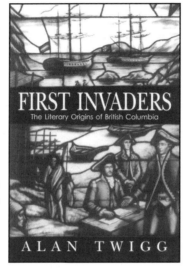

Nominated
for Hubert
Evans
Non-Fiction
Prize, 2005

Honourable
Mention:
BC Historical
Federation
Awards

First Invaders is the first overview of the earliest literary works pertaining to British Columbia, complete with maps, illustrations and original photos. *First Invaders* recalls the drama and confusion arising from the initial contacts between Europeans, Americans and the First Nations on Canada's West Coast.

$21.95 CDN; ISBN 978-1-55380-018-7

"Engrossing..." — DAVID COLTERJOHN, *VANCOUVER SUN*

"I got lost and found in it."
— EDITH IGLAUER,
AUTHOR OF *FISHING WITH JOHN*

"Fascinating... Studded with scads
of maps and illustrations..."
— LYNNE VAN LUVEN, *TIMES COLONIST*

"...the most enjoyable book
on B.C. history that I have
read for years."
— JIM CHRISTY, *GEORGIA STRAIGHT*

"There is absolutely no
substitute for this panorama of
our shared beginnings."
— MARK FORSYTHE, *CBC ALMANAC*

RONSDALE

Published by Ronsdale • www.ronsdalepress.com

Volume 2

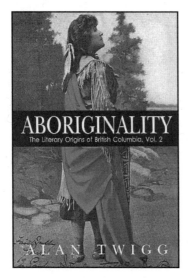

Volume 3

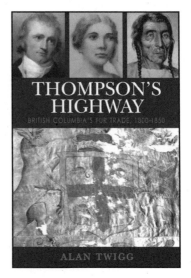

Aboriginality is the first overview of all literary works pertaining to 170 aboriginal authors and illustrators of British Columbia, including references to 300 titles and many original photos.

$24.95 CDN
ISBN 978-1-55380-030-9

"Twigg's new book alters the face of Canadian literature. It is a must-read."
— **WENDY WICKWIRE, HISTORIAN, UNIVERSITY OF VICTORIA**

Thompson's Highway traces the writings of David Thompson, Alexander Mackenzie and 30 of their peers, mainly Scotsmen, who managed more than 50 forts west of the Rockies prior to 1850.

$24.95 CDN
ISBN 978-1-55380-039-2

"Twigg is the Ali Baba of Canadian literary studies. He finds literary gems from the often silent and discursive past and brings them to life."
— **BARRY GOUGH, BIBLIOGRAPHIC SOCIETY OF CANADA**

RONSDALE

Published by Ronsdale • www.ronsdalepress.com